Lawrence of Arabia

Lawrence of Arabia

A Biography

RANULPH FIENNES

PENGUIN MICHAEL JOSEPH

UK | USA | Canada | Ireland | Australia
India | New Zealand | South Africa

Penguin Michael Joseph is part of the Penguin Random House group of companies
whose addresses can be found at global.penguinrandomhouse.com

First published 2023
001

Picture credits can be found on page 305

Set in 13.5/16pt Garamond MT Std
Typeset by Jouve (UK), Milton Keynes
Printed and bound in Great Britain by Clays Ltd, Elcograf S.p.A.

The authorized representative in the EEA is Penguin Random House Ireland,
Morrison Chambers, 32 Nassau Street, Dublin D02 YH68

A CIP catalogue record for this book is available from the British Library

HARDBACK ISBN: 978–0–241–45061–1
TRADE PAPERBACK ISBN: 978–0–241–45062–8

www.greenpenguin.co.uk

Penguin Random House is committed to a sustainable future for our business, our readers and our planet. This book is made from Forest Stewardship Council® certified paper.

To Eduardo Goncalves, a champion of animals!
Eduardo has dedicated his life to the defence of
endangered species worldwide
I salute you Eduardo!

Contents

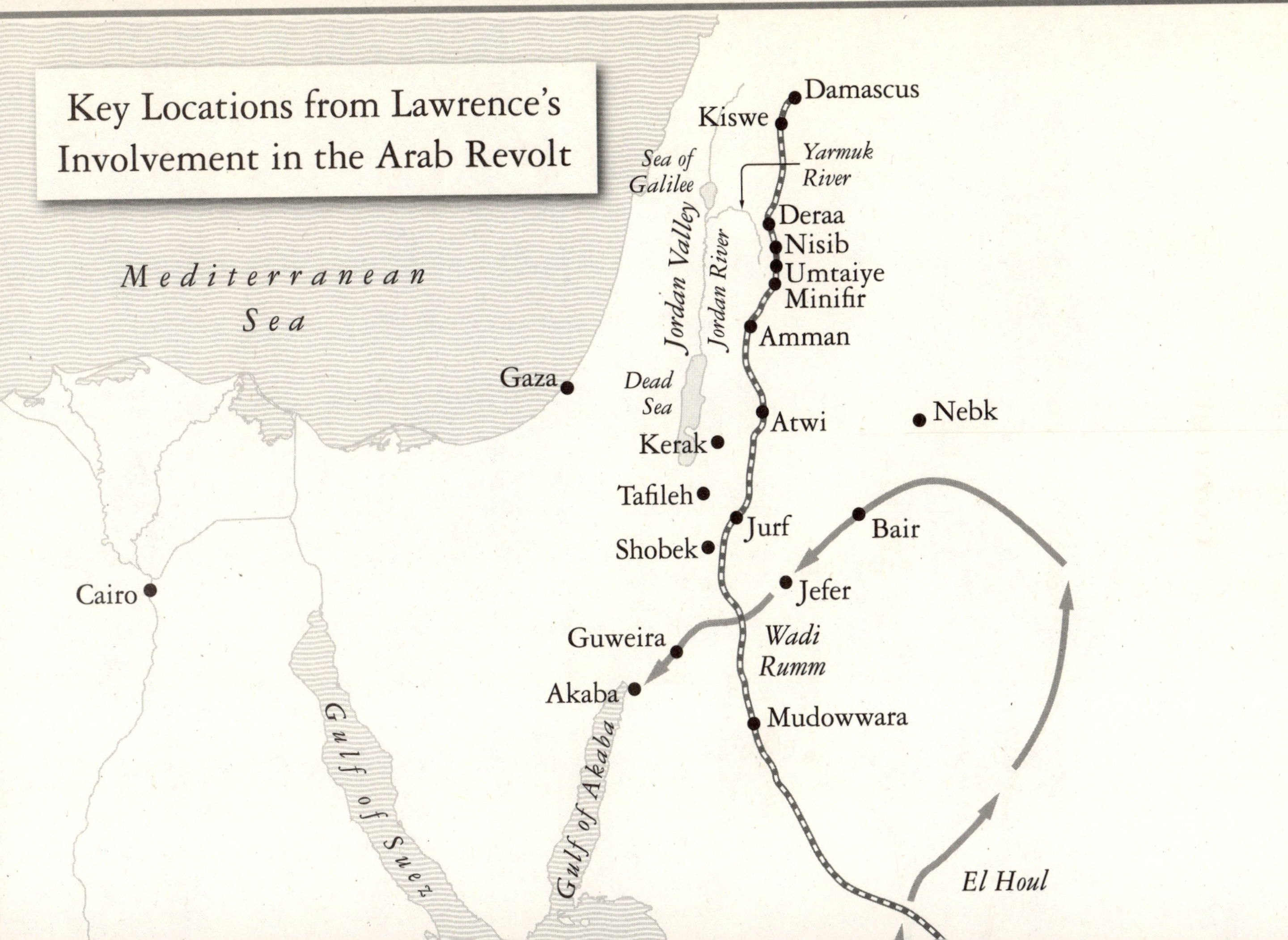
Key Locations from Lawrence's
Involvement in the Arab Revolt
Mediterranean
Sea
Damascus
Kiswe
Yarmuk
River
Sea of
Galilee
Jordan Valley
Jordan River
Deraa
Nisib
Umtaiye
Minifir
Amman
Gaza
Dead
Sea
Atwi
Nebk
Kerak
Tafileh
Jurf
Bair
Shobek
Cairo
Jefer
Guweira
Wadi
Rumm
Akaba
Mudowwara
Gulf of Suez
Gulf of Akaba
El Houl

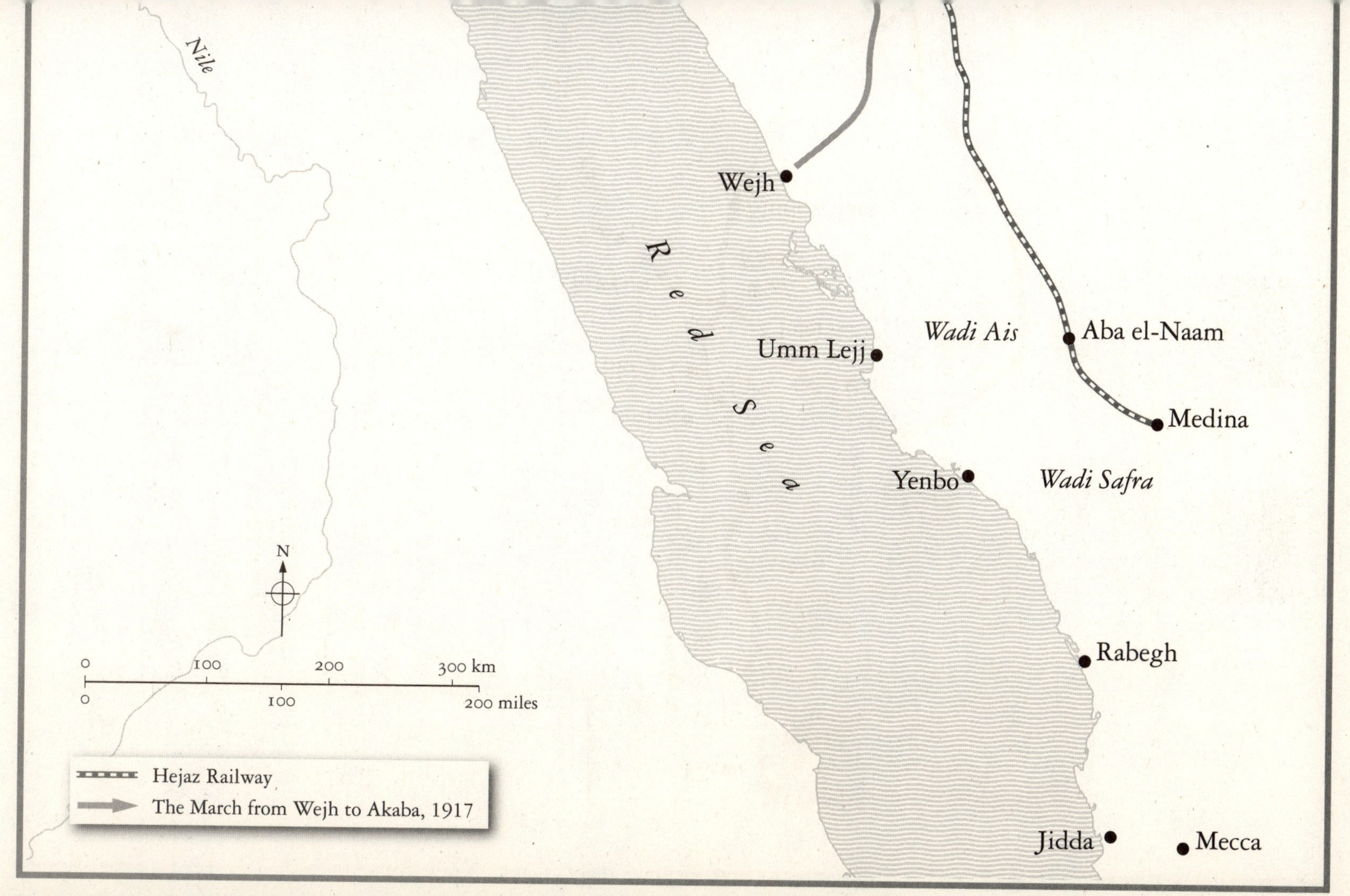
Nile
Wejh
Red Sea
Umm Lejj
Wadi Ais
Aba el-Naam
Medina
Yenbo
Wadi Safra
Rabegh
Jidda
Mecca
N
0
100
200
300 km
0
100
200 miles
Hejaz Railway
The March from Wejh to Akaba, 1917

Introduction

In the summer of 1967, I was facing a personal crisis. Five years previously, I had joined the Royal Scots Greys as a tank troop leader, hoping to see some action. It was the height of the Cold War, and everyone seemed to be on red alert. But instead of being thrown into the excitement of battle, I spent most of my time in the muddy Prussian plain of Westphalia. We barely saw any Marxists, let alone fired a weapon in anger. I was bored stiff and, at twenty-three years old, already wondering what on earth I was going to do with the rest of my life.

And then, out of nowhere, came a letter. It was from a major in my regiment who had spent the last twelve months on a posting to the Omani Army. His letter told of desert patrols in unexplored regions, terrorist arms caches found buried in the sand, and daily fights with Marxist rebels alongside Arab tribes. More officers were needed, he said. Why didn't I apply for a posting?

His life there certainly sounded colourful, a far cry from the mud and greasy tank engines of which I was heartily sick. Yet all I knew about Oman was that it was somewhere in Arabia. But that one thought immediately conjured up an exciting image: the legendary T. E. Lawrence thrillingly leading the Arab tribes on his camel, his white robes flowing behind him, roaring them into action against the Turks. In fact, the image in my head was that of actor Peter O'Toole, who had so brilliantly played Lawrence in the movie of his life released just five years earlier. Like many others, I loved the movie and revelled in Lawrence's adventures in the desert. Now here it was, an opportunity for me to also fight side by side with Arabs in a far-flung country, and actually see some action against the Marxists, no less. Suddenly, my blood was pumping with excitement. Without further thought, I immediately went to the orderly room and filled in the relevant application form. To my surprise, the colonel eagerly signed it, which I found slightly disconcerting.

Soon after, I joined eight other officers from various regiments at an Army school in Beaconsfield. We were there to learn Arabic, of which I didn't speak a word, and to understand what we would face in Oman, of which I knew very little.

'Fiennes, have you had any experience of action?' the instructor asked, sensing my fresh-faced innocence.

'No, sir,' I answered. 'None.'

His bulging biceps twitched in his well-ironed shirtsleeves.

'Do you know anything at all of the current situation in Oman?'

'Not really, sir,' I replied, sensing the rest of the class sigh in dismay.

Muttering under his breath, and with a shake of his head, he walked to a map on the wall and set me straight.

In June 1967, under Harold Wilson's expert guidance, Britain withdrew from Aden. Within three months, the

Russian and Chinese imperialists moved into the resulting power vacuum and looked to spread Marxism as far and wide as possible. Dhofar, a province of Oman, was their nearest target, where they found a receptive audience.

Many Dhofaris were already rising up against the aging Sultan of Oman, who they blamed for their country's impoverished living standards. Oil had been discovered in 1964, and the country suddenly received huge revenues, but the Sultan had retired to his palace and kept the country in the dark ages. The Dhofar Liberation Front was subsequently formed, and, after being infiltrated by Marxists, the guerrilla fighters were sent to Moscow and what was then known as Peking to be trained and supplied with state-of-the-art weapons. Soon there were over 2,000 insurgents supported by the Soviet Union fighting the Sultan's meagre forces in the Dhofar mountains. Revolution looked inevitable. And once Dhofar fell, Oman would follow, along with the rest of southern Asia.

'Would this be a problem, Fiennes?' the instructor asked.

I squirmed awkwardly, spluttering that any win for the Soviets was a problem for us.

'No, Fiennes, it would be a total disaster,' he bellowed, now staring at the rest of the class to ensure they also understood the gravity of the situation.

Over two-thirds of the oil requirements of the free world were derived from countries in the Persian Gulf. To deliver the oil, giant tankers had to pass through the Strait of Hormuz in the Gulf of Oman. This was the only sea passage available to the open ocean, with one tanker passing through it every ten minutes, every day of the year.

With the gates of the Persian Gulf under their control, the Marxists could blackmail the West with threats to oil supplies. It was therefore critical that the Soviet Union and its guerrillas did not succeed in taking Dhofar and Oman. The very lifeblood of the West hung on this.

'Your job, Fiennes, will be to lead an Arab platoon in Dhofar against the adoo.'

'The adoo, sir?'

'The enemy,' he replied, increasingly exasperated by my naivety. 'They're born mountain fighters who know every inch of their land. You'll have to teach your men mountain guerrilla warfare tactics before you go.'

Not only had I never seen any action before, I had also never commanded troops on the ground in any sort of conventional warfare, let alone in the mountains against guerrilla fighters.

'They're multiplying, and they're good,' the instructor continued. 'My God, they're good. Without well-trained soldiers, you'll be asking for trouble.'

I was not to know just what a rabble my Arab troops would be, or that they hated each other as much as the Marxists.

Unsurprisingly, I failed the passing-out exam as convincingly as the other eight passed it. No one seemed to mind. There wasn't even any need to retake the exam. I was going to Oman come what may. Again, this made me wonder what I was letting myself in for. I would soon find it was beyond anything I could have comprehended.

Like T. E. Lawrence, I led an Arab platoon in a fight for their country. Also, like Lawrence, it was an experience that would take me to the edge. Before my adventures in Oman, I already counted him as one of my heroes. Yet it was only after treading in his footsteps and embarking on similar adventures that I realised the man's true greatness. His example often inspired me to victory in life-or-death situations, and I found myself in awe at some of his decisions. I could also sympathise when he found himself falling short, up against impossible military and political odds, as well as confronting personal scars.

As I've grown older and reflected on these experiences, I've realised just what a debt I owe to Lawrence. For that reason, I sought to understand as much as possible about him. While there are some interesting parallels between us, I've often found that he is a man without equal. His adventures in the desert were enough to stir the blood, but the complexity of his character also held me in his grip. There have been few like him, before or since.

There have, of course, been many great books written about Lawrence, including his own acclaimed memoir. And yet, with the benefit of my experience in Oman, I believe I can offer a unique perspective on his fascinating life. As such, while this book will be somewhat educational, I hope that most of all you will enjoy joining me on one of the most awe-inspiring stories of all time, as a young British officer set the desert on fire and emblazoned his name in the pages of history.

Prologue

1913: Carchemish

Under the setting sun, a crowd of Arab tribesmen gathered amongst the ruins in expectation of a verdict. Before them, a wise man, standing at just 5 feet 5 inches tall and dressed in gold- and silver-threaded robes, considered the competing arguments of another blood feud. He was well versed in such tribal matters. For the previous three years he had travelled far and wide across Syria and beyond, taking in many of its great cities and far-flung villages, immersing himself in different tribes' cultures and customs. Not only was he fluent in Arabic, but in most cases had also mastered the various dialects between the tribes, and was able to speak in many tongues.

Some thought he was a magician or some sort of god, both for his much-admired grasp of justice and his reputation as a medicine man. Arabs travelled from all over to be treated by him for scorpion bites, cholera, malaria, and all manner of diseases and ailments. His name and reputation were known in the bazaars of Aleppo, as well as in villages far and wide. Even nomads of the desert knew of him.

Such a man was usually old and well established, a native of these parts who had earned respect over many decades.

And yet the man to whom the Arabs came flocking for justice was a twenty-five-year-old blue-eyed blond-haired Brit from Oxford, who still resembled a teenage boy.

Thomas Edward Lawrence had arrived in Carchemish just three years earlier, after completing his studies at Jesus College, Oxford. Reading history, he had been taken under the wing of David Hogarth, a professor and archaeologist who was an authority on the Middle East. Lawrence first visited the region in 1909, an experience that exhilarated him, with his subsequent final-year thesis earning him a first. His tutors were so impressed by his work that they even hosted a dinner party in his honour.

Following his studies, Hogarth arranged for his star pupil to supervise a British Museum archaeological dig at the ancient Hittite city of Carchemish, an area split between Turkey and Syria. Initially clad in shorts and a buttonless shirt, held together by a Kurdish belt covered in tassels – a symbol that he was seeking a wife – Lawrence had over 100 Arab workmen at his disposal. He watched over and encouraged them as, using nothing more than brute force, ropes, and crowbars, they excavated the remains of walls, houses, sculptures and rare artefacts.

Unlike other Brits, Lawrence did not adopt an air of superiority over the Arabs nor rule by force. He was genuinely interested in all of his men, from their many different tribes, and took the time to sit and talk with them. He also earned great favour by dressing in Arab robes, including a headdress known as a 'kufiya', eating their food, and even sleeping out in the open, waking at dawn to bathe in the Euphrates. Learning of their likes and dislikes, he came to know each tribe well, which was furthered by his extensive travels in the region.

Cut off from the materialism and self-interest of the West, he came to envy the Arabs' simple lives and sought to protect it at all costs. In a letter home, he wrote, 'The perfectly hopeless vulgarity of the half-Europeanized Arab is appalling. Better a thousand times the Arab untouched. The foreigners come out here always to teach, whereas they had much better learn, for in everything but wits and knowledge, the Arab is generally the better man of the two.' Adopting their dress and mannerisms, Lawrence virtually lived as an Arab of the desert, writing to his mother, 'I will have such difficulty in becoming English again, here I am Arab in habits and slip in talking from English to French and Arabic unnoticing.'

The men soon came to love Lawrence, not only for his childlike enthusiasm but also for his generosity in paying handsome bonuses for any discoveries. Yet his sense of fairness in all matters truly won their respect. Should arguments break out between the Arabs, often over a slight, or an affair with another's wife, Lawrence quickly calmed matters with punishments that were seen as just by all parties. Such was the Arabs' reverence towards him that he was soon invited to arbitrate all manner of tribal feuds, leaning on his knowledge of tribal customs and his own sense of empathy and fairness. When his brother Will visited in 1913, he wrote that Lawrence had become 'a great Lord in this place. Ned is known by everyone, and their enthusiasm over him is quite amusing.'

Admired by the Arabs and doing a job he loved,

Lawrence was happy and content in Carchemish. This simple life was all and more than he had ever envisaged for himself. But then, in the summer of 1914, Archduke Franz Ferdinand was assassinated in Austria, and war quickly spread across Europe. Forced to return to England, it seemed his adventures in the Middle East were over, and the battlefields of France awaited. Little did he know that events in Syria would soon change the course of the war, and the hopes and dreams of an Arab prince and much of the Middle East would rest on his shoulders.

21 May 1916

For Sherif Feisal bin Hussein the situation in Damascus was quickly spiralling out of control. War had set Europe ablaze for the past two years, and now he was planning to bring it to the Middle East; if he managed to survive that long, and that was by no means certain.

The thirty-one-year-old was the third son of Sherif Hussein Ibn Ali, the esteemed Emir of Mecca, who ruled the Hejaz (a region situated between modern-day Saudi Arabia and Egypt). As his father's representative to the Turkish Ottoman Empire, Feisal spent most of his time in Damascus, pushing the cause of his people.

Ever since the Ottomans invaded the Middle East in 1517, the Arabs of the Hejaz had long agitated for their independence. However, the Ottomans' superior armed forces had always been able to suppress any uprising with ease. An uneasy truce therefore persisted until the tide began to turn in the eighteenth century. In a series of wars with Russia, France, and Britain over the next 150 years, the Ottomans suffered significant territorial losses. With the Arabs vociferously expressing their desire for independence, the ruler of the Ottoman Empire, Sultan Abdul Hamid II, recognised the urgent need to take action.

Rather than use force against the Arabs, the Sultan thought revolutionising travel through the desolate Hejaz desert might win him favour. Pilgrims to Mecca usually had to endure a forty-day march to reach their holy land. A train could shorten that journey to just three days. Therefore, in 1908, with the help of German engineering expertise and donations from Muslims all over the world, the first phase of the Hejaz Railway was built. Initially covering the 800 miles between Medina and Damascus, there were plans to extend it to Mecca. But the move backfired.

The Sultan didn't realise that the Bedouin tribes of the Hejaz would not hail this supposed leap in progress. If anything, they were violently opposed to it. Many Bedouins survived by providing guides, camels, and tented camps for pilgrims along the Hejaz desert route. Moreover, some made a very comfortable living by robbing them. If the railway were to reach Mecca, then it would destroy their livelihood. To most in the Hejaz, this was a further sign of just how out of touch the Ottomans were. After violent protests, the planned 280-mile extension of the railway was scrapped.

However, the Arabs' victory was short-lived. In 1913 Sultan Abdul Hamid was deposed by a group of nationalists known as 'The Young Turks'. Having seized control,

Mehmed Talaat Pasha was installed as the grand vizier (prime minister) and minister of the interior; Ismail Enver Paşha became the minister of war, while Cemal Pasha was the minister of the navy and autocratic governor-general of Syria.

After consolidating power, the Young Turks became determined to assert their dominance over their Arab lands. In an attempt to 'Turkify' the region, they ordered the Koran to be translated into Turkish, and decreed that Turkish become the official language in schools and public administration. Compulsory service in the Ottoman Army was also enforced to try to ensure loyalty. Unsurprisingly, demands for Arab independence became louder than ever.

Despite these provocations, Feisal appeared to be willing to look for a peaceful solution with the Ottomans. As a member of the Turkish parliament, he was a born diplomat, charming almost everyone he met with his intelligence and soft but firm manner. Almost regal in appearance, tall and slim, with a neatly trimmed beard, he stood out from the crowd in his elegant white robes and always seemed to have a diplomatic solution at the ready. His education at the hands of the Turks in Constantinople certainly helped. He seemed to instinctively understand the Turkish culture and frame of mind, knowing when he could push hard for a cause and when to pull back.

For all of this, Feisal was well-liked by the Young Turks. They implicitly trusted him and always made him welcome in Damascus, where he lived as an esteemed guest of Cemal Pasha. Unlike the other, 'uncivilised', Arabs of the Hejaz desert, Feisal appeared to be a worldly, educated diplomat they could count upon. And yet all the while, Feisal was working from within, plotting an uprising against his Ottoman masters and their grip over the Hejaz.

Since the rise of the Young Turks, Feisal had been meeting with secret rebel societies in Damascus, hoping to organise an effective opposition against the Ottomans. However, this proved to be difficult. There was no national Arab army to call upon, and many of the disparate Arab tribes that needed to come together to fight hated each other, let alone the Turks. There also appeared to be no outside forces who might be willing to help their cause. Yet their hand was strengthened in 1914, when war erupted in Europe.

As the Germans and the French engaged in trench warfare on the fields of France, Russia made moves to claim vast swathes of the Ottoman Empire. Urgently requiring an ally to fend off such a mighty foe, the Young Turks looked to Germany to come to their aid. This alliance more than suited the Germans. With German assistance, the Ottomans could occupy the Russians and divert their troops from fighting on the Polish and Galician fronts. This would then allow the Germans to steamroll their way across Europe. But things didn't go to plan.

In 1915, British and French forces tried to take Constantinople and knock the Ottomans out of the war. In an attempt to defend their capital, Ottoman forces fought desperately in the Dardanelles Strait and on the Gallipoli peninsula. The resulting stalemate saw both sides lose hundreds of thousands of troops.

Feisal saw this as an opportunity. As the Ottomans

continued to suffer enormous losses, they became more vulnerable to an Arab uprising. Better still, the Allied Powers realised that the more stretched the Ottoman forces became, the more difficult it would be for them to help the Germans. The British therefore tentatively offered the Arabs an initial 2 million rounds of ammunition and 5,000 rifles.

This commitment finally set the wheels in motion. An Arab Revolt was no longer a dream but was fast becoming a reality. While negotiations for more support from the British continued, Feisal instructed his brother Ali to raise as many troops as possible in the Hejaz. Just in case any tribes loyal to the Turks informed them of this, Feisal told Cemal Pasha that the tribes were to be put at the Ottomans' disposal.

As preparations gathered pace, on the afternoon of 6 May 1916, Feisal's plans were suddenly interrupted. While staying at a farmhouse outside Damascus, a messenger approached, crying and screaming. Breathlessly, he told Feisal that all of the prominent members of the secret society whom he had been meeting with in Damascus had been arrested. Cemal Pasha not only knew of their plan but was about to publicly execute the supposed traitors in Central Square.

Feisal always knew this was a risk, but now that the moment had arrived, he was unsure what to do. Did Cemal Pasha know of his involvement? Should he quickly escape to Mecca before he was captured? Or should he plead ignorance and stay in Damascus? Before he could make any plans, the decision was made for him. A posse of burly

Ottoman guards arrived at his door and gruffly informed him that he was being taken to see Cemal Pasha.

Upon arriving at Central Square, Feisal braced himself to be accused of treason and executed along with the other traitors. To his surprise, Cemal Pasha instead greeted him as a friend and invited him to join him on the balcony. Down below Feisal saw his friends from the secret society being led towards the gallows. He turned to Cemal, who remained expressionless, not yet revealing if he knew of Feisal's clandestine meetings. Nevertheless, as Feisal silently watched his co-conspirators being executed to the cheers of the crowd, he was very much aware that this was a message to him and his father. If there was any thought of betrayal, this was the price that would be paid.

Watching the executions with satisfaction, Cemal asked Feisal how his brother Ali had fared in gathering a fighting force in the Hejaz. Feisal told him he had amassed as many men as possible, who were all ready to fight on the Ottomans' behalf. Cemal smiled. Perhaps it was time, he said, that he and Enver Pasha accompanied Feisal back to the holy Hejaz city of Medina, where they could inspect the troops for themselves.

Suddenly, the Arab Revolt was hanging by the slenderest of threads. More than ever, Feisal needed a powerful friend. Someone who could help him, and the Arabs, turn the tables on the Ottomans in their most desperate hour of need. No one could have foreseen who that friend would be.

I

In November 1914, following the Ottoman Empire's alliance with the Central Powers of Germany and Austria-Hungary, the British declared war on the Turks. Almost immediately they began to protect their domains in the Middle East. Of primary concern was defending their oil interests in Basra, while also securing the vital shipping lane of the Suez Canal, which helped bring much-needed supplies from India. As a result, British troops quickly flooded into Egypt (which had been under British occupation since 1882) and there was an urgent need for intelligence officers who knew the Middle East and spoke Arabic. This was how Lawrence came to be in Cairo in late 1914. On paper, at least, he certainly fitted the bill. Indeed, few were better equipped for such a role.

Lawrence's intelligence had stood out since he was a young boy. It was said that he could recite the alphabet by the age of three, while he could also read the newspaper upside down before he was five. He soon became fascinated by military history, devouring all manner of books on the subject, including all thirty-two volumes of Napoleon's correspondence. As a teenager he even travelled to France to study its great castles and fortresses, becoming particularly engrossed in the stories of the Crusades.

His time studying at Oxford and working at Carchemish

meant that he was also well versed in the Middle East. Indeed, his experiences had seen him forge a strong dislike of the Ottoman Empire and its hold over the Arabs. During the empire's disastrous Balkan War in 1913, he wrote, 'As for Turkey, down with the Turks! Their disappearance would mean a chance for the Arabs.' And in a letter to the wife of the British consul in Aleppo before war with the Ottomans was declared, Lawrence wrote, 'Turkey seems, at last, to have made up its mind to lie down and be at peace with all the world. I'm sorry because I wanted to root them out of Syria, and now their plight will be more enduring than ever.' In a 1915 letter to David Hogarth, he wrote of the various tribes, 'I want to pull them all together and roll up Syria by way of the Hedjaz in the name of the Sherif. You know how big his repute is in Syria.'

When war with the Ottomans was announced in 1914, it was Hogarth who helped arrange for Lawrence to join him in Cairo, where he was also working in intelligence. From his education and experience, it is clear why Lawrence was seen as an asset. Despite this, his first two years in Cairo primarily involved drawing maps of the landscape and pinpointing enemy positions. He was also adept at winding up many of his colleagues.

Following his time at Carchemish, where the Arabs treated him like a god, Lawrence considered himself an authority on the Middle East. He therefore had little time for those in Cairo who disagreed with him, and was not afraid to speak his mind. With his slight figure dwarfed by his khaki uniform, often missing his Sam Brown belt, and wearing his peaked cap askew, he would fix his superiors with his piercing blue eyes and eloquently lecture them in his cultured Oxbridge accent on the weakness of their argument. It is no wonder he reduced one exasperated officer to ask, 'Who is this extraordinary pip squeak?'

While some believed he had too much to say for himself, any dreams Lawrence might have had of leading an Arab rebellion against the Ottomans seemed a distant fantasy. In any event, he rarely ventured close to a battlefield. If he wasn't chained to his desk, he spent his spare time reading history books and exploring mosques and the local bazaars, often alone.

However, when Hogarth and General Sir Gilbert Clayton established the Arab Bureau in 1916, things began to change. Consisting of a small group of experts on Arab affairs, the bureau was responsible for collecting information on the Ottoman Army in the Middle East. Once again, Hogarth thought that Lawrence's intelligence and experience might be a valuable asset. Brought into the fold, Lawrence was soon doing far more than just sitting behind his desk.

Thanks to his ability to speak Arabic, he was tasked with interviewing Turkish prisoners of war. This gave him a unique insight into the Ottoman positions and the strengths and weaknesses of its forces. Such knowledge of the region, and the Turkish troops, also saw him edit the *Arab Bulletin*, a magazine for senior officers that shared intelligence on the Arabs and the Ottomans. This role also allowed Lawrence to push his pro-Arab independence agenda in Cairo, as well as in London. His memos on the subject were even forwarded to Sir Henry McMahon, the British high commissioner in Egypt. Clayton said of his work, 'Lawrence is quite excellent on this and many other subjects, and you may take his stuff as being good.'

While he continued to rub colleagues up the wrong way, Lawrence's intelligence and desire to work harder than most saw some senior officers prepared to indulge him. Ronald Storrs, the thirty-four-year-old oriental secretary of the British Agency in Cairo, was certainly a fan. In his book, *Orientations*, he recalled that Lawrence seemed to 'gulp down all I could shed for him on Arabic knowledge . . . I told him things sometimes for the mere interest of his commentary. He was eager . . . I found him from the beginning an arresting and an intentionally provocative talker, liking nonsense to be treated as nonsense and not civilly or dully accepted or dismissed.' Lawrence was also a fan of Storrs, knowing of his vital role in supporting the Arabs' plans.

Throughout 1915 and 1916, Storrs regularly met with the Arabs to discuss how the British could help them. However, this was a delicate situation. While the British government wanted to support the Arabs, it also had to be careful not to inspire the hundreds of millions of fellow Muslims in India to rise up against British rule. Any sign that it was actively helping the Arabs of the Hejaz to seek independence could cause a ripple effect across the continent and create yet another issue the British would have to confront when they were already stretched to the limit. One provincial governor in India even stated that if the British were to supply soldiers to Hussein in the Hejaz, 'a flame of fire [would] undoubtedly be lit in India'.

For now, at least, supplying British troops in the Hejaz was a non-starter. Instead, the British War Committee agreed to pay Sherif Hussein £125,000 a month to help meet any costs of the Revolt, in addition to the antiquated weapons it had already provided, some of which had last been used in the Boer War.

On 10 June 1916, Hussein heralded the start of the Revolt in Mecca by firing once at the Ottoman barracks. Quickly overwhelming the holy city, the Arabs forced the 1,500 Ottoman soldiers to flee. The result delighted Lawrence. This was just what he had hoped to see. On 1 July, he wrote home and said of the fledgling Revolt, 'I hate the Turks so much that to see their own people turning on them is very grateful. I hope the movement increases . . . This Revolt, if it succeeds, will be the biggest thing in the Near East since 1550.'

Soon after, with the help of the Royal Navy, the Arabs quickly took the key ports of Jidda, Yenbo, and Rabegh, and set their sights on Medina. However, without the help of the Navy, they lacked the heavy weapons required to overwhelm the walled city and the entrenched Turkish garrison. With no explosives and antiquated guns that frequently jammed, the Arabs were not only outgunned but also outnumbered, often by more than ten to one.

Manpower was a real issue. Thousands of Arab men had been conscripted into the Ottoman Army, while many of the tribes still regarded each other as the enemy and refused to join together to fight. The uncertain success of the Revolt saw some tribes fear Turkish reprisals if it was swiftly crushed. Religion was also proving to be a deterrent. The Ottoman Sultan, 'Caliph of the Muslim World', was still enormously influential, and his call for Muslims to wage jihad against the British saw some reluctant to join forces with the supposed enemy. There was also little money available to pay any tribesman who might have been considering joining the Revolt. The Arabs did, however, manage to enlist some 700 Arab Ottoman soldiers who had been captured and were eager to change sides. They became known as 'the regular troops' and included Iraqi officers Nuri Said and Ali Jawdat, whose experience and military training would prove invaluable in time.

With the Turks resisting the Arabs in Medina, they also finally won the brutal battle in Gallipoli against the British. This freed up more of their forces for operations in the Hejaz, and they now descended on Yenbo and Rabegh. The situation quickly became desperate. If the Arabs lost control of the ports, they would not be able to receive many of the supplies and reinforcements promised by the British. Conversely, the ports would be used to supply the Ottomans. Lawrence was particularly scathing of the situation and blamed poor leadership by the British and Arabs. 'Things in the Hejaz went from bad to worse,' he wrote. 'No proper liaison was provided for the Arab forces in the field, no military information was given to the Sherifs, no tactical advice or strategy was suggested, no attempt made to find out the local conditions and adapt existing Allied resources in material to suit their needs . . . The Arab Revolt became discredited.'

Soon after, General Clayton was replaced as director of intelligence in Cairo by Thomas Holdich. While Clayton would continue to head up the Arab Bureau, Holdich would oversee all matters, taking his orders from Sir Archibald

Murray, the general in charge in Egypt. Both men had little interest in supporting the Arab uprising, and it quickly became apparent to Lawrence that Holdich had little interest in him. In Lawrence's opinion, Holdich was 'excellent in O. [operations] and fatal in I. [intelligence].' By October 1916, Lawrence's influence on Arab affairs appeared all but over. Far away from the action, he was instead ordered to fulfil the mundane task of designing a set of postage stamps to reinforce the apparent success of the Revolt.

While this perceived demotion frustrated him, the death of his brothers Will and Frank on the battlefields of France also plagued him. 'They were both younger than I am,' he wrote to a friend, 'and it doesn't seem right, somehow, that I should go on living peacefully in Cairo.' However, when Lawrence learned that Ronald Storrs was due to meet Sherif Hussein's son Abdulla in Jidda, he spotted the opportunity he was looking for. 'I decided that I must escape at once,' he wrote. 'A straight request was refused, so I took to stratagems. I became, on the telephone, quite intolerable to the Staff on the [Suez] Canal. I took every opportunity to rub into them their comparative ignorance and inefficiency in the department of intelligence and irritated them yet further by literary airs, correcting Shavian split infinitives and tautologies in their reports.'

No doubt happy to see the back of him, Lawrence's request to accompany Storrs was finally approved. So, on 13 October 1916, Lawrence boarded the *Lama*, a small converted liner, and began the 650-mile journey to Jidda, hoping to reignite the Revolt, all the while carrying a dark secret with him.

2

At last free from the shackles of Cairo, Lawrence set off for Jidda with far more than just a joyride with Storrs in mind. Rather than be sidelined from influencing Arab affairs, as Holdich had intended, Lawrence now hoped to thrust himself right into its heart.

He confided that his visit 'was really to see for myself who was the yet unknown master-spirit of the affair, and if he was capable of carrying the Revolt to the distance and greatness I had conceived for it'. So far, Lawrence had been dismayed by the lack of leadership in the Arab Revolt. In meeting with Abdulla, he hoped to find the man who could inspire the Arabs to victory. With this knowledge, he believed that the British could then back a man they could depend on to get the job done.

Yet Lawrence's dreams for the Arab Revolt weren't just due to his attachment to the Arabs and his hatred for the Ottomans. There was a far deeper significance to all of this that he had long tried to keep a secret.

Before Lawrence was born, his father, Thomas Chapman, had been a baronet in Dublin. However, after having an affair with Sarah Junner, the family maid, his wife refused to grant him a divorce. Fleeing from Ireland in shame along with his mistress, the couple changed their name to 'Lawrence' and spent the next few years moving between Wales, Scotland and France, finally settling in Oxford in 1896. During this time, they had five boys, with Thomas Edward Lawrence the second born.

Raised in a strict Christian household, Lawrence was ten years old when he worked out he had been born out of wedlock, and that his parents were still unable to marry. While Lawrence found it hard to accept that his parents had been 'living in sin', polite Victorian society also shunned those who were illegitimate. Children born out of wedlock could not attend certain schools, were unwelcome in some social groups, and were barred from entering certain professions, particularly in government. It is no wonder that Lawrence kept the secret of his illegitimacy to himself.

With Lawrence riddled with shame, and feeling dirty, almost impure, his mother's reaction didn't help. Out of her five boys, Sarah Lawrence saddled him with the burden that he was special, and that he alone could redeem the family's tarnished reputation. He later wrote, 'I always felt she was laying siege to me, and would conquer, if I left a chink unguarded.' His friend David Garnett described her as 'a terror', someone who could devour people 'like a lion'. If Lawrence displeased his mother in any way, she would whip him, hoping to keep him on the straight and narrow. This was not a punishment she gave to his brothers. Years later, Sarah remarked that the reason Lord Astor's horses never won was because he wouldn't whip them. Lawrence's younger brother Arnold later wrote, 'The strongest impression I have is that his life has been injured by his mother.'

This insistence that Lawrence could redeem the family, and restore them to their rightful status, coincided with his obsession with the Crusades and medieval legends. He later told a biographer, military strategist and author Liddell Hart, that he had studied war when he was younger because he was filled with the idea of freeing a people, while his ambition had been 'to be a general and knighted by the time he was thirty'. With this complex background, the Arab Revolt was just the cause he sought to satisfy his mother's demands and restore his family's honour. Indeed, in a letter Lawrence wrote in 1919, he said he became involved with the Revolt because 'I thought that freedom for the race would be an acceptable present.'

I have some insight into how Lawrence might have felt. My own father died before I was born while fighting in the Second World War with the Royal Scots Greys. For that reason, it had always been my ambition to follow in my father's footsteps and join the regiment. I certainly did not endure the same pressure from my mother as Lawrence did, but something within me wanted to help cement my father's legacy after he had been killed so young. This was one of the many reasons that led me to Oman. He had died fighting for freedom, and I thought this was a worthy goal to follow.

However, it wasn't just Lawrence who was harbouring secrets on the trip to Jidda. Ronald Storrs also had information that, if it became public knowledge, could blow the Revolt apart.

In the event of an Arab victory, sixty-three-year-old Sherif Hussein not only expected Britain to recognise the

Arabs' independence but that he would then rule an empire encompassing the Hejaz, Syria, Mesopotamia and Arabia. Yet Hussein's Arab rivals, Ibn Saud and Ibn Rashid, also claimed those lands. If Hussein were crowned king, they would almost certainly oppose him. Moreover, France, Britain and Russia also had their eyes on Ottoman territory and were already carving up the spoils.

Since December 1915, talks had been underway about how to divide the Ottoman Empire in the event of victory. Sir Mark Sykes and François Georges-Picot were the men in charge of the negotiations. Thirty-six-year-old Sykes was a Conservative Member of Parliament who was regarded as an authority on the Ottoman Empire because of his extensive travels to the region and the publication of his book *The Caliph's Last Heritage: A Short History of the Turkish Empire*. On the other hand, Picot was a former lawyer and consul in Beirut who fiercely advocated French colonial interests in the Middle East.

The two had wildly different objectives, but together they thrashed out a document known as the Sykes–Picot Agreement. In short, it was agreed that in the event of victory, France would control southern Turkey, Syria, the northern Levant and part of northern Iraq; Britain would administer the provinces of Palestine, Jordan and Iraq, while Russia would acquire Istanbul and Armenia. It was also agreed that the holy land of Palestine would be shared among all three. As the director of military intelligence in London quipped, 'It seems to me we are rather in the position of the hunters who divided up the skin of the bear before they had killed it.' Some also felt that the whole agreement was a waste of time as there was little hope of an Arab victory.

For now, Sherif Hussein was unaware of the Sykes–Picot Agreement, and the British intended to keep it that way. Requiring the Arabs to fight the Ottomans, the foreign secretary, Sir Edward Grey, told McMahon: 'The important thing is to give our assurances that will prevent Arabs from being alienated, and I must leave you discretion in the matter as it is urgent and there is not time to discuss an exact formula.'

Rather than outright denying Hussein's demands, McMahon therefore carefully worded his response and appealed to Hussein's vanity. Letters from McMahon to Hussein usually began 'To the excellent and well-born Sayyid, the descendant of the Sharifs, the Crown of the Proud, Scion of Muhammad's Tree and Branch of the Quarayshite Trunk'. Buried within McMahon's overblown and vague passages was a statement that any decisions regarding land allocation would have to be decided at a peace conference following the war.

Storrs was well aware that when meeting with Abdulla, should the subject of the Arabs' independence be brought up, he needed to tread very carefully. As if this wasn't enough, he was also bracing himself to be the bearer of bad news. The British had previously promised Sherif Hussein a flight of fighter aircraft from the Royal Flying Corps to counter Turkish planes. Yet the RFC would not send the planes without British troops. As things currently stood, there was still no prospect of stationing a British brigade in the Hejaz to avoid inflaming tensions with

Muslims in India. The responsibility now fell on Storrs to tell Abdulla that there would be no planes, nor would there be the £10,000 he had requested to pay his beleaguered troops. Storrs knew Abdulla would not take the news well, especially as the Arabs were already facing defeat in Medina, Yenbo and Rabegh. The whole house of cards was about to crash down, and he was in the firing line.

On board the *Lama* and deciding to rest before what promised to be a difficult conversation, Storrs was taking a much-needed nap when he was interrupted by the sound of gunshots. Leaving his quarters to investigate, he found Lawrence on deck shooting at a row of empty bottles with a Browning pistol. Rather than reprimand him, Storrs watched in awe as he shot down bottle after bottle. He knew Lawrence to be a peculiar but highly intelligent character. What he didn't know was he was also a crack shot with a rifle. As always, there was more than met the eye when it came to Private Lawrence.

Soon after, amidst the haze of the fierce heat, white-washed buildings suddenly appeared on the horizon like a mirage. They had finally reached the town of Jidda, an important port on the Red Sea and for so many, the gateway to Mecca.

After disembarking, Lawrence and Storrs, in his trademark white tropical suit, made their way to the British Consulate through the narrow streets of the walled old town. In the blazing heat, their shirts stuck to their skin while they swatted flies from their faces, trying to ignore the traders from the fruit market who were shouting and manically thrusting produce in their direction. Finally spotting a tattered Union Jack barely fluttering outside the consulate, they were grateful to be shown into a shaded room where they could catch their breath and cool down.

The greeting from their host matched the cooler temperature. As the British representative in Jidda, Lieutenant Colonel Cyril Wilson had already had many disagreements with Storrs over their dealings with the Arabs. At the same time, he had no idea what Lawrence was doing there. They were to meet with Abdulla to discuss the progress of the Revolt. As far as he was concerned, a lowly intelligence officer like Lawrence did not need to be involved. In his early forties, Wilson was renowned for being irritable, abrupt and to the point. His mood wasn't helped by the extreme heat and trying to overcome another bout of dysentery. He certainly had little time to waste on sharing small-talk with the likes of Lawrence and Storrs. Indeed, Wilson would later describe Lawrence as 'a bumptious young ass' who 'wants kicking and kicking hard at that'.

Trying to conceal his frustration, Wilson kept to formalities and gave a quick briefing before Emir Abdulla finally arrived. It was the first time Lawrence had seen Abdulla in the flesh, and he was impressed. 'He was short, strong, fair-skinned,' he remembered, 'with a carefully trimmed brown beard, a round smooth face, and full short lips.' Greeting each other politely, Wilson led the party to his stifling office, where Storrs quickly cut to the thrust of their meeting. He informed Abdulla that, contrary to their promises, the British would not now supply the Arabs with any aircraft to fight the Turks. Abdulla paused to consider his response, then took a telegram out of his pocket and unfolded it. He explained that he had just received it from his brother Feisal, who was trying to stop the Ottoman forces from retaking Rabegh. Reading it aloud, Abdulla said that unless the two Turkish aeroplanes were driven off, the Arabs would disperse. He looked up and stared at Storrs, then put the letter back into his pocket. For a moment there was silence, before Lawrence calmly replied, 'Very few Turkish aeroplanes last more than four or five days.'

Abdulla turned to this stranger and looked him up and down. He was almost unworthy of a response. Turning back to Storrs and Wilson, the true power-brokers, he complained that the British should have cut the Hejaz railway to disrupt Turkish supplies and the transport of their troops. Before anyone could speak, Lawrence once more interjected. He told Abdulla this was impossible, as his own father had asked the British not to cut the line so he could use it for his victorious advance into Syria. Moreover, Hussein didn't want to offend the millions of Muslims who had contributed to it. Again, Abdulla tried to counter, but no matter his objections or complaints, Lawrence had an answer to hand. Taking centre stage, he detailed the enemy positions, even outlining precisely where each unit was stationed. Astonished, Abdulla finally turned to Storrs and exclaimed, 'Is this man God, to know everything?'

Lawrence might have impressed Abdulla, but the feeling wasn't mutual. Lawrence had come to Jidda hoping to meet the man who could inspire the Arabs to victory. Abdulla was not that man. 'As our conversation proceeded,' Lawrence wrote, 'I became more and more sure that Abdulla was too balanced, too cool, too humorous to be a prophet, especially the armed prophet whom history assured me was the successful type in such circumstances.'

Although Lawrence did not believe that Abdulla was the man who could lead the Revolt, he still held out hope that one of his brothers might. He therefore asked Abdulla if he might venture inland to assess the situation at Rabegh himself and, in doing so, meet his brothers, Emir Ali and Emir Feisal. This was not, however, a simple request.

Any Europeans or Christians found within the Hejaz took their lives into their own hands. Such was the danger that on Storrs's first trip to the region in 1914, he was offered the severed heads of seven Germans. The fact that Lawrence was British and technically an ally did not matter.

I faced a similar issue in Dhofar when I was expected to hunt down the adoo in the vast Hajar mountain range. On arrival, I was told that this interior plateau had not been seen by European eyes until 1835, when two British lieutenants had been lucky to escape with their lives from the fierce mountain tribesmen. A handful of others had since travelled within the interior, but it was always risky. Inhabitated by the fanatical Ibadhi sect, these plateau Omanis were liable to execute trespassing infidels without qualms: nor did they pay much heed to the edicts of their coast-bound Sultan. Even as late as 1950, Wilfred Thesiger, the greatest of European travellers in Arabia, was unable to enter inner Oman, such was the danger to his life. Although things had somewhat improved when I arrived in 1968, I was told that, given half a chance, the tribes were still likely to slit a white officer's throat. Matters weren't improved when the maps I was provided with contained several question marks where villages should be located. The areas had never been mapped before, much less visited by a British officer.

This filled me with trepidation, but Lawrence was unconcerned by the dangers involved. Nevertheless, he still needed permission to proceed. Abdulla therefore called his father in Mecca to outline the situation. The sherif initially refused to give the trip his blessing until Storrs informed him that only after a British officer had personally assessed the situation at Rabegh might he then be able to provide more reinforcements. This finally broke the impasse.

Although Hussein reluctantly gave Lawrence his blessing, no one thought to ask for permission from Cairo. Instead, Lawrence simply sent a telegram to Clayton saying 'Meeting today: Wilson, Storrs, Sharif Abdulla, Aziz el-Masri [Chief of Staff of the Arab regular army], myself. Nobody knows real situation Rabegh so much time wasted. Aziz el-Masri going Rabegh with me tomorrow.'

On this journey, he hoped to finally meet the man who would 'set the desert on fire'.

3

Travelling on an old steamer, Lawrence and Storrs soon arrived in Rabegh, an ancient Hejazi town of mud huts on the eastern coast of the Red Sea. Strategically it was an important port for both the Arabs and the Ottomans. Not only was it relatively close to Mecca and Medina, but its railway station connected it to Damascus. Whoever controlled the port also had easy access to much-needed supplies for their forces. It was therefore crucial that the Arabs repelled any Ottoman advance if they were to have any chance of victory.

After arriving at the shimmering harbour, Lawrence and Storrs boarded a Royal Indian Marine ship called the *Northbrook*. In a tented enclosure on deck, they found Emir Ali, the Sherif's oldest son, waiting to greet them. Ali was only thirty-seven, but owing to a bout of tuberculosis, Lawrence recalled that his frailness and soft voice made him appear 'a little old already'.

Following polite introductions, Lawrence asked Ali about the current situation. Ali explained that it wasn't good. His brother Feisal was with the bulk of the Arab army in the desert, about 100 miles to the north-east, trying to protect the route to the port. But reports indicated that Turkish reinforcements would soon arrive, with significantly more numbers than the Arabs, and far superior firepower. The only way to prevent them defeating Feisal and taking Rabegh, Ali said, was for the British to supply them with modern weapons and more gold, which might help persuade other Arab tribes to join the struggle. If they did not, he believed that the Arabs would be massacred and Rabegh lost for good.

Over three days of discussions, Lawrence 'took a great fancy' to Ali. He was intelligent, well mannered, and made an excellent host. But he was not what Lawrence was looking for. Specifically, he lacked the 'force of character' and ambition to lead the Revolt. Lawrence also met with Ali's half-brother Zeid during his stay and reached a similar conclusion. Zeid was still only nineteen, and while Lawrence could see he 'would be a decided man when he had found himself', he did not yet have the experience or gravitas to be a leader of men. Lawrence had now met three of Sherif Hussein's four sons and had found them all unsuitable. Feisal was his last hope.

In preparing to meet with Feisal in the desert, Ali graciously offered Lawrence his own 'splendid riding camel' for the journey. The camel is the ultimate mode of desert transport. Not only is it able to travel great distances in blistering temperatures, as it doesn't even raise a sweat until its body reaches 104 degrees Fahrenheit, it can also conserve water for days on end, while acting as a mobile milk bar for any rider long after his water has run out. I recall one of my men telling me, 'God's greatest gift to man is surely the camel.' While I appreciated this, the reconnaissance platoon I commanded in Oman was no longer camel-borne but used Land Rovers instead. Yet this was a luxury we would soon have to do without.

To guide and protect Lawrence, Ali supplied him with Tafas, a reliable tribesman, along with Tafas's son Abdulla. It was an Arab belief that those charged with protecting a stranger must do so with their lives. However, they would have their work cut out to protect a Christian in the wilds of the Hejaz desert. With this in mind, Ali insisted that Lawrence leave under cover of darkness so that no one would see an Englishman riding into the interior. If word got out, he might be followed and murdered.

Ali also gave Lawrence an Arab headcloth (the 'kufiya') and cloak to help disguise himself. Unlike other British officers, Lawrence was quite used to wearing Arab dress. During his archaeology days in the desert, he had often worn a kufiya and learned it would protect his face from the fierce sun and sandstorms. Despite this, not all British officers were as amenable to wearing Arab dress. When Wilson was advised to wear such items by Sherif Hussein, he commented in a letter, 'I absolutely refuse to disguise myself as an Arab . . . If I'm scuppered, I propose to be scuppered in my own uniform.'

Finally, Ali warned Lawrence against talking to anyone he might meet along the way. Although Lawrence could speak Arabic, his accent would still sound unusual. If anyone became suspicious and looked closer, it wouldn't take them long to see his blond hair and blue eyes and mark him as a European. Even with Arab guides, this might invite hostility, if not death.

As the sun set in a date palm grove on the outskirts of

the town, it was finally time to depart. Saying goodbye to Ali and thanking him for his help, Lawrence awkwardly mounted his camel and followed Tafas and his son into the desert.

Lawrence might have been aware of many of the dangers ahead, but two years of desk work in Cairo had not prepared him for riding a camel across the rough desert landscape. Even during his previous visits to the Middle East, he had rarely ridden a camel and was somewhat of an amateur. Bouncing up and down in the saddle, he tried to avoid falling off, but his back soon ached, and he developed saddle sores between his legs.

The weather that first day also proved more of a challenge than he had anticipated. It was clear it would be hot, with temperatures rising to 120 degrees and above in the ferocious midday sun. What Lawrence hadn't reckoned with was the sand reflecting the sun like a mirror directly into his face. This made it feel like he was being held against an oven, and burned his fair skin. He also had to squint his eyes in the blinding glare, and could not see where he was going. In such conditions, it was little wonder that all the thorn trees he passed were dead, burned, and black.

Grimacing in the heat, there was suddenly a mighty roar like a tidal wave, whipping up sand particles and filling his mouth, ears, and nostrils. Lawrence tried to shield his eyes in the blurred yellow gloom of a sandstorm, unable to see, feeling as if splinters were being thrown into his face. All the while, he clung desperately to the reins of his camel, fearing being lost in the storm if he was to fall off. It was little wonder that this assault on his senses left him exhausted. He was so tired that at one point he dozed off and only woke when he found himself slipping sideways, quickly grabbing the saddle post to avoid crashing to the ground.

With the temperature now soaring to 125 degrees, Lawrence became severely dehydrated. To his horror, Tafas said they were not carrying any food or water. By apparent way of explanation, he told Lawrence that the journey to the first well was only sixty miles. This was a comparatively short distance for an Arab of the desert but an eternity for a relative novice like Lawrence.

Finally, at around midnight, Tafas could see that Lawrence could continue no more. Calling a halt, he allowed Lawrence to sleep in a hollow in the warm sand for a few hours. Yet until they reached a well, there was still no water. As the darkness softened with the haze of the orange sun, Tafas woke Lawrence so that they could travel in the lower morning temperatures. Thankfully, the well was not far away. After climbing the length of a great field of lava, they finally reached it in the early morning. As they approached on their camels, a gaggle of Bedouin tribesmen stared at them menacingly from the remains of a stone hut. Not wishing to betray themselves, Lawrence rested in the shade while Abdulla climbed into the well and brought up water in a goatskin.

Eagerly gulping down the cold water and splashing it over his face, Lawrence slipped back into his saddle unnoticed and continued following Tafas and Abdulla to Feisal's desert camp. Passing through a barren black landscape, which gradually morphed into fine white sand, Lawrence saw smoke on the horizon. Tafas told him it was the village of Bir el-Sheikh, where they would stop to rest.

Upon reaching the tiny cluster of 'miserable' rock huts, Tafas purchased some flour and immediately lit a fire. Lawrence watched as he mixed the flour with water, patted and pulled at the wet dough, then spread it into a disk about 'two inches thick and six inches across'. Placing it within the fire until it was golden and crisp, Tafas took it out, wiped the cinders away, then served the warm bread to Lawrence and Abdulla.

Lawrence was grateful for a delicacy of the desert and the rest, but an hour later they were on the move again. By now, Tafas had become more talkative. Speaking tentatively about the Revolt, he revealed the existence of a small village of date farmers loyal to the Turks, only a few hours from Rabegh. No one had previously thought to mention this, but Lawrence recognised it was crucial information. From that position, the Turks could attack the flank of Feisal's army and then march south, going from well to well to first isolate Rabegh and then move on Mecca. The Arabs had pleaded with the British to place a brigade in Rabegh. Yet even if one was provided, Lawrence now saw that a single British brigade could not hold the twenty-mile front needed to deny the Ottomans access to the wells. The journey into the desert was worth it for this information alone. Lawrence could only imagine what other vital intelligence he might gather on his adventure.

Continuing on through the moonlit night and into the glare of day, they passed a 'garrulous old man' on a camel.

Lawrence kept his head down and said little, but in a supposed act of friendship, the old man offered them some of his 'unleavened dough cake'. Generosity is the rule of the desert, and I often recall those with nothing, close to starvation, offering us the last of their milk or meat. You might never be able to return their favour, for you might not see them again, but each person is expected to follow this example in turn.

Despite the old man's generosity, Lawrence suspected he was in the pay of the Turks and kept talk to a minimum. But during their brief conversation, the man revealed that Feisal 'had been beaten out of Kheif in the head of the Wadi Safra' with some casualties, and had fallen back on Hamra. This was not good news.

Leaving the old man behind, they rode over sand-rippled dunes like waves on the ocean, before stopping at the village of Wasta for fresh dates and bread. When the worst of the heat had passed, they set off on the final stage of their journey. By now, Lawrence was tiring badly, and his saddle sores had become red raw and bloody, not helped by his salty sweat seeping into the wounds. He was therefore relieved to see a buzz of activity in the distance.

Riding closer, they heard the sound of baying camels and smelt a waft of excrement. Then they saw a mass of tents, with Arabs moving to and fro or sheltering from the sun. At last they had reached Feisal's camp.

Dismounting, they held their camels by the reins as Tafas led Lawrence to a small house on the hillside. There they found the entrance blocked by a black slave wielding a sword, which glinted menacingly in the sunlight. Explaining their purpose, the slave made way so that Tafas and Lawrence could enter a second, inner courtyard. Suddenly Lawrence saw, 'standing framed between the posts of a black doorway, a white figure waiting tensely for me'. It was Feisal.

Tentatively entering a small dark room, Lawrence silently passed a crowd of people sitting on a carpet on the floor. He was very much aware that all eyes were on him. For many, he was the first British officer they had encountered, let alone one wearing Arab dress. He might as well have come from the moon. Making his way to the front, he sat before Feisal and adjusted his eyes to the dim light. Finally, Lawrence could make him out for the first time. He was 'almost regal in appearance . . . very tall and pillar like, very slender, dressed in long white silk robes and a brown headcloth bound with a brilliant scarlet and gold cord. His eyelids were drooped, and his close black beard and colourless face were like a mask against the strange still watchfulness of his body. His hands were loosely crossed in front of him on his dagger.' Lawrence also couldn't help but notice that he looked similar to one of his heroes, Richard I.

Feisal smiled and gestured around the room. 'And do you like our place here in Wadi Safra?' he asked.

After a pause, Lawrence replied, 'Well, but it is far from Damascus.'

This response fell 'like a sword into their midst'. All those in the room held their breath, waiting to see if Feisal took offence. Damascus was the Arabs' ultimate physical and spiritual goal. As the seat of the Umayyad Caliphate, the first Arab-led Islamic empire that ruled over much of the Middle East and North Africa in the seventh and eighth centuries, it carried huge historical significance. At the same time, it remained a major cultural and religious centre for all Arabs. If the Arabs of the Hejaz were victorious over the Turks, Damascus would serve as the capital of their grand new Arab state, of which Sherif Hussein would be crowned king. With all of this in mind, Lawrence was, in effect, saying to Feisal that the efforts of the Arab Revolt thus far had left them well short of their dream.

Thankfully, Feisal merely smiled at the comment. 'Praise be to God,' he replied. 'There are Turks nearer us than that.' Lawrence smiled in return. It was just the answer he hoped to hear.

For the next two days, Lawrence and Feisal discussed the many issues facing the Revolt. While the Turks were gathering en masse to isolate Rabegh and advance on Mecca, Feisal did not appear overly concerned. Like his brother Ali, he claimed that if the British could supply better weapons, he could stop the Turks in their tracks. When up against the Turks' modern German field-guns and howitzers, the Arabs had little chance with their antiquated shotguns. I know just how they felt. In Oman, I was shocked to find that despite the importance of our mission, we were expected to fight with bolt action .303 rifles, which had to be cocked after each shot. This dampened my men's morale, especially as we were up against huge new guns from China and the most modern weapons the Soviets could supply. These included Shpagin guns, which boasted 12.7mm bullets, some with high-explosive heads or armour piercers that could go through Sydney Harbour Bridge.

Between their discussions, Lawrence took time to speak to Feisal's officers. He found the Arab fighters were particularly horrified by the inhumanity of the Turks. When one of the local tribes had offered to surrender 'if their villages were spared', the Turks proceeded to rape the women and children in front of the men before setting fire to their houses and throwing their still-alive bodies into the flames. This act of great cruelty ensured the message of the Turks' savage brutality was spread far and wide. If any Arabs should betray the Turks, this was the punishment that would rain down upon them. Little wonder it left many Arabs reluctant to fight, especially as the Turks were far more numerous, had more arms and received military training.

The Marxist rebels in Oman did something similar. They had a carefully trained execution squad, the Idaara, led by a scar-faced Dhofari called Salim Amr. His work was not only to eliminate class enemies but to do so in such a fashion that each execution had a profound psychological effect. Why shoot a man behind a rock when he can be thrown over a cliff before his fellow villagers. And why make it an isolated incident when you can throw villagers over the cliff at hourly intervals until the survivors agree to support your cause. When people heard of these executions, they often agreed to support the Dhofar Liberation Front without further persuasion. I must admit, it also rattled me.

During Lawrence's time at the camp, it was obvious that the cobbled-together Arab tribes would be no match in any fixed attack on a well-trained military force like the Ottomans. Having inferior weapons was a significant issue, but virtually none of these men had been taught to fight as a unit. And those that had tried their best to teach them often found it impossible. One of Feisal's most trusted officers, Maulud el-Mukhlus, who had previously served with the Turks and had twice been 'degraded' for his pro-Arab views, told Lawrence that discipline was a major issue. The men only seemed to listen to the instructions of their own tribal leaders, and even then they pretty much did as they pleased. Lawrence was also horrified to hear stories of many men leaving the camp to return to their villages to feed their camels or goats. In return, they might send back a son or a brother with a rifle to take his place, but this often left the Arabs with uncertain numbers and made it impossible to prepare. In Oman, we particularly struggled during the date season, as many soldiers took leave to help their families harvest their only source of income for the year. I also found superstition did not help matters. If men felt an evil spirit haunted an area, they refused to go any further. On one occasion while on patrol, two of my men fell to the floor, shrieking and screaming that their souls had been stolen. While one of them quickly recovered, the other was sent to hospital, never to return.

On the face of it, things looked bleak, but Lawrence's primary purpose in coming all this way was to appraise Feisal. Could he be the man the British could trust to lead the Arabs to victory? He certainly spoke a good game, but Lawrence wanted to know more about his actions on the battlefield. During his talks with some of the officers, Lawrence was told that while under heavy fire from the Turks, Feisal had ridden up and down the Arab line, in full sight of the Turks, and urged his men to stay and fight. In response, not one Arab fled. Lawrence was impressed. This was a true sign of courage and leadership in the white heat of battle. A keen student of Napoleon, it reminded him of the French general's actions at Rivoli in 1797, where he had inspired his fleeing soldiers by grabbing a flag and waving it in the face of enemy fire. It nearly cost him his life, but the act of bravery immediately boosted the morale of his men, who were inspired to fight on and overcome a numerically superior enemy.

Lawrence saw that Feisal possessed many other vital qualities. He seemed to carry a natural magnetism and charisma, making him 'the idol of his followers'. The men could tell that he was the real deal and were all prepared to fight alongside him to the death. Lawrence appreciated that this was a rare attribute. It was something you could not fake.

At last, Lawrence felt a rush of optimism and claimed that he 'had found the man whom I had come to Arabia to seek'. Here was a man behind whom the many different (and often mutually hostile) Arab tribes might unite, a man with all the attributes of a leader, and, last but not least, one who would satisfy the British that their money was being wisely spent. In Feisal he found everything he had been searching for politically and personally. Both men were dreamers, but both also possessed the rare capacity to make their dreams come true.

However, Lawrence realised that if the Arabs were to succeed under Feisal's leadership, they still required far more support from the British. Although he was only a temporary second lieutenant and had no authority to make any promises, he recklessly told Feisal the British would supply him with more artillery, light machine guns, and gold.

Soon after, he left the camp, promising to return laden with goods, having no idea if he could deliver such promises. If he failed, he knew trust in the British would collapse, and the Arabs would be left at the mercy of the Turks. His return to Cairo could therefore make or break the Revolt for good.

4

After travelling through the desert, now with an escort of fourteen tribesmen, Lawrence finally reached the port of Yenbo, a little town with a long seafront of whitewashed houses. It would, however, be four days until the Royal Navy arrived to return him to Jidda. As Yenbo was known to contain pro-Turkish elements, Lawrence had to conceal his identity carefully. Until the Navy arrived, he was forced to hide in the home of one of Feisal's supporters.

Rarely venturing out, Lawrence instead made good use of his time. Feverishly writing a 17,000-word report, he forensically described the situation at Feisal's camp and what was required to help the Arabs. He also wrote down snippets of other invaluable information, such as the position of the wells and where the Turks could outflank the Arab or British forces.

At last, on 1 November, Captain William 'Ginger' Boyle and HMS *Suva* arrived to transport Lawrence to Jidda. There, anchored in the shimmering harbour, was HMS *Euryalus*. Better still, the commander-in-chief of the Egyptian Squadron, Vice-Admiral Sir Rosslyn Wemyss, was on board. After introducing himself to the monocle-wearing admiral, Lawrence informed Wemyss of his meeting with Feisal and what he had observed, particularly highlighting the need for more weapons. As his parrot cawed 'Damn the Kaiser! Damn the Kaiser!' in the background, Wemyss realised this was the first report of a British officer from the battlefield. Recognising its vital importance, he told Lawrence that he should accompany him to Port Sudan to meet with Sir Reginald Wingate, the governor-general of the Sudan and 'sirdar' of the Egyptian army at Khartoum.

The chance to speak directly with a man like Wingate seemed a great opportunity. However, Wingate didn't suffer fools. Barrel-chested, with a waxed moustache that flicked out at both ends like spears, he was renowned for his ferocious quick temper. He also had significant experience of desert warfare in Sudan and Ethiopia. An amateur soldier such as Lawrence, who had never seen any action, would be treading a fine line in making recommendations to such a man. Luckily for him, Wingate was an ardent supporter of the Arab Revolt, and read Lawrence's report with much interest. He was particularly interested in his proposal that the Arabs didn't need thousands of British soldiers to prop them up. At the time, manpower was already stretched to the limit, as wave upon wave of British soldiers were slaughtered on the Western Front. On the first day of the Battle of the Somme alone, there were over 60,000 casualties. Even if it had not been politically unpalatable to place British soldiers in the Hejaz, there was constant pressure to send more and more men to the grinder in France. Knowing this, Lawrence suggested that all that was required to help the Arabs were a few Arabic-speaking British technical advisers, along with explosives and a modest number of modern weapons.

Wingate glanced up from the report and took in the diminutive young lieutenant before him. Lawrence confidently met his stare. Wingate was impressed. This was a man who certainly seemed to know what he was talking about and had realistic expectations.

With Wingate promising to do all that he could, another event helped to further Lawrence's cause. While in Khartoum, Sir Henry McMahon was recalled from Cairo to Britain. Wingate was subsequently informed that he was to replace him as British high commissioner in Egypt. Not only did Wingate like and trust Lawrence, as well as support the Revolt, he was now the man in supreme control of Egypt. Lawrence had been virtually sidelined when he left Cairo just a few weeks before. Now he could return with the high commissioner on his side, feeling confident that all the support he had offered Feisal might soon be forthcoming. But things were not as easy as he hoped.

Back in Cairo, word had spread that the Turks were about to attack Rabegh and recapture Mecca. This would surely end the Arab Revolt before Lawrence had even had a chance to send reinforcements to Feisal. Yet Lawrence wasn't convinced that an attack was imminent. Indeed, he attributed much of the fearmongering to Colonel Edouard Brémond, the grey-bearded head of the French military mission. Lawrence was well aware that the French were pushing for their North African Muslim soldiers to be based in Rabegh to guard their proposed territory. It therefore suited them to make the situation sound more desperate than it actually was. For now, the British were anxious to keep the French out of what they regarded as a

British sphere of interest. If French soldiers were to capture any towns or regions, getting them to relinquish their grip would be very difficult.

Having just returned from meeting Feisal in the Hejaz, Lawrence was in a more informed position than most. He told General Clayton, his boss at the Arab Bureau, that while the Turks were planning to attack Rabegh, it was by no means imminent. Clayton ordered Lawrence to write a robust memorandum, dismissing Brémond's claims and stating that British or French troops were not required to repel the Turks so long as Feisal and his army were urgently given the support he had requested.

Within the hour, Lawrence handed the report to Clayton, who immediately cabled it to the office of the Chief of the Imperial General Staff (CIGS) in London. Although Lawrence was just a second lieutenant in Cairo, his report turned some heads, particularly as he was the only officer who had been in the desert to ascertain the actual situation. Even the French couldn't argue with that. It also helped that it was just what the CIGS wanted to hear. In fact, they were so impressed that they wanted Lawrence to play a more central role. Rather than remain stuck behind a desk in Cairo, they suggested that he be sent to Rabegh as a temporary adviser 'to train Arab bands'. In addition, he would serve as a liaison officer to Feisal until he was relieved by Colonel Stewart Newcombe, who Lawrence knew from his days surveying the Sinai.

This wasn't quite what Lawrence had in mind. While he quickly gave his opinion on the Arab Revolt and was happy to meet with Feisal, he had no wish to be on the front line.

'I urged my complete unfitness for the job,' he wrote, adding, 'I hate responsibility . . . I was unlike a soldier: hated soldiering.' Against his protests, Clayton informed him that it might take weeks, if not months, for Newcombe to arrive, by which stage the Revolt might well be over. In the circumstances, he was the only man for the job.

Lawrence had spent the last two years freely giving his opinions on the status of the Arab Revolt. Now he had to prove he wasn't all mouth, just as the Turkish forces were gearing up for an almighty assault to knock the Arabs out of the war once and for all.

5

'Well, here you are, Ranulph,' my commander said, introducing me. 'These are your trusty men.'

The atmosphere hung heavy as a group of Arabs stared back at me. They looked a ragtag bunch, unshaven, grimy, their uniforms appearing as if they had been thrown together from a jumble sale. I despaired. Like Lawrence, I was now expected to train and lead them to victory against a far superior enemy. As was the case in the Hejaz, the future of Oman depended on it. Yet, while Lawrence was vastly experienced in the language, culture, and traditions of Arabs, I was a total novice.

'This is your new Recce Sahb,' the commander said to the men, as my shirt and the crotch of my trousers became damp with sweat. There was no response, not even a hint of acknowledgement. If anything, they looked at me with disdain. I later found out that a British officer had just been sent home after accidentally blowing the mess-boy's head off when cleaning his rifle. Unsurprisingly, this led to some ill-feeling towards us in the camp, but it was nothing like the hate they had for each other.

I had been told that my Recce Platoon would consist of native Omanis and Baluchi mercenaries. The latter might have been Muslims like the Omanis, but they spoke a dialect of Urdu, not Arabic, and had very different cultures and beliefs. I barely spoke Arabic, and none of them spoke English.

'In just six months, you'll be let loose in Dhofar to fight the Marxists,' the commander continued. 'Before then, your new sahb will train you and make sure you are prepared.' Staring at their sullen, disinterested faces, I knew it would be suicide to go anywhere near adoo territory with this bunch in their present state. The commander looked at me to say something. In response, I uttered one of the few Arabic phrases I knew: 'Inshallah' – 'God willing.' This was a phrase I would return to time and again when I didn't know the answer.

The thought of giving these men articulate and detailed orders made me shiver. My main worry was a total lack of knowledge of my prospective job. I was already concerned that I would prove inadequate with the Arabs. This feeling of inadequacy was no doubt something Lawrence also shared as he made his way back to the Hejaz. It was all very well talking from behind a desk or imagining great adventures, but things are suddenly different when a group of hostile men, whom you are meant to be leading, glare at you with contempt.

On 2 December 1916, Lawrence returned to Yenbo, the key strategic port on the Red Sea coast. Although he was not overly enthused, his return coincided with all his promises to Feisal being fulfilled, along with the arrival of explosive expert, Major H. G. Garland.

Before the war, Garland had worked as a metallurgist, cleaning and preserving ancient Egyptian artefacts. Now he had somehow pivoted to become the British explosives expert in the Middle East, a position he held with relish. He had been sent to Yenbo to teach Lawrence and the Arabs how to use explosives to damage the railway. It was hoped that disrupting Turkish supplies to Medina would slow the Turks down, if not disable them altogether. Therefore, Garland's lessons focused on blowing up culverts and bridges, while he urged Lawrence to focus more on destroying curved rails, as these were in short supply and harder for the Turks to replace. He also suggested using a hammer to smash the screws holding the damaged rails together, which again would give the Turks great difficulty trying to remove them. But while destroying the rail track was crucial, a locomotive was the best target of all. These were almost impossible to replace as they had been imported from Europe before the war. The only way replacements could now be delivered to the Middle East was via the Mediterranean, which the British had since blockaded.

Thanks to Lawrence, a flight of four RFC aircraft had also arrived in Rabegh. Crucially, these were under the command of an officer who spoke Arabic and were guarded by 300 Egyptian soldiers. While the RFC flight would only carry out aerial surveillance, their presence was still a significant boost to the Arabs. Lawrence was also delighted to find that General Wingate had managed to forward whatever light artillery he could get his hands on. Most of it was antiquated, but it was still better than nothing.

Relieved to see his reckless promises were being kept, Lawrence rode with a guide to Wadi Yenbo to meet once more with Feisal. Arriving in the dead of night, Lawrence found the camp quiet. After a recent downpour, scores of wet men, their cloaks wrapped around them, were huddled around tiny fires or trying to sleep next to the warmth of their camels in the mud. From the downbeat mood and relative silence, it was clear that everyone was tired and fed up. When Lawrence finally located Feisal's tent, he saw a series of Arab tribal leaders impatiently waiting outside to speak to him, all with various complaints. Passing them by, Lawrence entered the tent and found Feisal sitting on a carpet, a slave holding a lantern above his head, as his secretary read a report to him. Lawrence saw that whatever was being read clearly concerned Feisal. Yet upon seeing Lawrence, he offered him a smile. He had come just in time.

Feisal explained that they had moved camp after the Ottomans had outflanked his army, with the Turks now ready to march on Rabegh and Mecca, and to take the area around Hamra with its precious wells. In the circumstances, Feisal had thought it best to cut his losses and retreat far enough so that he could fall back on Yenbo if the Turks continued to attack. Lawrence found all of this extremely concerning. Not only was it a disaster for the Arabs, but he had staked his reputation by telling Wingate, Murray, Clayton, and the CIGS in London that no attack by the Turks was imminent. Now it seemed that Colonel Brémond had been right. He looked like a fool.

Despite this, Feisal seemed in good spirits. He was confident that with Lawrence now by his side, along with British explosives, advisers, aircraft, and gold, things would soon improve. Lawrence marvelled at his optimism. He failed to see much reason for cheer. Things looked dire.

After a restless, cold night, with a wet mist filling the wadi, Feisal decided to move his army onto higher, drier ground. As the men mounted their camels and formed in two wings in the morning light, great drums were beaten, signalling a war-like march. Riding down the wide central alley, Feisal was followed by flag-bearers, the inmates of his household, and 800 of his bodyguard. Riding alongside Feisal, Lawrence thought that the rabble at last resembled some sort of army, in appearance anyway.

Less than forty miles from Yenbo, Feisal called a stop. This would now serve as their new camp. With camels baying and tribesmen bickering, the Arabs erected their tents while Feisal positioned himself on a hill above them.

Although the Arabs had suffered another humiliating retreat, Lawrence was beginning to feel more optimistic. He might have been wrong about the Turkish advance, but the more time he spent with Feisal, the more he became convinced that his initial judgement about him had been correct. He already knew that Feisal's own men respected him, but he found that other tribes also appreciated his diplomacy and good nature. 'I never saw an Arab leave him dissatisfied or hurt,' Lawrence wrote, '– a tribute to his tact and to his memory; for he seemed never to halt for a loss of fact, nor to stumble over a relationship.' If the Arab tribes were to unite as one fighting unit, then Lawrence remained confident that Feisal was the man who could bring them together.

Lawrence also found Feisal thoughtful and generous.

As a gift, he presented Lawrence with white, gold-threaded robes that made him stand out from the other tribesmen, who typically wore brownish robes. This also indicated his esteemed status within the camp. It seemed he took more care wearing these robes than of his British uniform in Cairo, which was often creased and missing items. He was undoubtedly aware that just by wearing them, he was not only ingratiating himself to the Arabs but also marking his authority. In time, they would become Lawrence's trademark.

Feisal also gave Lawrence a British short-barrel Lee-Enfield rifle. He stared at it, bemused. This was the standard .303-caliber weapon of the British Army, and he had no idea why an Arab prince should wish to gift it to him. Feisal was undoubtedly aware that these weren't in short supply for a British officer. However, this particular rifle had a unique history. It had initially been issued to a soldier with the Essex Regiment, before being captured at Gallipoli by the Turks, where it was gifted to Enver Pasha himself. After the receiver was inscribed in Arabic with 'Part of our booty in the battles for the Dardanelles', Enver Pasha in turn gave the weapon to Sherif Hussein as a present, although it was also a tactful reminder of Turkey's victory over the British. At the outbreak of the Revolt, Hussein passed the rifle to Feisal, and now it was being symbolically passed to Lawrence, a British officer, to kill the Turks in revenge. Appreciating the significance of this, Lawrence carved his initials into the stock and then planned to cut a notch above the magazine for each Turk that he killed.

After settling into life at camp, where mornings always began with a call to prayer by the army iman, word soon reached Feisal that a Turkish column had surprised his half-brother Zeid, along with his 800 tribesmen. Having abandoned much of their baggage and equipment, they were now in full retreat to Yenbo. With no opposition to block their way, the Turks were also moving rapidly on Feisal's position.

There was no time to waste. Lawrence immediately sent a messenger to Yenbo and asked the RFC to make a reconnaissance flight to determine where the Turks were located and in what strength. He also requested Captain Boyle to urgently send naval support. Following this, Lawrence decided that he should also return to Yenbo to help oversee the 'amphibious defence of the port' and to speak to Zeid.

Riding on a 'magnificent bay camel', with an escort provided by Feisal, Lawrence completed the journey in just six hours and was ready to see Zeid the following morning. What he heard left him astonished and dismayed. The Turks had been able to ambush Zeid's camp after he had neglected to organise any night patrols. But there was worse news still to come. A message arrived that the Turks were now engaging with Feisal and his army and had also sent them fleeing to Yenbo.

Although they had been overwhelmed by the Turks, matters weren't helped by the Juheina tribe, on Feisal's left flank, leaving the battlefield. 'It looked like treachery and a real defection of the tribes,' Lawrence remembered. Many of the British guns that had been supplied also failed to fire owing to damp shell fuses. In short, it had been a disaster.

Lawrence watched as Feisal and his 2,000 ragged troops descended on the port, the Turks in hot pursuit. He feared the Arab Revolt was about to meet its end and, along with it, his reputation. The Turks taking a key port like Yenbo would be a catastrophe. Worse still, most of the Arab fighting forces were now bottled up there. In just one stroke, the Turks could wipe out the Revolt once and for all and concentrate their efforts on the war in Europe.

Convening at a house, Lawrence and Feisal were desperately trying to work out some sort of defence when their meeting was suddenly interrupted by one of the leading members of the fleeing Juheina tribe. While it was feared that the tribe had defected, the man explained that they had only momentarily left the battlefield to 'make ourselves a cup of coffee' and had returned to fight. They hadn't realised that their break in fighting had caused Feisal's forces to be overwhelmed. It was this kind of disorganisation that was costing the Arab Revolt dear.

Rather than reprimand the man, Feisal gave the Juheina a chance to redeem themselves. Ordering them to advance on the Turks and harass their line of communication with sniper fire, he hoped this might slow their advance on Yenbo and buy them some time.

Meanwhile, Lawrence desperately tried to come up with a strategy. Like myself, Lawrence had never seen any action before and had also received no military training. Later, he admitted to Liddell Hart that he 'was not an instinctive soldier, automatic with intuitions and happy ideas'. He had, however, read countless military books and studied castles and fortifications. This meant that when he took a decision, 'it was after studying (or doing my best to study) every relevant – and many an irrelevant – factor. Geography, tribal structure, religion, social customs, language, appetites, standards – all were at my finger-ends. The enemy I knew almost like my own side.' He just had to pray that, in this instance, it would be enough.

Putting all these qualities to good use, Lawrence looked out over Yenbo and saw that it was built on a coral reef that rose twenty feet above sea level. He realised that, with the port surrounded by water, the Turks could only reach Yenbo by crossing salt flats beneath the reef. If the Arabs targeted all their artillery and machine-gun fire on the flats and fortified the town, they might be able to force them back.

Lawrence and the Arabs quickly got to work. Reinforcing the town's existing walls, they packed them with earth and covered them in barbed wire, while Egyptian gunners and naval machine-gun parties were placed at crucial defensive points. Boyle arrived in the nick of time, bringing with him five naval ships which he anchored close inshore. They included HMS *M31*, whose 6-inch guns were directed towards the salt flats.

After so much noise and excitement, reports reached Feisal that the Turks were now just three miles away and an attack was imminent. As the sun went down, the ships turned on their searchlights and aimed them at the vast salt flats. If the Turks were to approach, they would at least see them coming. Still, no one dared to sleep. At any moment, fighting could erupt, and the town and the entire region could be lost. In one swoop, the Turks could defeat the Arabs and return their focus to helping their German allies in Europe. It was a critical moment for the Arabs, the French and the British. And Lawrence was well aware that, if the Arabs should fall, he would receive a large share of the blame.

Yet as the hours passed and the sun began to rise, no attack came. Some proclaimed it was a miracle, but Lawrence knew better. On seeing the brightly lit salt flats, the commander of the Turkish advance had hesitated. He recognised that not only would the Turks be seen approaching Yenbo, but the Arabs also held the high ground, with artillery and naval guns ready to pick them off. Fearing a rout, the Turks decided to retreat.

Lawrence's strategy had worked. Somehow, the Arabs had held firm without a shot being fired. Better still, Feisal's army had survived to fight another day. Lawrence would later write that the Turks had missed their opportunity to wipe them out, and it 'had cost them the war'.

For now, the Arab army was saved, but they remained in a precarious situation. The Turks still outnumbered them, and this had only been a strategic retreat. They would certainly return, and so far the Arabs had failed to defeat them in any head-on battle, certainly not without the help of the British Navy. Things clearly could not continue as they had. Something had to change, and fast.

6

While Lawrence contemplated the next stage of the Arab Revolt, the war back home took a new direction. After a nervous breakdown and a collapse of confidence in him, Herbert Asquith stepped down as prime minister. His rival, David Lloyd George, subsequently took his place. Lloyd George wasted little time in setting his sights on the Ottomans, knowing that losing a key ally would not only be a blow to Germany but would also provide many opportunities for Britain in the Middle East. As far as possible, the Arabs were to be given Britain's full support.

This came at the perfect time for Lawrence, who was now advising the Arabs on their next move. With the Royal Navy providing assistance, Lawrence wanted Feisal's forces to head north and attempt to take the port of Wejh. This would not only allow the Arabs to cut off another vital supply line to the Turks but also extend their flank. Most important of all, having a base in the north would be a significant move towards Damascus and the huge political prize that Syria represented.

To screen their advance and to keep the Turks occupied, he wanted Abdulla and his forces to head fifty miles north and base themselves at Wadi Ais, which boasted numerous wells. With this ready water source, they could continually attack the railway line to Medina, cutting off the Turks' supplies in the process. He also wanted Feisal's brother Ali to make a feint attack towards Medina, so that the Turks would concentrate their forces to defend it rather than strike out in an attempt to take Rabegh or Mecca.

Reaching Wejh itself was an enormous gamble. The march was over 200 miles, and there would be few reliable wells or springs along the way. Unless they took Wejh, the Arabs would be in danger of dying of thirst. Moreover, as they moved north they needed to inspire local tribes to join them if they were to have the manpower to take the port. But this was far from certain. Many of the tribal feuds went back decades, if not centuries. Lawrence also knew that while Feisal possessed the charm and respect to persuade some of these tribes to join them, others needed a more alluring incentive than just the distant prospect of a victory against the Turks. Sacks of British gold would, therefore, be required to help to pave the way. Even this offered no guarantees, as I found to my cost.

Following my awkward first meeting with the Recce Platoon, I decided we urgently needed more men before we commenced training. Not only were there only fifteen men available to me, most seemed even less prepared than I was for the mission at hand. Yet the only way we could recruit more men was to head into the mountains and villages and attempt to persuade them to join us.

Even before we set out, there was a violent quarrel among the Omani and Baluchi platoon members. Unable to understand anything but the most basic Omani Arabic, I was left out of the arguments altogether as words flew, hot and bitter, about the platoon room. 'You idle sons of pigs,' one of the Bedu swore. 'You come to our country for money and to fill your fat bellies. But work is too much for you.' In return, a young Baluchi spat in their direction. Suddenly the room crackled with tension as I saw the men's splayed knuckles flex over their rifle butts.

Quickly, I moved between the men and, in broken Arabic, said, 'Allah has no place for violence. Why do you shout at each other?' They must have understood what I said as this diffused the tension, for now at least. If things were this volatile with fifteen men, I dreaded to think what it would be like with more.

Soon after, we set off into the villages, where the locals eyed us with open dislike as we handed out our recruiting pamphlets, encouraging them to join the fight against the Marxists. Our cause was not helped by the fact that most of the men in the villages could not read. Some villagers were also clearly supporters of the adoo. They shook their rifles at us, their voices shaking with anger, warning that they 'did not want Sultanate dogs on their land'. Even those villagers who were keen to join us had plenty of reasons not to do so. Most men needed to stay home to fend for their families. Others were too scared. In explaining himself, one villager lifted the back of his dirty cloak to reveal a jigsaw of dark purple weals over his back and chest.

'The adoo did this to you?' I asked. He nodded his head.

'I sold some goats to the Sultan's soldiers,' he explained, 'and someone told the adoo. They tied me to a tree and beat me with a strand of wire. No one dared cut me free afterwards for many hours. If I join the army, they will kill me and my family.'

Wherever we went, this was a familiar tale. These people were poor, and some supported the Sultan, but even the prospect of decent pay could not persuade them. We left without a single villager willing to join us. If Lawrence was going to take Wejh, he would face many of the same issues, especially as the Arabs were equally terrified by the Turks.

Moreover, while Lawrence was widely read in military history, like myself he had still not seen any action. For most of the last two years, he had been drawing maps behind a desk in Cairo. If he was going to help lead an Arab army into war, he had to understand what he was up against.

Before the march to Wejh commenced, Lawrence gave himself and thirty-five Arab tribesmen some raiding practice. Their target was an old blockhouse well near Nakhl Mubarak. In the dead of night they set off, climbing over steep 'knife-sharp' rocks in the dark and down into the crevices of a precipice. As the blackness of night softened, they finally made out the Turkish encampment below. At this, Lawrence gave the signal to open fire.

In his *Arab Bulletin* notes, he recalls, 'This turned out a crowd of Turks from all directions. They leaped into trenches and rifle pits each side of the road, and potting them was very difficult . . . They fired in every direction except towards us, and the row in the narrow valley was so awful that I expected to see the Hamra force turn out. As the Turks were already ten to our one, this might have made our getting away difficult, so we crawled back . . . and bolted off down the valley.'

While this was only a small-scale assault, it was Lawrence's first actual attack on the Turks. It had all gone as well as he might have hoped. Both he and the Arabs were flush with excitement and laughed at the fear they had instilled in the Turks, and also at their own nervous escape.

On their return, their spirits were lifted further when they picked up two Turkish prisoners, whom Lawrence described as 'the most ragged men I have ever seen, bar a British tramp'. The men confessed that their state was indicative of many in the Turkish forces. It was a rare sign of weakness, in what had previously seemed an impregnable armed force.

On 2 January 1917, Lawrence joined Feisal and his 10,000 men as they set out on the 200-mile march towards Wejh. To avoid detection by the Turks, they intended to stay close to the sea, using the hills and mountains to screen their movement. Meanwhile, Abdulla and his men had been tasked with attacking the railway at Wadi Ais, seventy miles from Medina, to occupy the Turks and create a diversion.

Drummers played the beat of a march as a vast mass of tribesmen on their camels advanced in a line a quarter of a mile long. At the front, three banners of purple silk were held aloft, where Lawrence rode alongside Feisal, surrounded by over a thousand bodyguards, all dressed in various bright colours and chanting war songs.

Although the march was visually impressive, Lawrence observed it also served a far greater purpose. It was the first time that such a large number of tribes had joined together for a significant march, hoping to bring others to the cause. Such an endeavour immediately boosted morale and saw Arabs remark, 'It is not an army but a world which is moving on Wejh,' and 'We are no longer Arabs, but a nation.' If they had any chance of defeating the Turks, this feeling within them was vital. It was a lesson I was to later learn myself. When recruiting others to your cause, it first helps to put on a united and successful front.

Equally important was Lawrence's role in the march. To lead the Arabs to first take Wejh, and hopefully beyond, he knew he had to tread carefully. Before the war, he had spent significant time in the Middle East and was accustomed to the Arab culture and beliefs. He had now also spent time within Feisal's camp and had proven his worth in defending Yenbo. But if he were to act as a typical British Army officer, and believe he was above the Arabs, then he knew they would not respect him or allow him to lead.

Resplendent in white robes, he was already attempting to look like them while also at one with their hopes and dreams for independence. Yet to truly succeed, it was the little things that would count. As Lawrence said himself, 'They taught me that no man could be their leader except he who ate the ranks' food, wore their clothes, lived with them, and yet appeared better in himself.' To be truly accepted, he had to uphold Arab standards even more than the average Arab. This was an extraordinarily difficult thing to do, especially in the heat of battle.

Many had already found such feats impossible. Famed explorers like Richard Burton and Charles Doughty had tried to live with the Bedouin and were never truly accepted. Lawrence not only had the necessary experience and understanding of what was required but also had another rare talent at his disposal.

The shame of his illegitimacy and finding that 'Lawrence' was not even his real name meant he was never comfortable in his own skin. At times he even hated himself. To escape, he had long tried out different roles and personalities to find a part that fit. His brother Arnold said that, like a chameleon, 'When he had just been with someone or was just going to see someone, Lawrence tended to take on the characteristics of that person.'

Morphing into another personality, and being accepted in another group, is a great skill. But even more than that, Lawrence could become that group's most loved and admired member. His friend John Buchan said of this, 'I loved him for himself, and also because there seemed to be reborn in him all the lost friends of my youth.' Lawrence had this effect on many of the men he worked with. His trick was not just to mimic them but to truly make them believe that he was everything they looked for in a friend and leader. To succeed with the Arabs, and lead them to victory, he would need to use all of his experience and talents.

Lawrence's example in this regard was one I soon knew I had to follow in Oman, particularly as other British officers had already shown the alternative. One had been sent home in disgrace after shooting the mess-boy's head off. Another tried to lead by sheer force, which led to his men hating him. He was a Royal Marine and was not good at making allowances, jumping upon those who did not meet his own standards. This authoritarianism held no appeal for the Arabs. Eventually there was a mutiny, and he also had to return home.

Trying to lead the Arabs through sheer force, especially when they were already so divided, was not the solution. But I also found following Lawrence's example very difficult. Unlike him, I had no great experience working and living with Arab tribes and barely spoke Arabic. To understand my soldiers' culture and way of life, I was quiet at first, not giving away too much of myself, just observing them, and copying them as I went along. I noticed how they only ate with their right hands, as the left is used for unsanitary issues, and sat with their legs tucked underneath so that their soles could not point at another man – for this would be an insult to a Muslim. During Ramadan, I also sought to eat and drink only during the sunless hours, just as they did. I also picked up some of their slang and could join in with their jokes or at least laugh in the right places. A good sense of humour can help any situation, but I carefully observed what they laughed at. You can throw a stone in jest at a British soldier if he's lagging, and he'll laugh. Throw one at the wrong Arab, and you'll be shot through the back, maybe two years afterwards.

Perhaps most importantly of all, I treated Omani and Baluchi soldiers equally. They performed the same duties, received the same punishments, and lived and slept in the same quarters. I wanted them to identify themselves as the Recce Platoon and not by race.

I must admit I also made some mistakes along the way. One night a giant black spider landed on my head in the shower and slithered down my neck. When I knocked it off, I saw it was at least seven inches in span and had a curved beak for a mouth. I screamed and hammered it with my clenched fist as it came for me again. The following morning, one of the Arabs saw the spider's body on the floor. Unsticking it from the concrete, he held it in the palm of his hand and said, 'Did you kill this, Sahb? It is no good thing to crush such an insect for a chapter of the Holy Book is given to its honour.' He glanced at me disapprovingly and then removed the corpse on his tea tray.

There was also the time Neil Armstrong became the first man to walk on the moon. The following morning, I told one of our men this momentous news. 'What!' he exclaimed. 'It cannot be. The moon is a holy place known only to the Prophet. No man can go there. No aeroplane can carry enough petrol.' I explained as best I could what a spacecraft was, and when he saw that I was definitely not joking, the man grew angry, glaring skywards. 'The blasphemers! How dare they trespass on holy ground. I will pass the word about, and tonight we will shoot many rounds at the moon.'

Picking up these little things was not a quick process. I can't claim to have ever fully immersed myself to become an 'Arab', as Lawrence aimed to do, but over many months I at least earned their respect, and that was enough for me to begin to lead them.

As if to emphasise the effectiveness of Lawrence's

approach, he was soon joined by another British officer who did not share the same sensibilities.

While Lawrence joined the Arabs for the first stretch of the journey to Wejh, he had to momentarily return to Yenbo to supervise loading stores on board one of the British ships. He was delighted to see that, once again, his promises to the Arabs were being kept. Amongst the shipment were 8,000 rifles, 3 million rounds of small arms ammunition, and 2 tons of high explosive. With this job complete, Captain Boyle took him up the coast by sea to reconvene with Feisal and the Arabs at Um Lejj, a small port halfway between Yenbo and Wejh. For the journey, Lawrence was joined by Major Charles Vickery, who had previously fought in the Sudan desert and spoke fluent Arabic. Until Colonel Newcombe eventually arrived to relieve Lawrence, it was hoped that Vickery could supply some actual military experience to the Arabs, having served in the armed forces for over sixteen years.

After arriving at Um Lejj on 15 January 1917, Lawrence, Boyle, and Vickery made their way inland to Owais to reconvene with Feisal and his men. There they were greeted by a lavish meal of rice and boiling mutton fat. However, Vickery and Boyle were shocked and disgusted by 'the absence of any sanitary precautions around the camp'. With barely concealed horror, they watched as each guest reached with his right hand into the stew and ladled out a portion. This was, of course, the accepted Arab way of eating, though this provided little comfort to them. The smell of human and camel faeces drying in the blazing sun did nothing to improve their appetite.

I recall an Arab host presenting me with a plate of dates

crawling with flies that had risen from a nearby mound of faeces. Buzzing around them was what also looked to be giant wasps, the like I had never seen before. When the dates were offered to me, I recoiled and shook my head. A fellow officer, far more experienced than me, nudged me and whispered, 'Take some, or you'll offend him.' As I reluctantly reached towards the plate, he whispered, 'But watch the *dibees*. Their sting is as bad as an African hornet's.' Despite this, I carefully ate every last one.

Vickery was an example of a Brit who had no concern for such matters. To help come to terms with these conditions, he took a long swig from a pocket flask full of whisky and offered it around. It might have been an act of friendship, but Lawrence and Boyle flinched at the ill-advised gesture. Alcohol was of course forbidden to Muslims, and Lawrence thought that a man of Vickery's experience should have known better. After all, he had served in the Sudan and was by no means ignorant of such Arab customs.

Things quickly went from bad to worse. When Vickery wore his Arab head cloth over his pith helmet, one of the Arabs pointed, 'Mashallah, the head of an ox!' As all the Arabs laughed, Vickery saw Lawrence joining in. He had hoped to stamp his authority on the camp and be treated with respect. Now he was the target of their jokes. Just a day in, Vickery was already less than enamoured with the Arabs, and, more importantly, with Lawrence. When it was decided that Boyle would take 500 of Feisal's men aboard one of his ships and land them at Wejh to create a pincer movement, Vickery was more than happy to depart the camp and go with them.

As Boyle, Vickery, and the Arabs set off for the ship, Feisal's army recommenced their march to Wejh. As they sang songs and recited poems, their camels strode over the vast dunes, some hundreds of feet in height. Before long they saw two horsemen coming in their direction. While one of the men was an Arab, Lawrence soon saw that the other was wearing a British khaki uniform and was red-faced and sweating profusely. Colonel Newcombe had arrived at last.

Lawrence was happy to see him. The two men had worked closely together in the Sinai, they got on well, and Lawrence knew Newcombe's experience would greatly benefit the Arabs. However, while Lawrence admired Newcombe, he also felt uneasy seeing him. Newcombe was supposed to be in command of British military support to the Arabs, as well as Feisal's senior British adviser. Technically, this meant that Lawrence should now be sidelined and could even be sent back to Cairo. Just a few weeks before, this was exactly what he had wanted. But now he was in the thick of the action, he was reluctant to return to his desk job. Thankfully, Newcombe recognised that Lawrence was a significant asset. Feisal and the Arabs seemed to like and respect him, while his plan to take Wejh seemed well thought through, if ambitious. For now, at least, Newcombe decided to let things continue as they were.

Newcombe was less impressed with the Arab forces. They had no sense of urgency and their ponderous pace infuriated him. Significant time was also spent by Feisal attempting to encourage other tribes to join them. Such matters could not be rushed. Before they could get down to business, Feisal and the tribal leaders had to observe Arab customs. More often than not, this included conversations about anything other than the war over countless cups of coffee, mint tea, and delicacies. Newcombe could barely contain his frustration. But it was time well spent; Feisal persuaded Sherif Nasir, brother of the Emir of Medina and a respected Shia Muslim figure, to join them, along with many of the local Billi tribes, who 'came to swell the advancing host'. Without the tribes joining the march to Wejh, the Arabs had no chance of taking it.

However, all of this meant that by the time the Arabs reached the Wadi Hamdh, they were already two days behind schedule. Growing impatient, Newcombe decided he needed to inform Boyle of the delay if they were to coordinate their attack. He therefore rode ahead to reach HMS *Hardinge*, which was anchored about twenty miles south of Wejh.

When the Arabs finally reached the *Hardinge* on 24 January, Lawrence was grateful to find it waiting. They were severely dehydrated and had barely drunk for days. Now they could drink the water supplied on board while preparing themselves for the attack on Wejh. Yet, while Boyle was aboard, Lawrence was confused to find that Vickery and the 500 Arabs were not. To his amazement, Boyle said that Vickery had lost patience and had already landed the 500 Arabs at Wejh, while the guns of his other naval ships had begun pounding the town.

Determined to find out what was happening, Lawrence set out for Wejh immediately. As he arrived, he found the town in a state of chaos. The Turks were fleeing en masse, as the Arabs grabbed and looted whatever they could lay their hands on. Lawrence recalled, 'They robbed the shops, broke open doors, searched every room, smashed chests and cupboards, tore down all fixed fittings, and slit every mattress and pillow for hidden treasure.' Passing the dead lying on the ground, he saw that the British naval guns had also decimated large parts of the town, reducing it to smouldering ruins. If it were going to be used as a base, much rebuilding would have to be done. He was also angry that the mosque had been shelled. This was sure to upset some of the townspeople, who were already shouting and gesturing at their sinking boats in the harbour, which they relied on to trade with Egypt.

Lawrence was furious, particularly when he was told that twenty Arabs had died in the fighting. If Vickery had waited for Feisal's men to arrive as planned, the Turks would have been surrounded. With nowhere to go, they would have eventually surrendered without any loss of life. Barely able to conceal his temper, Lawrence confronted Vickery, but he was unrepentant. Dismissing the losses, as if the death of twenty Arabs was a price worth paying, Vickery told Lawrence that all that mattered was they had achieved their objective.

For many British officers, the war had made them almost immune to mass death. The tens of thousands being killed nearly every day on the Western Front meant that the likes of Vickery saw the death of 'only' twenty Arabs as a good result. But Lawrence knew the Arabs treated death differently. It would deal a significant psychological blow if they suffered too many losses. It would also discourage more tribes from joining the Revolt. Unlike other officers, Lawrence did not see the Arabs as a means to an end. They were not expendable. 'Our men were not materials, like soldiers,' he wrote, 'but friends of ours, trusting in our leadership. We were not in command nationally but by invitation, and our men were volunteers, individuals, local men, relatives, so that a death was a personal sorrow to many in the army.' If he was to be trusted by them, then he sought to keep death to an absolute minimum. For this reason and many more, the Arabs liked and respected Lawrence.

While Vickery and Lawrence saw things very differently, the taking of Wejh was a significant result. The Arabs now had a base north of Medina. From here, they could target a 250-mile stretch of the railway, cut off supplies, stretch and isolate the Turks, and then eventually move on to the grand prize: Damascus.

7

Victory over the Turks had long seemed a distant dream to so many of the Arabs, especially when the Turks were descending on Yenbo and ready to wipe the Arabs out. But now the Arabs had captured a key port in the north and were closer to Damascus than ever before.

Sensing the tide was turning, more tribes now flocked to the cause, including the Juheina, the Billi, and the Beni Sakhr. One of the most important tribes expressing interest was the Howeitat, with Feisal inviting their leader, Auda Abu Tayi, to meet with him at Wejh. The Howeitat tribe was one of the largest and most powerful in the Hejaz. They were not only renowned fighters but also well equipped with horses, camels, and weapons. If they agreed to join the Revolt, this would be a real coup.

The Arabs were also delighted to welcome another new recruit. Jaafar Pasha was a Baghdadi officer who had fought in the Turkish and German armies. After being captured by the British, Jaafar had learned of the Arab Revolt and was eager to defect. Feisal and Lawrence knew of his reputation and felt he would be an ideal commander-in-chief of their regular troops, mainly consisting of other former Ottoman Arab POWs who had changed sides. Jaafar's military experience, ability to lead, and knowledge of the Turkish armed forces were just what was required.

Despite this stunning turn of events, Lawrence was unsure if his grand adventure in the desert would continue. As he returned to Cairo, he braced himself to be relieved of his duties by Colonel Newcombe. He was somewhat consoled that he had made a difference, even if he could not see the Revolt through to the end. However, Newcombe and the other powers-that-be felt that Lawrence had more than proved himself. Feisal and the Arabs trusted him, and his strategy to target Wejh had been a success. At the moment, he was far more useful in the field than behind a desk. He would therefore continue to serve as Feisal's liaison officer, while Newcombe focused on commanding a series of daring raids on the railway line.

If the Arab Revolt was going to continue its momentum, Lawrence knew that they required more guns. Yet this presented a problem. The British had already given all that was available. They also had no modern artillery that could be easily disassembled and carried by camels. Conversely, the French were well supplied with such weapons. While they were eager to make them available to the Arabs, Colonel Brémond demanded that they could only be handled by his French North African troops. Again, this created an issue, as the British were still uncomfortable with a significant French military presence in the Hejaz. As a result, the offer was turned down.

Despite this, Brémond now recognised that, as Feisal's right-hand man, Lawrence was beginning to hold more power in dictating Arab policy. He therefore engaged in a charm offensive. Congratulating Lawrence on the assault on Wejh and his military talent, he suggested that the allies should now target Akaba, the only Turkish port remaining in the Red Sea. More than that, it was the nearest port to both the Suez Canal and the Hejaz Railway. By taking Akaba, the Allies could severely restrict Turkish supplies to Medina and have a crucial strategic base from which they could target Damascus.

Although Lawrence was wary of Brémond's intentions, his advice made some sense. When mapping the region before the war, he had visited Akaba and knew the town well. It had a natural harbour and was surrounded by mountains. Yet, for this reason, he felt Brémond's idea was flawed. To storm the town, any Anglo-French force would have to land on the beach. From there, they would be quickly gunned down from the surrounding hills. Even if some troops somehow survived this artillery barrage, they would then have to climb the granite hills, thousands of feet high, all while under attack. In short, attacking Akaba in this manner was not only impossible but also madness. It sounded like Gallipoli all over again.

Lawrence had another idea. If Akaba was attacked from the interior, they might stand a chance. But marching across hundreds of miles of desert to reach the port would be a significant challenge for French or British forces. Yet the Arabs might be able to do it. When Lawrence suggested this, Brémond almost choked. If the Arabs were to take Akaba, he knew there was a real chance they could push on into Syria and stake claim to the lands the French wanted for themselves. For Lawrence, this was just the idea.

Eager to spoil such plans, Brémond told Lawrence he was heading to Wejh to meet with Feisal. But Lawrence beat Brémond to the punch. Before Brémond arrived, laden with gifts and persuasive talk, Lawrence had already fully briefed Feisal. Subsequently able to counter the Frenchman's suggestions, Brémond 'had to retire from the battle in good order' while Lawrence sat 'spitefully smiling'.

Soon after Lawrence had seen off Brémond, he was handed an urgent telegram from General Clayton. The British had intercepted a message that seemed to call for the evacuation of Medina and the transfer of Turkish troops to Maan. With British forces looking to target Gaza, the addition of two or three more Turkish divisions on the Gaza–Beersheba line would almost certainly prevent an attack. It was, therefore, of utmost importance that the Arabs try to stop the Turkish troops from being transferred north. As such, any plans for the Arabs to target Akaba would have to wait.

While Lawrence promised to do the best he could, in a message to Colonel Wilson he wrote, 'I'm afraid it will be touch and go . . . it's fearfully short notice.'

Lawrence immediately decided to ride from Wejh to Wadi Ais to encourage Abdulla to attack the Turks should they leave Medina, or to cut off the railway. This could not be done by message alone, as he was also growing concerned that Abdulla 'had done nothing against the Turks for the past two months'. He therefore needed a forceful prod in the right direction.

However, before setting out, Lawrence fell ill with dysentery and was 'feeling very unfit for a long march'; nevertheless, there was no time to rest or feel sorry for himself. Time was of the essence. With no choice but to try and overcome his ailments, he set off on the 100-mile journey to Wadi Ais, along with an escort of men from different tribes. This was a recipe for disaster. The tribes had long feuded with one another, and right from the start there was bickering and arguments. It was clear that it would not take much for the situation to boil over, but Lawrence had other issues on his mind.

As the effects of dysentery worsened, boils on his back caused him considerable pain, leaving him unable to ride more than four or five hours at a time. The rugged landscape was often too dangerous for Lawrence and the men to stay mounted on their camels. They, therefore, had to dismount and walk for miles alongside them. All of this left Lawrence exhausted. Matters weren't helped when he found that the water in the few wells they visited en route had turned salty.

Despite all of this, Lawrence did not want to show that he was in any pain. Not only did he not want to lose the respect of the tribesmen, who always seemed to continue no matter their illnesses or ailments, but he was also terrified of one of them trying to 'cure' him. Treatment for most ailments usually saw the Bedouin burn a hole in the patient's body on the spot that was assumed to be opposite the site of the illness. Following this, a boy would urinate into the wound. Not only was this treatment useless, but it was often more painful than the disease it was meant to treat.

In Oman, I recall watching in horror at how some villagers treated a little girl who had been bitten by a snake.

While the bitten limb was badly inflamed, her other leg held my attention. From the ankle to the knee were a series of deep, pustulous burns that had been brushed over with fresh camel dung for supposed antiseptic reasons. Our medic tried to treat the poor girl with antiseptic, dressings, and morphine, but it was too late, and she died soon after. There were countless other occasions when I saw villagers burn and blind a patient in a misguided attempt to cure them rather than seek out any proper medical attention. However, some strange treatments did have their uses. I was incredulous when one of my men told me a broken arm could be healed with a melon. I assumed they meant by rubbing the fruit on the broken limb. Instead, they burned a hole in a long melon from end to end and then placed the arm inside to keep it straight until it was healed. The one issue with this was that the arm would often fix itself in that position, and the patient could not bend it ever again. Still, it beat amputation, which was often the alternative.

After days of sickness, Lawrence could stand it no more. His head was pounding, and he was beginning to feel as if he might faint. Ordering a stop for the night, he hoped he might feel better in the morning. Crawling under the lee of a 'steep broken granite' cliff, he tried to get some sleep when the sound of a gunshot suddenly woke him. At first he thought one of the party had been shooting at game in the valley. However, as he closed his eyes, one of the men quickly roused him. He was needed at once. There had been an incident.

Led to a hollow in the cliff, Lawrence saw the body of

one of the Ageyl camel-men sprawled on the ground. The man had been shot in the head. He was told that a man from another tribe known as 'Hamed the Moor' was the culprit. The Ageyl were excitable and angry, swearing revenge against Hamed and the Moors, ready to lynch him if necessary. 'This need not have happened this day of all days when I was in pain,' Lawrence wrote. Yet it was a matter that could not be dismissed. If he ignored it now, the tribes would undoubtedly attack each other. This might also not be an isolated incident. When word got out, it could spark reprisals throughout the Arab forces.

Scanning the camp in the darkness, he caught sight of Hamed picking up his saddlebags and preparing to run away. Drawing his pistol, Lawrence aimed it at him and forced him to stop.

The Ageyl men quickly descended upon the stammering and scared Moor, demanding they be allowed to execute him. Lawrence had to quickly make a decision. In my early days in Oman, I tried to settle one particularly violent feud between tribes by naively offering them a coin and telling them to toss it. They looked at me as if I had gone mad. Thankfully, Lawrence was more experienced in such matters. After all, in his days at Carchemish before the war he had been invited to arbitrate disputes between the tribes. He was, therefore, well aware that 'blood for blood' was the accepted code of the desert. However, he also knew that if the Ageyl carried this out, the feud with the Moors might explode. Again, this would be a disaster for the Revolt. And yet it was clear that the Ageyl would somehow have to be satisfied.

Lawrence finally knew what had to be done. He would have to execute Hamed himself. He was not aligned with any one tribe and could therefore deliver justice without causing offence. After some discussion, both the Ageyl and the Moors agreed.

Soon after, Hamed was marched at gunpoint into a narrow crevice in the cliff where he was to meet his fate. Lawrence raised his gun as Hamed curled into a ball, crying and screaming for mercy. Suddenly, Lawrence felt uneasy. He had never killed a man in battle, let alone executed one of his own. Yet he knew it had to be done. There was no other choice that could be made. Ordering Hamed to get to his feet, he took a deep breath, tensed his finger on the trigger, and shot him in the chest.

Hamed fell to the ground, 'shrieking' and writhing in the dust. He was still alive. In a panic, Lawrence shot him again, but his hand was shaking so violently that the bullet hit Hamed's wrist, leading to yet more howls of agony. This was now turning into a horrifying ordeal. Lawrence had to quickly put an end to it. Taking no chances, he approached Hamed, put the muzzle of his pistol to his neck, and pulled the trigger. Hamed's body jolted backwards and then fell face forward into the dirt. At last, there was silence.

Lawrence was unable to sleep that night. While he continued to feel unwell, he could not get the images of Hamed out of his head. He had looked a man in his eyes and shot him dead. One of his own, no less. The incident upset him, but he realised he had had no choice.

I well remember a similar troubled feeling after killing a

man for the first time. During a fight with the adoo in the mountains, I cornered one of the adoo and pointed my gun at him. 'Drop your weapon, or I will kill you,' I shouted in Arabic. Ignoring my warning, he moved with incredible speed, twisting at the knee and bringing his Kalashnikov to bear in a single fluid movement. Before he could get off a shot, I squeezed my trigger automatically. On impact, the man's face crumpled with surprise as he was slammed back as though caught in the chest by a sledgehammer. I had often shot at people hundreds of yards away – vague shapes behind rocks who were busy firing back – but never before had I seen a man's soul in his eyes, sensed his vitality as a fellow human, and then watched his body ripped apart at the pressure of my finger. I tried to force away the image of his destruction, but his scared face stayed watching me from my subconscious. A part of me that was still young and uncynical died with him, spreadeagled on a thorn bush, with his red badge glinting in the hot Qara sun.

Lawrence also knew that a line had been crossed. He now had blood on his hands. The execution of Hamed might have won him the respect of the Arabs, but it came at a great cost to his soul. From here, there would be no going back.

8

After two more days of torturous travel Lawrence finally arrived at Abdulla's camp at Wadi Ais. He was in no state or mood for small-talk. After greeting Abdulla, he explained the problem of Medina before he was shown to his tent and collapsed into a ball. He did not emerge for the next ten days, as he suffered 'a bodily weakness that made my animal self crawl away and hide till the shame was passed'. While the effects of dysentery, as well as malaria, hit him hard, so did the flashbacks of the execution of Hamed.

Between his fitful sleep and hallucinations, a moment of clarity also came to him. Drenched in sweat and being pricked by flies, he suddenly realised that what many perceived as the Arabs' greatest weakness might actually be their greatest strength. In a letter to his family in February 1917 he wrote, 'The Arab Movement is shallow, not because the Arabs do not care, but because they are few – and in their smallness of number . . . lies a good deal of their strength, for they are perhaps the most elusive enemy an army ever had, and inhabit one of the most trying countries in the world for civilised warfare.' As he had seen for himself, 'In mass they were not formidable, since they had no corporate spirit, nor discipline nor mutual confidence. The smaller the unit the better the performance. A thousand were a mob, ineffective against a company of trained Turks; but three or four Arabs in their hills would stop a dozen Turks.' Therefore, rather than expecting the Arabs to operate as a typical disciplined army, able to defend ports and towns and attack as a unit, he now recognised they could be more effective attacking in smaller numbers on specific guerrilla operations.

Lawrence's thoughts on utilising the Arabs in such a manner seemed to match renowned military theorist Carl von Clausewitz, who had proposed in his classic book *On War*: 'The war must be fought in the interior of the country; it must not be decided by a single stroke; the theatre of operations must be fairly large; the national character must be rough and inaccessible, because of mountains or forests, marshes or the local methods of cultivation.'

Clausewitz might as well have been describing the Arabs in the Hejaz. They might be smaller in number than the Turks, but they had a superior knowledge of the desert landscape. For many of the Turkish soldiers, fighting in the desert was entirely alien. The Arabs, therefore, had to force them out of their comfort zone in the towns and villages, and draw them into the vast, inhospitable, scorching heat of the desert, where the Arabs were far more at home.

They could achieve this by aggressively targeting locomotives, railway cars, telegraph wires, sources of water, bridges and culverts. The Turks would have to venture into the desert to defend these targets, spreading themselves thinly, and in doing so would not be able to defend the 140,000 square miles of Arabia. Small groups of Arabs could attack them when they least expected it, 'drifting about like a gas', then vanishing back into the desert. Not only would such attacks have a practical effect on the Turks, particularly in cutting off supplies, they would also take a huge psychological toll. In the unfamiliar desert landscape, the Arabs could prey on their worst fears. Knowing they could be attacked at any moment would eat away at the Turks and destroy their morale. Conversely, these small victories and signs of progress would boost the Arabs and make them realise that David could defeat Goliath. This surge of confidence might then attract other tribes to the Arab cause.

The memory of the loss of the twenty Arab fighters at Wejh also continued to torment Lawrence. He understood that if the Arabs were to fight in bigger battles and perish in large numbers, their confidence would desert them. With this the entire Revolt could fail. By attacking in small numbers and then disappearing, they could avoid this. Indeed, as Lawrence said himself, the Arabs were supposed to be fighting for freedom, 'a pleasure only to be tasted by a man alive'.

Lawrence also understood the psychology of many of the tribesmen. A large number had made their living as thieves of the desert. The opportunity to attack the Turks, and relieve them of whatever booty they had, would be very enticing. Indeed, with money and resources tight, many would be happy to join the cause just for the chance to rob and loot alone.

With all of this in mind, Lawrence realised that irregular guerrilla warfare rather than standard military tactics might just be the key to victory. It was a critical turning point in the Revolt and proved to be a vital example for me to follow in Oman.

One day the colonel called me into his office and said, 'NFR's Recce Platoon has been ambushed and is written off for a while. There is no one to cover the desert north of the mountains. Can your men be ready to replace them within six weeks?'

This was months ahead of schedule. We were still under-strength and had not even begun to train properly yet, let alone for mountain warfare. But there was no option. We had to get started at once.

As well as five years with Centurion tanks in Germany, I had been trained in the basic arts of an 'elusive saboteur' by the 22nd Special Air Service Regiment. While this helped provide me with a framework, particularly utilising night-time operations whenever possible, I also had to improvise, especially if my men were going to respond. They were already not best pleased that in the mountains they would be on foot patrol and would have to leave their Land Rovers behind.

For weeks on end, we trained in the hills, often at night and using live ammunition. Hiding 12-inch white metal plates in the hillside, I had some of my men stand near them and shoot above our heads, leading to us having to hit the plates in return. Soon we were all crack shots. Advances over broken ground were practised again and again until the men were silent, while we also perfected twenty different hand signals, so talking and whispering were no longer necessary.

Many of the men found it tough. The sweat quickly

rotted our clothes, and sharp rock and camel thorns cut through footwear and tore at equipment. Some of the men had socks, but most wore only canvas gym shoes, however rough the country. There was plenty of moaning, but at least it was now in unison: a measure of harmony had crept in, for the common denominator was discomfort.

I also felt more confident in myself, and my Arabic had improved dramatically. It seemed the men could sense this. The mood was lighter, and they followed my instructions to the letter.

When the moon shone, the men moved with twenty yards between each of them, presenting no bunched target to a would-be marksman. When clouds came, each soldier closed up enough to see the man in front of and behind him. This also allowed them to identify the hand signals which dictated the types of formation in which the platoon would move through the changing terrain. Meanwhile, every item of equipment and clothing was painted green and brown, all watches were pocketed, radio aerials were covered by cloth tubes and their luminous control dials by adhesive tape. We had to blend into the landscape, just as the adoo did. But I was always conscious that the mountains were their home, and they knew the terrain far better than we did. This was why our training had to be so intensive. We had to become guerrilla fighters, just like them.

After another recruitment drive, with my men far more settled and preaching the virtues of the platoon, I soon had thirty men at my disposal. However, just like Lawrence, I could not afford casualties for practical reasons, let alone what it would do psychologically to my platoon and beyond. As far as possible, I tried to avoid engaging my men in direct battles but instead utilised psychological tricks to frighten the enemy away. If we were near a hostile village, I told my men not to attack but to display our arsenal's power nearby. More often than not, the adoo would watch and be scared away. This simple tactic was crucial. Soon, just like Lawrence and the Arabs, the building blocks of our success were in place.

When Lawrence's fever had finally passed, he went to Abdulla's tent and excitedly shared his strategy. However, Abdulla didn't appear to share his enthusiasm. Since arriving at Wadi Ais, he had made himself far too comfortable, reading poetry, hunting, and eating. He had little interest in leading any attacks on the railway, even if it would stop the Turks from leaving Medina to halt the British advance in Gaza. If Lawrence wanted to lead a raid, however, then Abdulla had no objection.

On 26 March, just as General Murray was mounting his first attack on Gaza, Lawrence set off for the railway station at Aba el-Naam. He took with him a group of thirty tribesmen, a number of explosives, two antiquated mountain guns, and a German Maxim machine gun on a sledge, drawn by a donkey. Abdulla's cousin Sherif Shakir also promised to assemble further reinforcements. He claimed he could raise another 800 men and told Lawrence they would meet him near the station. If Shakir was true to his word, then Lawrence believed they would have the manpower to easily overrun the Turks.

After a three-day march across the desert, Lawrence finally called a halt in the early hours of the morning. In the distance, he could make out Aba el-Naam station, along with a locomotive and nearly 400 Turkish troops. He also saw it was surrounded by higher ground, perfect for any attack.

However, before the attack commenced, he needed the extra 800 men that Sherif Shakir had promised. Waiting all day for them to arrive, he was dismayed to find that when Shakir finally turned up he had only brought 300 with him. This meant that the Turks would outnumber them. Lawrence was tempted to abort the operation but realised that there was a way they could still proceed. If he could plant some blasting gelatine on the track to the south of the station, he was confident that when the Arabs attacked the locomotive would look to retreat to protect itself. If it did this, it would run over the gelatine and explode. Should the locomotive's crew survive the explosion, the two mountain guns and the Maxim would be in position, ready to finish them off.

In the dead of night, he approached a deserted part of the track like a wraith under the moonlight, his heart beating against his white robes. Checking he wasn't being watched, he quickly planted 'twenty pounds of blasting gelatine'. He then cut the telegraph so that the Turks could not call for reinforcements.

With everything set, Lawrence gave the order to attack as the sun rose. Waking the Turks with a barrage of shells, he watched as the locomotive crew hurriedly backed it southward towards safety. This was just what he had hoped for. Passing over the gelatine, an explosion suddenly ripped through the air, leaving the train to vanish in a cloud of sand and smoke. At this the Arabs opened fire, blasting at the locomotive to finish it off, then, streaming through the smoke, ferociously wielded their weapons at the panicking Turks, who fled to their trenches. Lawrence decided to leave them there. He had already achieved his goal. The locomotive and track had been destroyed, with seventy Turks killed or wounded and thirty taken prisoner. In contrast, only one of Lawrence's Bedouin was slightly hurt.

The raid was an enormous success. The destruction of the track meant all traffic to and from Medina was stopped for three days, helping to protect General Murray's British forces, who were now attacking Gaza. While Lawrence had kept his promise to help, he had also proven that his guerrilla strategy could work. It was now time to do it on a much larger scale.

9

Lawrence had proven his strategy could work, and my time to do the same was soon upon me. Yet as my men prepared to move into the mountains of Dhofar, the Army's list of dead and wounded had lately become alarming. The game was turning sour. Emergency regulations were quickly implemented, and it was announced that a curfew would apply throughout Dhofar after dark. Soldiers could therefore fire at and kill any armed man seen to run away without first challenging him.

Night after night, we drove towards the mountains without lights. Then, on foot, we moved up the mouths of the great intermontane valleys where they debouched onto the plain: the Jarsees, the Arzat, and the Naheez, all wide and deeply forested. Soon these foot patrols became routine. Spreading out across a chosen wadi-bed, the platoon crept along its meandering course across the mountains. Long sharp thorns in the brush tore at our skin and ripped our clothes, while a ceaseless monsoon drizzle soaked us to our skin. In the wet clay, we slipped and fell, barely able to see each other in the darkness and the mountain mist, as ticks and mosquitoes continually nibbled away at us, leaving us constantly itching and red raw.

As soon as we saw any movement, we opened fire. Villagers knew the terms of the curfew, so everyone was considered fair game at this time of night. We knew the adoo kept to no set route or schedule, so we had to rely on intelligence wherever we could get it. Thankfully, some villagers were still willing to talk to us, especially when money changed hands. Sometimes we had to arrest men for further questioning, but this often left me uneasy. On one occasion, their women clung to my shirt, distraught and hysterical. Both talked at once in a bird-like chatter, begging us not to take the men away, for they would all die if there was no one to collect wood and buy food. But their men had been seen talking to the adoo, and we needed to know all they knew. Still, I felt uneasy. That night I drank two brandies back at the mess when I usually stuck to soft drinks.

Over the coming weeks, we stopped a camel train smuggling arms from Yemen, and hid in caves and ambushed the adoo when they took their women to have sex there. When we learned that the enemy was targeting the village of Mirbat and operatives were already working from within, we raided the mud huts and found a cache of 3.5-inch rockets, 3-inch mortars, and semi-automatic weapons.

I was proud of my men. We were beating the adoo at their own game and had proven our guerrilla strategy could work. But it seems this riled our enemy. One night our camp was attacked by mortars. Then, the following morning, two of our sewage-disposal lorries were ambushed near our gates, with one of the drivers seriously injured. We were instantly angered by this and set out to hunt down the adoo who were responsible. Taking the platoon forward to where the attack had taken place, a barrier of shock waves suddenly passed above and beside our heads with a crackle that sent all of us instantly sprawling to the ground.

Looking out, I saw their muzzle flashes 600 yards away. Well concealed in low sangars camouflaged with clay, they appeared to be mere extensions of the ant-hills. The weight of fire was stunning. Spurts of mud kicked up all about us, as we crawled into a ditch. One of my men jumped up, tried to return fire, then keeled over backwards, his rifle flying away. As his body thumped to the ground, I stared at him for any sign of movement, but there was none. He was dead.

I could hardly think. Fear took a firm hold of my mind. There was no way out, and we appeared to be surrounded. Then I realised what I had to do. Grabbing the radio, I called in air support. There was a nervous wait; with gunfire still erupting all around us, we didn't dare move an inch. Suddenly, there was a high whine above us. A Provost fighter screeched past, then moments later the ground shook as a 2.5lb fragmentation bomb exploded over the ant-hills. At last, there was silence.

Cautiously moving forward, we soon reached the adoo's position and found empty cases of machine-gun clips, and bloodstained rags. They had fled, but intelligence later told us that six of the adoo were killed and ten wounded. The attack was a wake-up call. So far, our guerrilla strategy had been effective, but the adoo were now striking back, and this had been a lucky escape. It was something that Lawrence would also soon have to come to terms with.

Following their attack on Aba el-Naam station, shots

were fired into the air to herald Lawrence and the Arabs' victorious return to Abdulla's camp. A party atmosphere quickly took hold as a huge feast was prepared in their honour. Lawrence ate happily and watched the Arabs tell tall tales of their feats while mocking and laughing at each other, as was their way. He let them have their moment, but there wasn't much time to celebrate. There was still much work to do.

The following morning, Lawrence set off to mine the tracks, joined by forty Juheina tribesmen and a machine-gun platoon. The conditions were dreadful. Battered by a sandstorm, Lawrence remembered that it

> tore our cloaks from us, turned our camels sometimes right around, and sometimes drew them together in a vortex, and large bushes, tufts of grass, and small trees were torn up clean by the roots, in a dense cloud of the soil about them, and were driven against us, or dashed over our heads, with sometimes dangerous force. We were never blinded – it was always possible to see seven or eight feet each side – but it was risky to look out since one never knew if one would meet a flying tree, a rush of pebbles, or a column of dust.

They were covered in sand and dust, then heavy rain and howling winds followed, along with a sudden drop in temperature. Lawrence and his party were left soaking wet and shivering, trudging through puddles of water. The conditions became so hazardous that, as they climbed a rocky crag, one of the men slipped and fell forty feet to his death.

Cold, wet, and tired, they finally reached the railway

track at ten at night, close to a small station and a Turkish garrison. This time, Lawrence was eager to experiment with a more complicated mine which could destroy a train going in either direction, but the conditions were so awful that it took him over four hours to make it. When it was finally finished, he crawled back to 'a safe distance' and joined the Arabs to wait for a train to pass. 'The cold was intense,' he wrote, 'and our teeth chattered, and we trembled and hissed involuntarily, while our hands drew in like claws.'

At sunrise, a small trolley carrying four men and a sergeant approached the mine. This was far from the prize Lawrence wanted to destroy. He breathed a sigh of relief when the trolley passed over the mine and it failed to explode. Lawrence reasoned that it had been too light to set it off.

Yet as they waited for another locomotive to approach, they saw a patrol of Turkish soldiers heading their way from the station. Lawrence was conscious that they had left their footprints all over the area, as they had been impossible to hide after the rain had turned the sand to mud. He was convinced the Turks would see them and then find the mine if they came much closer. Despite this, they passed the footprints and did not appear concerned.

Soon after, a larger train, fully loaded with civilians, many of them women and children, approached. Lawrence felt a rush of anxiety ripple through him. He had no wish to kill innocent victims such as these, but he could do nothing. With his heart in his mouth, he watched as the train passed over the mine, but again it failed to explode.

Lawrence dropped his head in relief, exhaling slowly, but he was also concerned. The first trolley might have been too light to set off the mine, but this locomotive surely should have done so.

There was no time to inspect the problem. The Turkish garrison had finally spotted Lawrence and the tribesmen, and opened fire from a distance. Fleeing into the desert, Lawrence contemplated returning to camp as the Turks would now surely be waiting for them. But after so much hard work, he was determined to understand why his mine had failed.

At nightfall, he returned to the track and found it deserted. In the moonlight, he hurriedly searched for the buried hair trigger, all the while on edge that the Turks might appear at any moment. There wasn't time to do any proper check. Instead he raised it one-sixteenth of an inch higher, hoping that this would fix the issue.

It was now far too dangerous to wait for another locomotive to arrive. Lawrence hoped that he still might achieve his goal, even if he was not around to see it. Leaving a scout near the station, he turned back to Wadi Ais. To ensure their mission wasn't a complete failure, on the way they managed to blow up a small railway bridge and cut over 200 rails, telegraph and telephone lines.

The next morning, as they rested at a well in Rubiaan, they suddenly heard a tremendous explosion. The scout who had been left behind arrived soon after. Sporting a wide smile, he told them the mine had destroyed a locomotive carrying spare rails. This effectively blocked the track to Medina for days. Lawrence was thrilled. Just as importantly, over the course of two operations, the Arabs had only suffered one casualty, and that had been the servant who had accidentally fallen to his death.

Lawrence knew that his plan to keep the Turks bottled up in Medina and cause maximum physical and psychological distress could work. Satisfied that the tribesmen at Abdulla's camp could continue to mine the tracks without him, Lawrence prepared to return to Feisal at Wejh as soon as possible.

10

On Lawrence's return journey to Wejh, he was accompanied by an Arab called Mohammed, who 'enlivened the march'. In his notes for the *Arab Bulletin*, Lawrence wrote, 'So he took most of his clothes off, got off his camel and challenged any of us mounted to race him to a clump of trees on the slope ahead, for a pound English. All the party started off at once; the distance turned out about three-quarters of a mile, uphill, over heavy sand, which I expect was more than Mohammed had bargained for, though he won by inches, he was absolutely done and collapsed bleeding from his mouth and nose.'

Always wanting to prove he was one of them, Lawrence enjoyed joining in some of these Arab high jinks himself. 'If you come up quietly behind a camel,' he wrote, 'poke a stick up its rump, and screech, it plunges off at a gallop, very disconcerting to its rider.'

Just a few months before, Lawrence had never ridden a camel. Now he was riding with the best of the Arabs, and more than keeping pace with them. Major W.F. Stirling, who was with Lawrence during much of 1918, later wrote:

> His powers of endurance, too, were phenomenal. Few of even the most hard-bitten Arabs would ride with him

> from choice. He never tired. Hunger, thirst and lack of sleep appeared to have little effect on him. He had broken all the records of the dispatch riders of the Caliph Haroun al Raschid which had been sung for centuries in the tribal sagas. On one occasion he rode his camel three hundred miles in three consecutive days. I once rode with mine fifty miles at a stretch and that was enough for me . . . His spiritual equipment overrode the ordinary needs of flesh and blood.

Lawrence returned to Wejh happy with his efforts at Abdulla's camp and feeling ever more a part of the Arabs. Quickly seeking out Feisal, he was brought up to speed on what he had missed while he had been away. Despite his efforts, the British assault on Gaza had been unsuccessful. The Turks had been expecting the attack for some time and in anticipation had dug trenches and built fortifications. The British were not prepared for this or any sustained attack. While they unsuccessfully tried to overrun the Turks, they also faced logistical issues, with a severe shortage of ammunition, water, and food. Despite considerable efforts to build a small-gauge railway to bring supplies and ammunition forward, and to lay a water line, neither was completed. Since the only way of securing water was to take Gaza, the British had a limited time to do so before facing disaster. With the Turks and Germans holding firm in their trenches and taking advantage of every piece of high ground, it soon became clear that Murray would have to order a retreat, but not before 3,000 of his men had perished.

While the British forces licked their wounds and regrouped, supplies continued flooding into the Arab camp at Wejh. Cars had arrived from Egypt, as had the RFC aircraft that had previously been at Rabegh, along with their Egyptian troops and their commander Lieutenant Colonel Pierce Charles Joyce. Lawrence was also delighted to hear that Newcombe was still hard at work attacking the railway. For the Arabs, at least, everything appeared to be well in hand. But then Lawrence was stopped in his tracks.

Feisal informed him that while he had been away, Sir Mark Sykes had visited him in Wejh. During their conversation, Sykes had tentatively mentioned the existence of the Sykes–Picot Agreement without going into any real detail. In fact, he had made it sound rather vague and of benefit to the Arabs. He certainly didn't reveal that the British, French, and Russians had already divided up the Ottoman Empire among them, excluding the Arabs from most of the areas they coveted. Feisal had been highly suspicious, while Lawrence was baffled. This was the first time he had heard of the agreement and he was determined to get to the bottom of it. Yet just as Lawrence was about to leave Feisal's tent, the guest-master rushed inside and whispered in Feisal's ear. A wide smile broke across Feisal's face as he announced, 'Auda is here.'

At this, the tent flap was drawn back, and in strode a tall, muscular figure with a haggard face, passionate and tragic. Feisal sprang to his feet while the man caught his hand and kissed it warmly. They then drew aside a pace or two and admired each other. Auda Abu Tayi was the tribal leader of the Howeitat who had previously pledged allegiance to Feisal. This was the first time they had met since promising to become allies.

The tales of Auda were legendary. He 'had married twenty-eight times, and had been wounded thirteen times', and he was revered as one of the most fearsome fighters throughout northern Arabia, Syria, and Lebanon. In his younger days, it was even said that he had cut out the heart of a rival and then taken a bite while it was still beating. When the Ottomans demanded he pay them a tax, Auda shot two officials dead. The Turks had since put a price on his head, but he had managed to outrun and outfight them at every turn. And no one would dare to betray him. Not only would that individual face severe repercussions from the Howeitat, but so would their family. Lawrence realised that Auda and his tribe were just what the Arab Revolt required.

Leaving the two men to speak, Lawrence decided that he needed to see Sykes at once. On 7 May, Lawrence and Colonel Wilson confronted Sykes over the agreement. Lawrence was astounded that such matters had apparently already been decided, especially while the Arabs were fighting to take the Hejaz and reach Damascus, believing it would secure their independence. The agreement meant that it might all be for nothing – they would be trading being ruled by the Ottomans to being ruled by the French.

Sykes tried to soften the issue by claiming that granting the Arabs immediate independence would only lead to 'poverty and chaos'. To placate Lawrence, he suggested that after ten years of British or French protection, the Arabs might then be in a position to form a nation. Struggling to contain his fury, Lawrence claimed that the Arabs had legitimacy to govern because they were fighting for their independence, and it was not for the British or French to make such underhand decisions. In return, Sykes said that now Lawrence was 'a great man he must behave as such and be broad in his views'.

Lawrence left the stormy meeting with a bitter taste in his mouth. Was all of this for nothing? Would the Arabs be better off laying down their arms rather than continuing to fight for something they would never get? This was also very much a personal issue. The Arabs had trusted Lawrence but had it all been a lie? Part of his motive in inspiring the Arabs to victory was to overcome his shame at his illegitimacy and to restore his family's honour, as his mother had demanded. Yet he had always been upset at how his mother and father never saw fit to be honest with him about their 'sin'. Now he felt that in lying to the Arabs, he was no better than them. His dream of redemption was irrevocably tarnished.

I well recall this feeling of conflict within me while serving in Oman. During a week's leave, I joined a fellow officer at the wired-off compound of Petroleum Development Oman Ltd, a subsidiary of Shell. We spent a weekend relaxing in a keyhole cove with soft sand. It was like something out of St Tropez, with its clubhouse, plentiful sandwiches, and cold beers. Looking around the facility, I saw the luxurious air-conditioned prefabricated bungalows for the employees, with fresh food delivered weekly in refrigerator ships from Australia. There was a private school, lavish bars, swimming pools, and even a private hospital, which mainly treated sunburn and stomach upsets. No patients from outside the compound were allowed in.

I was shocked. Throughout Oman and Dhofar, I had seen abject poverty everywhere I turned. If Omani oil could give such opulence to foreigners, when would they, the Omanis, taste similar fruits?

Although I was serving the British Army in protecting the Sultan of Oman, Said bin Taimur, I began to understand why so many wanted to oust him. By 1968 he was receiving millions of pounds in revenue from oil, but his countrymen continued to starve, living in conditions that were akin to the Middle Ages. Meanwhile, he continued to live in a palace, denying the Omanis their rightful inheritance.

The Marxist radio stations constantly urged the Omanis to

> throw off the harness of British Imperialism and take the wealth that is yours but is stolen by the Sultan. Why does he hide from you amongst his harem in distant Dhofar? Because he is ashamed that he has betrayed the Omanis. See what we revolutionaries have done in the People's Republic of Yemen. Here there are schools for our children, hospitals for our sick. With the help of our Russian and Chinese brothers, we are building a great future for our people. The road to success is revolt.

I was far from a Marxist, but I could understand why so many were now rising up against the Sultan. I felt dirty and ashamed for protecting him. His attitude to the Dhofaris particularly appalled me. He gave them nothing. To him, they were no better than animals.

The whole affair stank, and I resolved to resign from the Sultan's forces without delay. I had come here in ignorance of the true state of affairs. Now that the situation was unpleasantly clear to my conscience, I had no wish to stay on. However, when I told Staff Sergeant Abdullah of my decision, he urged me to reconsider: 'No, no, sahb. You make a serious mistake. Communism must not come here. They try to turn us from our God and that must never be.' His voice rose with the urgency of his words, and his grip was fierce on my shoulder. 'You must not think the British do wrong here, sahb,' he continued. 'They do not meddle with our way of life or our religion.'

The Marxists had sought to eradicate Islam by confiscating Korans and closing mosques. Anyone who refused to betray their beliefs had the soles of their feet burned away, or red-hot coals applied to their faces, backs, and genitals. Others were not provided with food or water until they admitted there was no God. Some refused and died of thirst and hunger. Young Dhofari men returned from the communist training camps, their long hair shaved off, reciting like machines, 'The Koran, the Prophet, and all other manifestations of Islam are inventions of the British imperialists who are running dogs and lackeys of the US.' If these converts found anyone opposing them, they would burn out their eyes in public with a fire-heated pocket knife, while reciting Karl Marx.

The man responsible for so much of this misery was Salim Amr. He had earned a reputation for exceptional cruelty; for instance, he was renowned for lowering male villagers over a fire with their legs spread apart so that their most sensitive parts would be kippered slowly but surely.

After telling me all of this, Abdullah at last lowered his voice. 'It is said that the Sultan's son Qaboos will rule before long,' he said. 'With the oil money that now pours into Oman, thanks be to God, he will give us all those things which the communists promise without changing our religion. If you British leave before that can happen, then the communists will take over without a doubt. They will force us to leave Islam or kill us.'

I was still troubled by the situation but understood that the best service our officers and men could offer was to keep the adoo at bay until Qaboos took over from his father and gave the people of Dhofar a better way of life.

While I came to terms with what I must do, Lawrence also realised that one option was still available to him. If the Arabs were going to have any say in what lands were to be theirs, then they needed to strike out on their own and claim them. 'I vowed to make the Arab Revolt the engine of its own success,' he wrote, 'as well as handmaid to our Egyptian campaign; and vowed to lead it so madly in the final victory that expediency should counsel to the Powers a fair settlement of the Arabs' moral claims.'

And the first prize they could target was the port of Akaba. This would see the Arabs further stretch the

Turkish forces in the Hejaz and bring the Arab Revolt within striking distance of Damascus and Jerusalem. But to do this, Lawrence would need to act alone, without his British superiors' knowledge, consent, or financial or logistical support. This wasn't necessarily a problem. He knew he could certainly rely on Feisal for men, camels, and money, and the arrival of Auda and the Howeitat tribe made it all the more possible. With Auda by Lawrence's side, they could move north, raising other, smaller tribes as they went, before attacking Akaba from the direction the Turks would least expect.

With this in mind, Lawrence excitedly outlined his plan to Auda and Feisal. In principle, they were enthusiastic, but they were also cautious. Reaching Akaba would involve a desert march of more than 600 miles, across some of the world's harshest and most challenging terrain. They would be unable to carry much in the way of guns or stores, and there were no water-skins to buy at Wejh 'for love or money', so any travelling party would be left dependent on wells along the way. Persuading other tribes to join them en route was also far from certain.

Despite all of these dangers, Lawrence, Feisal, and Auda understood the enormous importance of an unexpected Arab victory without the help of the British. It was extremely risky, but it was worth it. Preparations were therefore made for an operation that could transform the Arab Revolt and put their future into their own hands.

Before setting off, Lawrence wrote an apologetic letter to General Clayton in Cairo, informing him that his 'intentions were for the best'. Without waiting to receive a reply or even bothering to tell his superior officers of his plan, Lawrence set off with his Arab followers on his most epic journey yet. Now he was going rogue, and he had truly transformed into one of them. But only victory would be enough to help the Arabs get what they desired while protecting Lawrence from severe consequences.

11

In the early hours of 9 May 1917, Lawrence left Wejh accompanied by Auda and fewer than fifty tribesmen. Also joining them on the journey was twenty-seven-year-old Sherif Nasir, who would act as Feisal's spokesman to the tribes. As the brother of the Emir of Medina, he immediately earned a lot of respect. The Syrian nationalist politician Nesib el-Bekri was also along for the ride, hoping to make contact with Feisal's supporters in the north, and pave the way for the eventual move on Damascus.

Sweeping into the desert on their camels, each man carried forty-five pounds of flour, intended to last him for six weeks, as well as sharing the load of 22,000 gold sovereigns. Wherever necessary, these were to be used as tools of persuasion. As always, the men carried plenty of ammunition, blasting gelatine, fuses, and wires so that they could continue to target the railway.

Along the way, Lawrence rode next to Auda, hoping to get to know him a little better. Standing over six feet tall and with a long black beard, he was everything you might expect an Arab warrior to look like. But while he had earned a fearsome reputation on the battlefield, Lawrence also found him to be intelligent, quick-witted, and with a mind filled to the brim with stories of love, war and adventure, as well as legendary tales about the bravery of his tribal ancestors. His physique, deep voice, and natural confidence gave him a certain gravitas. Lawrence liked him at once.

Riding through the night and into the next day, the sun beat down upon Lawrence and the tribesmen, leaving them breathless. As the glare reflected from the white sand into their eyes, the rocks on either side of their path soon became 'too hot to touch and threw off waves of heat in which our heads ached and reeled'. A few days in, Lawrence was troubled by the same boils and fevers that had given him so much pain on his way to Abdulla's camp at Wadi Ais. 'The weight is bearing me down now,' he wrote on 13 May, '. . . pain and agony today.' Finally, he could take it no more. At his request, they rested briefly, with each man throwing a blanket over the branches of a thorn bush to try and get some shade.

After a while, they were on the move again, soon reaching an oasis where an old farmer was happy to sell them some fresh vegetables. Despite this, Lawrence and many of the Arabs were unable to continue. The heat was far too fierce. Resting for two nights to regain their strength, Lawrence began to question his judgement. If a hardened man of the desert such as Auda had urged caution against such a journey, surely it would be too much for a relative novice like him. But it was too late to turn back now. The Arabs were depending on him.

The rest at the oasis at least replenished their energy, but soon after setting off again, they were forced to dismount and climb 'a precipitous cliff'. Two camels fell and broke legs, while Lawrence dared not look below, salty

Thomas Edward Lawrence's birthplace in Tremadog, North Wales.

Lawrence *(left)* was born to Sarah Junner *(centre)* and Thomas Chapman, who left his wife Edith to be with Sarah. The couple did not marry, adopting the pseudonym Lawrence to live together.

A young Thomas Lawrence at Oxford High School for Boys, in 1901.

Thomas *(left)* with his brothers *(left to right)*: Frank, Arnold, Robert and William.

After graduating from Jesus College Oxford, Lawrence worked as an archaeologist in the ancient Hittite city of Carchemish.

I, too, had a taste of archaeology, while searching for the lost city of Ubar, the Atlantis of the Sands.

While in Carchemish, Lawrence struck up a close friendship with fifteen-year-old Dahoum *(above)*, who accompanied him on a trip home to Oxford. Much has been speculated about their possible romance – there is little doubt he was one of the few people Lawrence truly loved.

Lawrence in his British Army officer uniform – after enlisting in October 1914, he began his military career in Cairo.

Archaeologist Leonard Woolley *(left)* and Lawrence at their excavation house in Carchemish.

Soldiers carrying the flag of the Arab Revolt. Sherif Hussein and his allies commenced resistance against the Ottoman Empire in June 1916, but were soon outgunned and outnumbered. Eager to escape his dull duties in Cairo, Lawrence requested to join the British officials travelling to Jidda to meet Hussein's sons – his part in reigniting the Revolt was about to begin.

Sherif Hussein's sons *(left to right)*: Ali, Abdulla, Zeid and Feisal. Lawrence met with all four men in turn, and Feisal impressed him as being suited to lead the Arab Revolt, with his charisma and accounts of his bravery on the battlefield.

Feisal *(centre, seated)* and Lawrence *(crouched right of Feisal)* consulting with Bedouin sheikhs. After his report recommending Feisal, Lawrence was sent to serve as the prince's liaison officer and to train Arab bands.

Much of the desert warfare utilised camel cavalry, with the British Empire raising an Imperial Camel Corps Brigade in 1916.

Attacks on the railways and trains proved an effective strategy, disrupting the Turkish supply lines. Some of the trains and railways Lawrence was involved in destroying can still be seen in the desert today, over a century later.

Lawrence soon after the capture of Wejh – a significant result which boosted morale among the Arabs and gave them a base north of Medina.

Following Wejh, Lawrence, Feisal and Auda set their sights on the port of Akaba in southern Jordan, a 600-mile march across the desert. Here, a flag bearer mounted on a camel leads the entry march.

Auda Abu Tayi *(centre)*, Howeitat tribal leader, with his brothers. Auda's fearsomeness was legendary throughout Arabia, and just what the Arab Revolt required.

Arab fighters assemble in Akaba.

Discussing surrender terms in Akaba on 5 July.

Ruined buildings in Akaba following naval bombardment – British Naval ships can be seen in the background.

Lawrence *(standing)*, with his assembled bodyguard.

Like T. E. Lawrence, I led an Arab platoon in a fight for their country, in my time with the army of the Sultanate of Oman in the 1960s. Also like Lawrence, it was an experience that would take me to the edge. His example often inspired me to victory in life-or-death situations, and I found myself in awe at some of his decisions.

sweat dripping into his eyes as he fixed his stare ahead. At least the meat from the slaughtered camels brightened the group when they rested that night under the yellow moon.

When they set off at dawn, their silhouettes over the dunes took on a ghostly hue, the black merging into one with the orange sky. At last, they reached the Abu Raga encampment of Sherif Sharraf, a major figure in Sherif Hussein's court in Mecca. Sharraf was currently away, but Lawrence and Auda were told they were welcome to stay until he returned the following day. Once more, Lawrence was grateful for the opportunity to rest.

As he took a seat behind some sandstone blocks, relieved to find some shade, Lawrence saw a young Arab squatting beside him. The boy introduced himself as Daud. He explained that his best friend, Farraj, had burned their tent for a joke, and was now due to be beaten as a punishment. He pleaded for Lawrence to intervene, hoping that Farraj might be spared. Lawrence soon found out that the two boys were always involved in practical jokes, and there was little sympathy for them. Most thought it was time they learned a lesson. The best that could be offered was that Daud must also share the punishment. To Lawrence's surprise, this immediately cheered Daud up.

After the shared beating, Daud returned to Lawrence with Farraj by his side. Lawrence suspected that while they were inseparable as friends, they might also be lovers. 'They were an instance of the eastern boy and boy affection,' he wrote, 'which the segregation of women made inevitable.' Such relations were certainly not unusual in

Arab tribes. I recall sitting by a stream one day and watching two of my men squatting in the water nearby. Both were Baluchis, and while they defecated, they held hands and chatted in whispered tones. While this was shocking to any British officer at the time, many of the men I observed had an intimacy of this kind.

Daud and Farraj were grateful to Lawrence and pleaded that they be allowed to serve him on his mission to Akaba by way of recompense. Lawrence initially turned them down, but he soon found the pair's fun-loving personalities so infectious that against his better judgement he agreed that they could join him. He thought they might be good for morale, if nothing else.

Finally, after two days of waiting at Abu Raga, a celebratory volley of rifle shots signalled the arrival of Sharraf. Even Auda recognised the importance of the occasion. To greet the old man, he put on his best clothes, along with his prized elastic-sided boots.

Over a sumptuous meal of rice and mutton, Lawrence asked Sharraf if he could spare nineteen of his warriors for their mission. Ever loyal to Sherif Hussein, he not only agreed to Lawrence's request but also told him there were pools of rainwater in the dry, barren country ahead. This was excellent news.

Resuming their journey the next day, the camels stumbled and slipped as they passed over a black volcanic plateau. In the flickering haze of the heat, they suddenly saw another traveller walking towards them. Reaching for his rifle in case they might be from an enemy tribe, Lawrence was surprised to make out 'a fair haired, shaggy-bearded Englishman in tattered uniform'. It was Henry Hornby, one of Newcombe's men.

The two Brits were delighted to find each other in the middle of the desert. Lawrence learned that Newcombe and Hornby had been keeping four Turkish labour battalions occupied with their attacks on the railway line. 'These were legends,' he said of their efforts. Hornby was now almost deaf in one ear after a charge had exploded in his face, but he had zealously destroyed the railway like a man possessed. Such was his dedication, Lawrence wrote, 'Hornby would worry the metals [rails] with his teeth when guncotton failed.'

Leaving Hornby to his travels, they continued onwards, grateful for the fresh pools of rainwater to slake their thirst. Lawrence was also glad of the company of Farraj and Daud. Unable to remain serious, their cheery nature constantly made him smile. They also proved to be of some use, dressing his camel with butter to help relieve it of mange. He was glad that he had allowed them to join him. Life without them would undoubtedly have been far more boring, and they also appealed to his own juvenile nature.

Eleven days after leaving Wejh, the party finally reached the railway near Dizad. Pausing to place explosives 'with a child's first pleasure', they also pulled down the telegraph poles and wires. They then rode into the furnace of El Houl, known as 'the desolate place', where the superheated desert wind cracked and parched their lips and skin. Lawrence's notes record that it was 'a grey country utterly without trees or shrubs or any grazing – whence its name.

Horrible sand-blasts sweep across it, and sun heat and mirage are bad.'

Battling sunburn, heat stroke, and severe thirst, the men carried on in silence, the oven-like heat affecting their ability to speak, let alone think. They needed to conserve all of their energy to continue. For once, even Daud and Farraj did not say a word.

In these deadly conditions, they rode for three days and nights, 'the hammer strokes of the sun upon our bowed heads', before they at last reached a well. The water might have been 'slightly brackish', but that didn't prevent them from gulping down as much as their stomachs could hold, swiping away flies who tried to suck at the salty perspiration dripping down their brows.

Passing the towering, brick-coloured sand dunes at Nefudh, Auda led the group across the white mudflats, which reflected the heat and made it feel like their faces were being sizzled. It had been almost two days since they had last drunk any water, and the nearest well was still a day's march away. Lawrence almost blacked out, while even the camels slowed their pace, struggling to continue. Dismounting to give the camels a break, Lawrence suddenly noticed that one of the beasts was riderless. After a quick head count, he realised that the missing rider was Gasim, a 'gap toothed, grumbling fellow . . . bad tempered, suspicious, brutal, a man whose engagement I regretted'. Indeed, it seems nobody cared much for the surly stranger from Maan, hence why he had not been missed. Lawrence realised that he must have fallen off somewhere along their march, with no one noticing. Surveying the vast stretch of desert, Lawrence could see no sign of him. In these conditions, he feared he might already be dead.

It would have been easy for Lawrence to continue onwards and not be blamed for 'shirking his duty'. After all, he was still regarded as a foreigner who was not strictly bound by the Arabs' rules and morals. Indeed, most of the Arabs would have happily continued without Gasim. But Lawrence saw the bigger picture. If he was going to lead the Arabs into battle, he had to prove that he could meet their standards, even when they could not meet them themselves. Weighing up his options, Lawrence realised that, as little as he liked Gasim, he had to go back for him.

Turning away from the group, he rode back into the vast furnace of the desert. But finding Gasim, alive or dead, would not be easy. Lawrence had no idea how far back he had fallen and he himself was severely dehydrated. The further he retraced his steps, the further away the next well became. All the while, he battled exhaustion and heat stroke.

After an hour and a half of desperately scanning the barren landscape, he finally saw an object move. At first, he dismissed it as a mirage, but as he got closer he realised it was Gasim, 'nearly blinded' and stammering incoherently. Lawrence handed him the last of the tribe's water, which Gasim, wailing and mumbling, desperately splashed all over his face, his broken lips and hanging tongue lapping up the drops as they fell into his mouth.

Seating Gasim beside him, Lawrence set off on the long ride back, using his army compass to retrace his steps. Gasim continued to scream and babble, until Lawrence could stand it no more. Striking him in the face, he threatened to throw him off and ride on by himself. This eventually silenced the traumatised man.

After finally reaching Auda, the old warrior shook his head in disgust. 'For that thing, not worth a camel's price,' he shouted, striking out at Gasim. Yet as Lawrence had calculated, the episode earned him much good will amongst the Arabs. They knew that if he would risk his life for a man as worthless as Gasim, then he was a man they could trust and follow. Much like the execution of Hamed the Moor, the rescue of Gasim furthered Lawrence's reputation as being 'one of them'.

Still, there was no time for any fleeting thoughts of hero worship. They were now all out of water, and the temperature was rising. With sand blasting against their parched and burned faces, it became impossible to continue. They had no choice but to stop for the night without water or food, and prayed they could reach the wells the next day. If not, then they might well die of thirst.

Waking in the dead of night to take advantage of the lower temperature, they rode under the vast twinkling sky at a canter towards the wells of Arfaja. As the stars faded one by one, a soft orange light rose on the horizon as they finally reached their destination. To their relief, they found the water was 'creamy' and 'delicious'. There was also lots of foliage to feed the camels. In such surroundings, Lawrence decided they should stop and rest. The last few days had taken their toll on all of them, including Auda, who was unusually silent.

However, even in the wilderness they were not safe.

That night, as they gathered around a fire and drank coffee, yellow flashes lit up the darkness as gunshots suddenly rained down on the camp. A man called Assaf rocked back into the dirt, his coffee flying from his hands, as he was shot in the chest. Auda's cousin Mohammed quickly kicked sand over the fire while the others grabbed their rifles and furiously fired in all directions. Silence now greeted them in return. It appeared they had forced their attacker away, but they could take no chances. That night they dared not sleep, all fearing that the attacker might return at any moment.

In the safety of first light, they left the wells, and Auda led them to a Howeitat encampment where they would be safe. Receiving a warm welcome, they sat on rugs in a large tent as a copper bath was presented, full to the brim with rice and covered in the legs and ribs of a sheep, including its boiled head, 'the jaws opened to cracking point and yawning upwards,' Lawrence recalled, 'showing the open throat, the tongue sticking to the teeth and the bristling hair of the nostrils and jaw round the incisors, lips left full.' The guests of honour were allowed to enjoy the choice morsels of meat first, dipping their right hand into the tub and fishing around amongst the rice. If any of the Arabs should be lucky enough to find a good chunk of meat, they would first offer it to Lawrence or Auda before being allowed to consume it themselves. It had been a long time since they had enjoyed a feast like this and every man ate until he was fit to burst.

Before continuing their journey, it was decided that Auda should travel to see Emir Nuri Shaalan and present him with six bags of gold coins. Nuri led the desert tribes of Syria and the Lebanon known as the Rwala. They would need his blessing if they were to continue on his lands without facing substantial opposition. Agreeing to reconvene with Auda at Nebk, Lawrence and the tribes were soon on the move again. They were now deep behind Turkish lines, with a large part of the population favouring the Ottoman Empire or in its pay. By this time, Lawrence was also a wanted man, with a substantial sum offered for his capture, dead or alive.

Meanwhile, Farraj and Daud continued to delight and annoy Lawrence and the tribesmen in equal measure. Yet after playing a prank with snakes, even Lawrence had had enough and ordered them to be struck across the backside six times, hoping it might deter them. Of course, it didn't.

Finally arriving at Nebk, grateful for the plentiful water and grazing, they were soon joined by Auda, who brought with him ever more tribesmen, as well as the vital blessing of Nuri Shaalan. The path towards Akaba was now open to them. All seemed back on course when Sherif Nasir and Auda suddenly proposed a change of plan. Rather than continue on their path to take Akaba, they believed that with Nuri Shaalan on their side, they might be able to raise all the tribes of Syria and Lebanon and aim for Damascus itself.

Lawrence was alarmed. At this stage, it was doubtful that all of Syria could be raised against the Turks. They would surely be significantly outnumbered. Even if they could somehow take Damascus, they could not hold it for more than six weeks, certainly not until the British had broken through the Turkish lines at Gaza and the Arabs had taken Akaba.

To head off this lunacy, Lawrence tactfully played to each man's ego. He gently suggested to Auda that an advance on Damascus would see Sherif Nasir hailed as the all-conquering hero. Conversely, he told Nasir that raising the local tribes to advance on Damascus would put Auda in effective control of the expedition. With this, Lawrence managed to stave them off and convince them that for now they needed to focus on taking Akaba. Maybe then they might be in a position to talk of marching on Damascus.

All the bickering and political machinations left Lawrence on the brink. It was enough to argue with the British, let alone the Arabs. He was exhausted, both physically and mentally. The camp at Wadi Sirhan also wasn't helping his mood. He described it as 'Hideously green, unbearable, sour, putrid smelling, with the ugly, pitiless landscape, rich only in poisonous snakes, the "Leprosy of the world!"' The longer he thought about the situation, the more he convinced himself that his efforts were worthless. Ultimately, the French, British, and Russians had already decided what would happen to the Arabs and their lands. The conceit of encouraging them to fight without knowing the full picture was becoming too much to bear.

Finally he snapped. He needed to get away at once. In his notebook, he scribbled some words for General Clayton: 'Clayton, I've decided to go off alone to Damascus, hoping to get killed on the way: for all sakes try and clear this show up before it goes further. We are calling them to fight for us on a lie, and I can't stand it.'

With this, Lawrence disappeared from the camp, planning to 'chuck it'. At this point, the daily notes that Lawrence had been making during the journey cease, and the incident is only vaguely covered in just one short paragraph in his autobiography, *Seven Pillars of Wisdom*. While Lawrence writes that he 'planned to go off myself . . . on a tour of the north country', there is little detail other than 'a rash adventure suited my abandoned mood'. Years later, Lawrence told his biographer Robert Graves of this period: 'You may make public if you like the fact that my reticence upon this northward raid is deliberate, and based on private reasons: and record your opinion that I have found mystification, and perhaps statements deliberately misleading or contradictory, the best way to hide the truth of what really occurred, if anything did occur . . . I do not want the whole story to be made traceable.'

British and French intelligence reports later revealed that Lawrence may have undertaken an undercover mission into Syria to ascertain how much support there was for the Arabs' proposed invasion. It has been suggested that over the next few days he travelled to the outskirts of Damascus and met a prominent Arab nationalist called Ali Riza al-Rikabi. It seems Rikabi told him that conditions were not yet favourable for any uprising. The Turks were still far too strong within Damascus, and unless Lawrence had a very strong army with him, the chances of success were slim. From there, Lawrence is said to have met

Hussein el-Atrash, the leader of the Druse tribe, who was not only willing to support the Revolt but to take him to see Nuri Shaalan of the Rwala at the old man's camp near Azrak.

The old man's reputation alone was enough to earn the respect of Auda, and Lawrence soon found out why. He described the tribal leader as 'very old, livid and worn . . . Over his coarse eyelashes the eyelids wrinkled down, sagging in tired folds, through which, from the overhead sun, a red light glittered in his eyes and made them look like fiery pits in which the man was slowly burning.' He was certainly not a man to trifle with. While he was now in his seventies, he had previously killed two of his brothers to take control of his tribe. Despite his age, he was still very sharp and did not trust the British or the French.

During their meeting, Nuri passed Lawrence some documents containing Britain's promises to the Arabs over the past three years. Lawrence was embarrassed. They all seemed to contradict each other. No wonder so many tribal leaders were so cautious when dealing with the British and French. Lawrence did not want to lie to the old man or try to cover things up. If he did, he was sure Nuri would see right through him. Instead, he told him that it continued to be a fluid situation and only to believe the latest promise and disregard the rest. Nuri seemed satisfied by this explanation. Lawrence had not tried to lie to him, and at least shared the same cynicism he felt for the situation.

However, as Lawrence prepared to return to the camp

at Nebk, it was clear that many other tribal leaders, like Nuri, were beginning to question the Brit's intentions and whether supporting the Arab Revolt was worth their while. The only thing that could persuade them otherwise was if the Arabs were to take Akaba, yet there was still a long way to go and many more obstacles to overcome.

12

On 16 June 1917, Lawrence finally returned to Nebk. Whatever he might have done and wherever he might have been, he seemed refreshed and refocused. He also appeared to relish the opportunity to spend some time with his Arab friends. When Auda made a speech teasing one of the tribesmen, Lawrence proceeded to join in, not only poking fun at the man, but also mimicking Auda's epic storytelling style, leading to 'waves of laugher'. This only made the tribesmen warm to Lawrence more. Amidst the laughter and tall tales, Lawrence took in all the men who had put their faith in him. In the dying embers of the flickering firelight, he saw that some were thieves of the desert, some were simple men obeying orders or looking for a way to support their families, while others truly believed in the Revolt and were desperate to secure their independence. Whatever their motivation, he prayed he would not betray their trust.

These moments were also some of my favourite memories from my time in Oman. Over a fire, I remember watching my men talk into the small hours but never speaking derisively, trying to score over their neighbour in conversation, as is the way of British soldiers. They could express themselves without the need to swear or any alcoholic stimulus. I thought of other army nights by other fires: the clatter of empty beer cans, the filthy language punctuating every sentence, the crude laughter as someone rose to urinate into the flames. I felt happy, and at one with these Muslim soldiers in a way I had never experienced with my own kind. There was no ever-present barrier of self-consciousness, no superficial officer–soldier gap designed and perpetuated to prevent familiarity gnawing at discipline. Such a gap was unnecessary with the Arabs since they accepted an inch without coveting a mile. Their morals and manners were built in, as was their respect for authority. I, too, felt more at one with them than my own kin and just hoped what I was doing was right.

Setting out again on 19 June, with his army now over 500 strong, the Arabs began a two-day march to the wells at Bair. En route, Auda asked Lawrence to ride ahead with him to visit the grave of his son Annad, who had been killed in a feud with their Motalga cousins. However, as Auda crouched at his son's grave, they spotted smoke rising from the direction of the wells at Bair. Something was wrong. Riding towards them, they found the wells covered in rocks and mud. Closer inspection revealed they had been destroyed with dynamite. It could only have been the Turks.

Panic quickly set in. If they could not take water from the wells, their position would be grave. They were already pushing their bodies to the limit, and the success of the whole journey relied on these wells being available. Frantically searching the area, it seemed all of them had been destroyed. Just as things looked bleak, Auda shouted across to Lawrence. He had managed to find a hidden well that was undisturbed. But it was small. There was no way it could provide water for over 500 men, not to mention their camels. Looking back to the destroyed wells, they knew that they somehow had to get at least one of them open again. Inspecting them all one by one, Lawrence found a small gap amidst the rubble. He thought it might be big enough to squeeze a bucket through and lower it into the water.

A full-blown crisis was averted, for now at least, but Lawrence was sure this wouldn't be the end of the matter. Only good fortune had enabled them to drink from the wells at Bair. What of the other crucial water stops on their way to Akaba? They would have no hope of reaching the port if they had also been destroyed. Worse still, if the Turks were dynamiting the wells, then they surely knew of Lawrence and his army. Indeed, any number of Turkish supporters might have informed on them. If that was the case, they would no doubt have filled the interior with troops to defend their route to Akaba. Lawrence couldn't yet be sure of this, but if the operation had been difficult before, this might make it all but impossible.

Before they could contemplate such a disaster, they first needed to work out if it was possible to continue. Deciding to camp at Bair, they sent a scout ahead to the wells at Jefer to report on their condition. If the wells at Jefer were also destroyed, then not only was there no further water available, but the Turks surely knew of the Arabs' intentions to attack Akaba from the interior. In the meantime, rather than wait around, Lawrence decided to make use of his time and attack the railway. He hoped this would at least make the Turks look in the wrong direction and think that perhaps they had been wrong about the Arabs' target.

Setting off with 100 tribesmen and Auda's nephew, a feared raider known as Zaal, Lawrence finally found a stretch of rail near Minifir. It was unguarded, but better still it was curved. Lawrence knew that to replace any curved rails, the Turks would have to bring replacements all the way from Damascus. If they were to destroy it, the track might be out of action for days, if not weeks.

As Lawrence planted his explosives, the Arabs spotted over 200 Turkish mule-mounted infantry in the distance. Despite inferior numbers, Zaal and the tribesmen were eager to attack. Lawrence urged them to resist. Their main goal was to take Akaba. They needed to do all they could to avoid unnecessary combat or casualties. While the tribes were desperate for action and the booty that went along with it, Zaal managed to persuade them it was unnecessary. In any event, the operation was a success: the buried mines destroyed the curved track and then obliterated the locomotive that arrived from Damascus a few days later to repair it. Lawrence prayed it also focused the Turks' attention away from defending Akaba.

On their return journey to Bair, they encountered a young Circassian cowherd in the desert who they were sure was loyal to the Turks. If he were allowed to continue to his nearby village, he would surely inform on them. From there, it wouldn't be long before the Turks were in hot pursuit. This posed a problem. It seemed unfair to kill the cowherd, but at the same time they could neither take him with them nor turn him loose. Neither could they tie him up, since they had no rope to spare. And even if they could tie him to a tree or a telegraph pole in the desert, he would surely die of thirst. Finally, an unorthodox solution presented itself. Ordering him to strip off his clothes, one of the tribesmen drew his dagger and then swiftly cut the cowherd across the feet. At this, he was set free to crawl naked on his hands and knees to his village, which might take him an hour or two in his condition. This was all the time the Arabs needed to disappear. At the same time, the cowherd would live.

Making life and death decisions for supposed innocents, such as the cowherd, was a dilemma I also faced in Dhofar. While on patrol, my platoon was spotted by two villagers known to be hostile to the Sultan. Some of my men wanted to slit their throats, and I well remembered a horrifying story an SAS soldier had told me. While on an operation in the Radfan mountains of Eastern Aden in 1967, an old shepherd had seen their platoon. They knew he would inform the enemy of their presence, and some urged their commanding officer to cut his throat, but he refused. The old shepherd soon managed to escape, and before long the men found themselves surrounded by hostile tribesmen. Two of the men were captured, including the commanding officer, and their heads cut off and then paraded around the villages. The moral of the story was never to take any chances in such situations.

And yet, I also felt it would be unfair to kill the two villagers, who might have been innocent. Rather than slit their throats, I ordered that we use rifle slings to bind the men together back to back while taping their mouths shut. We then moved onwards, knowing they would be found in the morning when we were far away.

Soon after the Arabs left the Circassian cowherd to crawl back to his village, they came to the Turkish railway station at Atwi. This was a tantalising proposition. The chance for the Arabs to have some action, and booty, was always a big motivator. Better still, this station also had a herd of fat sheep alongside it. For days they had lived off a diet of hard-dried corn kernels. The sheep now represented the chance for a glorious feast. Lawrence was still reluctant to engage in any battle with the Turks, but on this occasion he thought the risk might be worth it. It would not only be good for his men's morale, but once more it would turn the Turks' attention away from Akaba.

Giving the signal to attack, Zaal shot the railway official on the platform before the tribesmen opened fire on the Turks. Thundering forward, they mowed them down as they tried to flee and then ransacked a building and set the station ablaze. Meanwhile, Lawrence destroyed more of the track and took down some telegraph poles.

With the Turks and the station decimated, the Arabs prepared to ride off into the desert, but only after slaughtering the flock of sheep. That night, Lawrence recalled, 'One hundred and ten men ate the best parts of twenty-four sheep.' Both the Arabs and Lawrence were satisfied with their day's work. They had suffered no casualties, the railway had been destroyed, and they had plenty of food and plunder to enjoy as a result. Just as Lawrence had intended, that night the mood was high, and the Turks were no doubt starting to look away from Akaba.

Following the raid, Lawrence and the Arabs returned to Bair at dawn, 'without casualty, successful, well-fed and enriched'. There was further good news to greet their arrival. The tribal leader Nuri Shaalan had sent them a message. About 400 Turkish cavalrymen were hunting for Lawrence's party in Wadi Sirhan. This might have seemed a disaster but the message also revealed that Nuri's nephew was helping to guide the Turks. As such, Nuri had instructed him to take the Turks by the slowest and hardest of routes, away from the Arabs' actual location and further away from Akaba.

However, bad news arrived soon after. The scout who had been sent to Jefer to report on the condition of the wells had returned. It was not good: the wells there had also been destroyed. Lawrence cursed their luck. Even if the Turks might now be looking the wrong way, it would be impossible to continue without water. It seemed the adventure would have to end here. Yet Auda was optimistic. The wells at Jefer were on his family property. As was the case at Bair, he was confident they would be able to find some that the Turks had not been able to destroy. They had little choice but to put their fate in the hands of this flimsy prospect. It was either that or return to Wejh.

After a day's march, they finally reached Jefer. The situation was just as the messenger had reported. All the wells looked to have been destroyed and were covered in rocks. It also seemed the Turks had done a more thorough job than at Bair. There appeared to be no hidden wells they had missed and no apparent gaps in the ones they had destroyed. Removing the rocks covering the wells also proved to be impossible. They were far too heavy, while the wells themselves were filled in. A sense of desolation came over Lawrence until he heard an echo behind him. Turning, he saw one of the Arabs hammering at a rock covering one of the wells. Listening closer, Lawrence realised that it sounded hollow below. If this was the case, then it might not be entirely filled in.

Under the glare of the hot sun, the Ageyl tribesmen frantically went to work. Digging around the soil, they pulled at the rocks with all of their might, hoping to reveal the cool, dark abyss below. It was relentless work, but just before sunset the rubble suddenly crashed into the deep chasm below, along with one of the tribesmen. Rushing towards the hole, the men saw him thrashing around in the water, crying out for help. Reaching for his hands, they fished him out as they laughed and cheered. Against all odds, they had water.

That night they drank from the well until it was dry. The Turks had been certain that they had ensured the Arabs would have no access to water on their way to Akaba. But they were wrong, and the Arabs were now within sight of their final goal.

One obstacle still remained. A Turkish blockhouse at Abu el-Lissal guarded the approach from the north, while the rail track also helped to supply Turkish garrisons along the way to Akaba. If they were to continue, the Arabs had no choice but to engage with the Turks and take the blockhouse. Lawrence therefore sent a pack of riders forward to overwhelm the post while he waited with the rest of the tribesmen in Jefer for news. The result of the attack would determine if and how they could proceed.

The following day a tribesman returned with news. The blockhouse at Abu el-Lissal had been taken but at a bloody cost. As the Arabs approached, they had been spotted by the Turks. While they fled for cover, the Turks approached a local Arab camp from where they thought the tribesmen had come. The retribution was barbaric. The Turks mercilessly murdered all of the women and children by slitting their throats. On hearing what had happened, the Arabs charged at the Turks, killing every last one.

At once, Lawrence and his men immediately set out for Abu el-Lissal. They not only swore of revenge but urgently needed to destroy all of the track to stop the Turkish posts on the way to Akaba from receiving any more supplies. However, luck was against them. A Turkish relief battalion had arrived in Maan just as the news came that Abu el-Lissal had been attacked. It was a coincidence, but the result was that the Turkish column had immediately advanced on Abu el-Lissal, and had now reoccupied the blockhouse and were blocking the advance to Akaba. Suddenly the fruits of two months of hard toil looked to be in real jeopardy.

With the Turks under Nuri's nephew searching for them in Wadi Sirhan, there was no chance the Arabs could turn back as they would surely be found. And yet the path forward also now looked to be blocked. Although he wanted to avoid a direct battle, Lawrence knew there was no choice.

Riding through the night, Lawrence and his men approached Abu el-Lissal in the early-morning haze. From a hilltop, Lawrence could see that the Turks still looked to be sleeping. It was the perfect time to attack. Quickly, he ordered Zaal and some tribesmen to cut the telegraph line to Maan, while the rest of the Arabs spread themselves out on the hills around the campsite. The Turks might have large numbers, but the Arabs had them surrounded.

Lawrence then gave the order to open fire from the high ground. As their tents were peppered with bullets, the Turks quickly arose and exchanged fire. The gunfight continued for hours, with the Arabs constantly on the move, refusing to give the Turks a fixed target and appearing larger in number than was the case. With the telegraph line to Maan cut, Lawrence was confident that the Turks would have no reinforcements on the way. He and his men therefore had to do all they could to wear them down and make them think their situation was hopeless. But as the sun rose, the searing heat soon meant that the Arabs' rifles were often too hot to touch, while the rocks and thorns of the rugged landscape burned and lacerated the soles of their bare feet. Worse still, they were growing desperately short of water, with some collapsing from heat exhaustion.

By late afternoon, Lawrence was also severely dehydrated. Such was his desperation that when he saw some wet mud in a small hollow, he lay down, placed his sleeve in it, and tried to suck out any moisture to relieve his cracked lips. As he did so, Auda approached, grinning. Apparently proud of the efforts of his tribe, he asked, 'Well, how is it with the Howeitat? All talk and no work?' Lawrence was not impressed. 'By God indeed,' he replied, 'they shoot a lot and hit little.' This infuriated Auda. Turning red with rage, he tore off his headdress and threw it to the ground. Running up the hill's steep slope, he called to his tribesmen to come to him. At first Lawrence thought that Auda might be pulling the Howeitat out of the battle. Instead, the old warrior glared at Lawrence and shouted, 'Get your camel, if you wish to see the old man's work!'

As Lawrence and Nasir mounted their camels, they saw Auda and his fifty Howeitat horsemen charge directly down at the rear of the Turkish troops, their robes flapping in the breeze behind them. At this, Lawrence knew it was time to strike the Turkish flank. With Nasir at his side, Lawrence led the charge of his 400 men, firing their revolvers from their saddles. The sudden charge of hundreds of men caught the Turks unawares. Then, just as Lawrence prepared to charge into them, his camel collapsed in a heap, sending him flying out of the saddle. With the bulk of his force rampaging behind, Lawrence braced himself to be trampled to death. Wrapping his arms around his head, hearing his men charging towards him, he was relieved to find them pass around him. Without realising it, the body of his stricken camel had sheltered him from any harm.

Dusting down his white robes, he regained his bearings and looked towards the station. He saw that the battle was all but over. The surprise aggression of the two charges had quickly broken the Turks' formation. As they attempted to flee for cover, the Arabs were merciless, no doubt remembering the murders of the women and children at the nearby camp. They shot until their rifles were empty, before hacking at the stunned Turks with their curved sabres, the blood shimmering on the blades in the sunlight. In just a matter of minutes, over 300 Turks were slaughtered, and 160 wounded were left moaning under the glare of the beating sun. In contrast, the Arabs only lost two men.

Fresh from victory, Auda approached Lawrence. His robes, holster, field-glass case, and even his sword scabbard were all pierced by bullets. Nevertheless, he was unharmed. With 'his eyes glazed over with the rapture of battle', he muttered incoherently, 'Work, work, where are words, work, bullets, Abu Tayi.' Despite this gibberish, it was clear he was satisfied that he had finally proven to Lawrence the might of his tribe. And with Abu el-Lissal finally taken, the prize of Akaba was now within sight.

As ever, water remained scarce between Abu el-Lissal and Akaba. Indeed, the men and animals had almost nothing more to give. Worse, there were still three major Turkish outposts they would have to navigate. If there were much delay in taking them, many of the Arabs would surely die of dehydration. To avoid this and engaging in any more battles, Lawrence had an idea.

Despite the killing frenzy at Abu el-Lissal, some Turkish officers had been spared. Lawrence ordered one of them, a former policeman, to write letters in Turkish to each of the commanders of the three outposts. In them, Lawrence promised that if they surrendered, they would be allowed to live, and taken to Egypt as prisoners. He prayed they would take the bait. If one of the Turkish posts offered serious resistance, then he was not sure the Arabs had enough in them to prevail.

Thankfully, as they approached the first outpost at Guweira, 120 Turks surrendered immediately. This opened up 'the gateway to the gorge of the Wadi Itm', which in turn led directly to Akaba. Yet food and water were running dangerously low. With two outposts still to encounter, they needed to ensure victory quickly.

The next day the garrison at Kethera proved far more resistant to surrender. However, the Turks quickly crumbled when the Arabs launched a night attack under the cover of a lunar eclipse. So far, all had gone like clockwork. They had quickly taken two of the outposts, in less than two days, without suffering any losses. All that now lay between them and Akaba was the Turkish outpost of Hadra, just four miles away.

Descending Wadi Itm, preparing for the final battle, they found the Hadra outpost empty. This seemed strange. Had the Turks fled in advance rather than surrender? That was wishful thinking. The remaining 300 Turks had instead fallen back to Khedra, preparing to defend Akaba with their lives. However, with the wells destroyed and the rail track cut, both sides were now running very low on food and water.

'We sent the Turks summonses,' Lawrence recalled, 'first by white flag, and then by Turkish prisoners, but they shot at both. This inflamed our Bedouin, and while we were yet deliberating a sudden wave of them burst up on to the rocks and sent a hail of bullets spattering against the enemy.'

Neither the invitation to surrender nor the shooting broke the impasse. The Turks were determined to stay put, and Lawrence was reluctant to order a full-scale assault. In the stalemate, the Arabs positioned themselves in gorges, which soon became unbearably hot. Without access to any water, their heads throbbed and their tempers frayed. A final and urgent attempt to persuade the Turks to surrender was therefore made. 'We had a third try to communicate with the Turks, by means of a little conscript, who said that he understood how to do it,' Lawrence recalled. 'He undressed, and went down the valley in little more than boots. An hour later he proudly brought us a reply, very polite, saying that in two days, if help did not come from Maan, they would surrender.'

For Lawrence and the Arabs, this was too long to wait. By then, they would surely be dead. Lawrence accompanied the messenger towards the Turkish position and called for an officer to talk with. He informed the Turks that the telegraph line and the rail had been cut. There was no relief coming to rescue them from Maan. The Arabs could also wait no longer. Unless the Turks immediately lay down their arms, they would attack, and there would be a massacre.

The Turkish commander realised that resistance was futile. On the morning of 6 July 1917, he duly ordered his men to cease firing and surrendered. At this, the last remaining force preventing the Arabs' march towards Akaba was gone.

While the Arabs looted the Turkish camp, Lawrence raced his camel four miles towards the undefended port and plunged headlong into the sea. It was a moment to savour. He had achieved the impossible. Against all odds, and perceived wisdom, Akaba, a critical port, was out of Turkish hands. And while he had killed or captured more than 1,200 Turks, he had lost only two of his own men. It was a scarcely believable triumph. He had promised to 'make the Arab Revolt the engine of its own success', and with Akaba now in Arab hands, without any assistance from the Allies, they had proven they were to be taken seriously.

However, the joy of victory didn't last long. By cutting the rails and therefore the regular Turkish supply caravan from Maan, the port was almost out of supplies. And Lawrence now had more than 500 men, 700 prisoners, and 2,000 local tribesmen close to starvation. Sooner or later, the Turks would also try to retake the port. Lawrence needed to immediately return to Cairo urgently, to inform them of the Arabs' monumental victory and to ask for urgent assistance.

Despite his success, he had no idea how his British superiors might react to his rogue operation. Before embarking on it, he had not sought their permission and, in victory, had strengthened the Arabs' demands for independence. If his superiors took a dim view of his actions, the Arabs might be left to fend for themselves. It might also turn out to be Lawrence's last moment in the war.

13

While Lawrence had spent the previous two months in the desert, he had missed a significant event. Furious at General Murray's failure to take Gaza, Prime Minister Lloyd George had replaced him with General Sir Edmund Allenby, a decorated Boer War veteran who had recently commanded in France. Allenby had been appalled at the senseless loss of life in the trenches, and had fallen out with Douglas Haig, the commander-in-chief of the British Expeditionary Force. Lloyd George thought it best to remove him from this situation. In doing so he realised that his experience, and alternative thoughts on military tactics, might actually be the perfect fit for the Egyptian Expeditionary Force (EEF) in the Middle East. Lloyd George also had a very specific request for him: to capture Jerusalem by Christmas. Considering the British Army had been stuck outside Gaza for two years, this was a tall order. Moreover, given the pressure on the Western Front, Allenby could expect no reinforcements. Yet Lloyd George felt that the capture of Jerusalem, which had last been in Christian hands in 1187, might deliver a blow to the Ottomans and provide a boost to an increasingly war-weary public.

As Allenby pondered this conundrum, Lawrence set off for Cairo along with seven men. Time was of the essence. Thousands were relying on them at Akaba to get help before the Turks returned to try and retake the port. After fifty hours of almost continuous marching, the exhausted party finally arrived at Shatt, on the Suez Canal.

Expecting to find a bustling port, Lawrence was perturbed to discover that it was abandoned. He did not know that a recent plague outbreak had caused everyone to flee. Riding down the deserted streets, he saw that homes and offices had been left as they were. It was like a ghost town. Lawrence began to worry. He had come all this way to get help, and now no one was around.

Searching the empty offices, he was relieved to find that one of the telephones still worked. Picking it up, he asked to be connected to the general headquarters at Suez, from where he requested a boat to take him across the canal. He was told that this was no business for the Army. He would have to call Inland Water Transport instead. However, when he informed Inland Water Transport of the situation at Akaba they were also of little help. Lawrence tried to outline the urgent situation and begged for a boat, until finally 'a sympathetic northern accent from the military exchange' came on the line. '"It's no bluidy good, Sir," they said, "talking to them fooking water boogars, they're all the same."'

At last, Lawrence was connected to a Major Lyttleton at Port Tewfik who handled cargo shipments for the Arab forces at Jidda, Yenbo, and Wejh. Lyttleton promised Lawrence that a boat would be at Shatt for him within the hour. As good as his word, Lawrence and his tribesmen were soon taken to Port Tewfik, where he was told that a train would be able to take him to Cairo the next morning. Until then, he could stay at the Sinai Hotel, where he enjoyed his first hot bath in months and luxuries such as iced lemonade, dinner, and a real bed. Meanwhile, his men were sent northward 'to the animal camp on the Asiatic side' in Kubri, and provided with rations and bedding. From his room, Lawrence wrote an urgent telegram to Clayton to ensure that he was fully briefed.

With no time to waste, Lawrence caught the train to Cairo the following morning. While changing trains at Ismailia, he recognised one of Admiral Wemyss's aides, Captain Rudolph Burmester, on the platform, and introduced himself. At first, Burmester didn't recognise him. Since Lawrence had been away, his weight had dropped to less than ninety-eight pounds, his thin face was blackened by the sun, while he was barefoot and in white Arab robes. However, the sensational news of the capture of Akaba quickly saw Burmester move into action. He promised to load a ship with 'all the food in Suez' and send it to the city at once.

Following this, Lawrence finally arrived in Cairo at noon on 10 July 1917 and went straight to the Savoy Hotel, where the Arab Bureau was located. Entering Clayton's office, travel-stained and in his robes, his boss merely glanced up and said 'Mush fadi' ('Go away'). When the figure didn't move, Clayton was ready to reprimand him when he suddenly stopped. He couldn't believe his eyes. It was Lawrence.

Having received Lawrence's telegram, Clayton was already well aware of the situation in Akaba. For now he ignored the fact that it had been an unauthorised operation and was hard at work reinforcing the position. He told

Lawrence that Burmester had ensured that HMS *Dufferin* was already en route to Akaba with the food and supplies, along with £16,000 in gold which was to be used to pay the tribal sheikhs who had provided men and access across their lands.

Lawrence was relieved that, for now at least, disaster had been averted. He was also happy that he seemed to have escaped any reprimand for his actions. But then he was summoned to meet General Allenby, a man known as 'The Bull'.

Allenby was a stickler for perfection, particularly when it came to every detail of military uniform, regardless of rank. Ronald Storrs recalled that if anything displeased him, the subject of his ire was made to feel like they were being blown from the muzzle of a gun. Despite this, Lawrence went to see him still wearing his white Sherifian robes and headdress. He claimed that moths had eaten his army uniform while he was away, so he had no choice but to continue to dress as an Arab. It is also likely that Lawrence wanted to display where his sympathies lay. For a first meeting with Allenby, this was quite a risk.

'He sat in his chair looking at me,' Lawrence recalled, 'not straight, as his custom, but sideways, puzzled.' It was as if Allenby was trying to decide how much of what he saw was 'genuine actor and how much charlatan'. But when Lawrence explained how he had taken Akaba from the interior with the Arab tribesmen, Allenby soon realised that the bedraggled figure might just be the real deal. Moreover, he might also be able to help him achieve his impossible goal.

Allenby had been pondering how on earth he could take Jerusalem by Christmas. He had quickly understood that advancing up the coast to attack Gaza for the third time would get him nowhere. The Turks had already repelled two advances from this route and would be well prepared for a third. Therefore, his plan was first to take Beersheba to secure its vital wells to supply his forces for the push towards Jerusalem. To achieve this, he needed a fast-moving force on his right flank to occupy the Turks. Such a force would be situated in the desert, so would need to go for long periods without ready access to food or water. He now realised that Lawrence and the Arabs could fulfil this role. They could isolate the three Turkish divisions at Medina, while at the same time smashing trains and railway lines, cutting the Turks' communications, and keeping their attention focused in the wrong direction.

Lawrence thought this also represented a tantalising opportunity for the Arabs. He therefore made a long list of demands, which included more food, small arms, ammunition, Lewis guns and instructors, Stokes mortars and instructors, armoured cars, flights of British aircraft, enormous amounts of high explosives, and even more camels and mules. He also asked for 'a fund of two hundred thousand sovereigns to convince and control the converts'. This seemed an extraordinary request, but Allenby recognised that if this was what it took to take Jerusalem, then it was a price worth paying. For Lawrence, it also ensured that the Arabs were finally fully supported by the British, and all within striking distance of Syria.

Following their meeting, Allenby immediately sent a

telegram to the War Office which read: 'The advantages offered by Arab co-operation on lines proposed by Captain Lawrence are, in my opinion, of such importance that no effort should be spared to reap full benefit therefrom.'

However, there was one difficulty that still needed to be overcome. Feisal's Arab forces would now need to move from Wejh and base themselves at Akaba, where they would come under Allenby's command. Unsurprisingly, Feisal's father, Sherif Hussein, was far from comfortable with this prospect. To help smooth things out, Lawrence volunteered to speak to him in Jidda.

Meanwhile, Lawrence's exploits in Akaba saw him recommended for Britain's highest decoration for bravery, the Victoria Cross. He was not, however, eligible for it, as no British soldier had witnessed his success. He was instead awarded the Companion of the Order of the Bath (CB), although this also presented a minor problem as a CB could not be awarded to an officer below field rank. To get around this, Lawrence was instantly promoted to major. He was still only twenty-eight years old. By comparison, Nelson had been thirty-nine when he received the same award, while the Duke of Wellington had been forty-four.

It was an extraordinary achievement, but Lawrence was embarrassed by the award and the many others that would follow. In a revealing letter to his father, he wrote, 'All these letters and things are so many nuisances afterwards and I'll never wear or use any of them. Please don't either. My address is simply T.E.L., no titles please.' With the Arabs' hopes of independence in the balance, he no doubt felt undeserving of any honours until he had rectified the situation. Perhaps then, at last, he might have fulfilled his mother's wishes, and brought honour back to the family. In such circumstances, he might be more willing to accept any awards that came his way.

Upon arriving in Jidda, Lawrence prepared himself for a difficult conversation with Sherif Hussein. Feisal had warned him that his father might not be amenable to the idea of the Arab forces coming under Allenby's command. Indeed, even at the best of times the British found Hussein to be unreasonable, intolerably long-winded and vain. Lawrence was grateful that Colonel Wilson would also be present for the meeting. After many years negotiating with Hussein, Wilson knew better than most how to deal with him.

The meeting initially proceeded as Lawrence had expected. King Hussein, dressed in his trademark black robe and white turban, offered them cups of cardamom-flavoured coffee and sweet sherbet, while making clear he was suspicious of Britain's intentions and of losing control. The conversation then turned to the Sykes–Picot Agreement; a subject Wilson certainly wanted to avoid. But Hussein quickly went off on a tangent to talk of religion and his hatred towards his rival, Ibn Saud. For a moment, the whole Revolt looked in jeopardy before Wilson appealed to the old man's vanity. He promised that by working in tandem with the British, the Arabs would soon be marching on Damascus. This set Hussein off, dreaming of the moment he would then be crowned king of the Arabs, as he believed he had been promised.

The crow's feet around his brown eyes twitched upward as he patted Wilson's hand and called him 'ya ibni' ('my son'), a sure sign of his approval. Feisal and his army could now move to Akaba, where they would fall under Allenby's command.

This was a real boost, but as they left the meeting Lawrence felt conflicted. On the one hand, he was relieved that the British and Arabs would now be working in tandem. However, that gnawing feeling in his stomach once more returned. It was again clear that the Arabs expected something very different from what the British and the French were prepared to give in the event of victory. Even if the Arabs did get what they wanted, Lawrence doubted Hussein's ability to rule. In a letter to his family, he wrote, 'Upon us as a people is the responsibility of having made him a ruling power, and he is pitifully unfit for the rough and tumble of forming a new administration out of the ruins of the Turkish system.'

My time in Oman also saw me face the man responsible for many of the country's problems. When presenting my Recce Platoon at the Salalah Palace, we were inspected by Sultan Said bin Taimur. As this slight and frail old man approached, I stiffened and saluted. He nodded with a small smile and shook my hand, his turban at the level of my shoulders. He moved as though he had recently recovered from an illness, and his gentle face was pale about the large brown eyes. For some reason, I had been expecting something of a tyrant, so his appearance and manner shocked me.

My thoughts about the man were most confused. After

seeing the kindness in his wrinkled old face and noticing his aura and dignity, I found it difficult to associate him personally with the misery and poverty so prevalent among his subjects. But one thing was certain from his appearance; as Abdullah had told me, he did not have long left to rule. We just had to ensure we kept the adoo at bay before his son took over. Then, we hoped, things would improve at last.

As Lawrence battled with his feelings concerning Sherif Hussein, an urgent telegram arrived from Cairo. The contents left him stunned. Auda Abu Tayi was in secret negotiations with the Turks.

14

Lawrence couldn't believe such treachery could be true. With his own eyes, he had seen Auda swear his allegiance to Feisal, and they had fought side by side to take Akaba. Besides, Auda hated the Turks more than anybody. Surely he wouldn't join them for a few pieces of gold? Yet if this was true, the Howeitat tribe and the Turks would indeed join forces and could already be well on their way to retaking Akaba. This would be a total disaster, not to mention an abject embarrassment. All faith in the Revolt would surely fail, from the Arab side and the British. He had to return to Akaba at once.

After three days aboard HMS *Hardinge*, Lawrence arrived in Akaba and quickly rode to confront Auda at his camp at Guweira. But Lawrence realised he had to tread carefully. If things went badly, he was surrounded by the Howeitat, who now worked with the Turks. Lawrence was also now a marked man with a price on his head. If the Howeitat had no issue betraying Feisal, they would not think twice about handing Lawrence over to the Turks.

After arriving at Guweira, Lawrence found Auda in his tent. Trying to appear relaxed, he greeted him warmly before revealing that he knew about Auda's correspondence with the Turks. So that he could not deny it, Lawrence then quoted phrases from the letters. To Lawrence's surprise, Auda erupted with laughter.

He explained that, unbeknown to him, one of his tribesmen had sent a letter to the Turkish governor under Auda's seal, seeking out terms for switching sides. The governor had agreed on a price and even a demand for a down payment. When Auda found out about it, he caught the messenger with the Turkish gold in the desert and robbed him 'to the skin'. The Turks had been stupid enough to believe he would swap sides and he had taken their money.

However, while Auda again pledged his allegiance to Feisal, it was clear there were still some remaining issues. After taking Akaba, he was angry that he had not yet received any reward, while no guns or troops had yet arrived in support. To calm the situation, Lawrence explained that gold, rifles, ammunition, and food, as well as Feisal and the Arab regulars under Jaafar Pasha, were all on their way. To keep Auda happy, he even made 'a down payment' on the gold. In Oman, we always found that wads of ten-rupee notes could usually calm matters, although sacks of flour, rice, sugar, tea, milk powder, and spices were just as valuable.

A crisis had been averted. Lawrence immediately sent a message to Cairo to soothe any concerns and declared that there was 'no spirit of treachery abroad'. The incident had, however, made Lawrence uneasy. While he might have had grand ambitions for the Revolt so that the Arabs could form their own nation, he recognised that some might put their own needs first. Serving with the Arabs in the desert, Lawrence had been well aware of this, but he realised that many of his superiors in Cairo could never understand it. 'The crowd wanted book-heroes,' he wrote, but in the heat of the desert Revolt, true, unvarnished heroes were hard to come by. No doubt he was also referring to himself. He had long hoped to be a hero, but even he was now tainted by the deceit of the British. His sense of sin was almost overwhelming, and he knew his only chance of redemption lay in leading the Arabs to their independence.

Things became more complicated when, soon after, Lawrence discovered that another party was also in talks with the Turks. A letter from Sir Mark Sykes revealed that the British government was secretly negotiating with the Ottomans, hoping to strike a peace deal. For the British, the situation on the Western Front was becoming desperate. Ceasing war in the Middle East with the Ottomans would allow them to transfer thousands of troops to France. It would also be a blessing for the Turks. They could keep their empire intact and regain control over the Arabs.

Lawrence was disgusted. In a rage, he wrote a withering letter to Sykes, lambasting him for stabbing the Arabs in the back. To avoid a diplomatic incident, Clayton 'spiked' the letter and assured Lawrence that he did not believe a peace deal would materialise. He also told Lawrence that with the Arab and British forces now under Allenby's control, he had faith that they would soon be able to advance into Palestine and then Damascus. With this, the Sykes–Picot Agreement would be obsolete. This somewhat consoled Lawrence, but he did not know who to trust any more.

As the Arabs continued to hold their position in Akaba, Feisal and his regular forces, under Jaafar Pasha, soon arrived. This encouraged thousands of other tribesmen to descend on the port, declaring their loyalty. In a letter to General Clayton, Lawrence wrote that the influx of Arabs had 'become immense, almost impossible, since Feisal arrived. He is unable even to see all the head sheikhs of the newcomers.' British vessels, aircraft, armoured cars, and thousands of troops also came flooding into the city, with Lieutenant Colonel Pierce Charles Joyce in command. A French contingent also arrived under the command of Captain Rosario Pisani, an experienced French colonial officer. At last, the Arabs and the Allies were engaged as one. Although much of this was most welcome, it also caused some issues.

The British and the Arabs came from very different cultures. Lawrence had been shrewd enough to realise he was a guest and to ingratiate himself with his hosts. Not only did he speak Arabic, but he was respectful of their culture and traditions. But some British soldiers weren't quite so willing to follow his lead. Others were ignorant that what they were doing might cause friction or even offence. In Oman, I recall officers reading *Playboy* magazine in front of Omanis, who appeared to be appalled and intrigued in equal measure. To help guide the British, Lawrence wrote an article in the *Arab Bulletin* giving twenty-seven pieces of advice that British soldiers should remember when working alongside the Arabs. He introduced them by saying:

> Handling Hejaz Arabs is an art, not a science, with exceptions and no obvious rules. At the same time we have a great chance there; the Sherif trusts us, and has given us the position (towards his Government) which the

> Germans wanted to win in Turkey. If we are tactful, we can at once retain his good will and carry out our job, but to succeed we have got to put into it all the interest and skill we possess.

Amongst the twenty-seven 'articles' was advice such as 'Be shy of too close relations with the subordinates of the expedition'; 'Your ideal position is when you are present and not noticed'; 'Magnify and develop the growing conception of the Sherifs as the natural aristocracy of the Arabs'; 'The foreigner and Christian is not a popular person in Arabia'; 'However friendly and informal the treatment of yourself may be, remember always that your foundations are very sandy ones'; and 'Wear an Arab headcloth when with a tribe.'

The articles proved that during his time in the Middle East, Lawrence had made a conscious effort to study Arab culture and psychology. Rather than focus on himself and his supposed superiority as a British officer, he had actively made the decision to try to fit in. He realised that only then would he be accepted and be able to lead. Indeed, he was aware that if the British did not try to, at the very least, respect the Arabs' ways and avoid causing offence, then the alliance could be shattered. His articles would be influential for years to come and helped to inspire how I mixed with the Recce Platoon.

As the Brits came to terms with their cultural differences, the Turks regrouped. Since losing control of Akaba, they had been reinvigorated by new supplies and the arrival of the experienced German general, Erich von

Falkenhayn, who had been sent to Syria following service in France. With 6,000 infantry and a regiment of cavalry, the Turks had based themselves at Maan and were now preparing to retake Akaba. Before Lawrence and the Arabs had a chance to move into Syria and the prize of Damascus, they first had to prepare for an all-out assault.

15

To avoid the prospect of the Turks besieging Akaba, the Arabs needed to keep their flank stretched and occupied. While RFC aircraft pounded Maan and other Turkish camps with bombs, Lawrence decided to raid Mudowwara, 'the great water station in the desert eighty miles south of Maan'. If Lawrence could take it or destroy it, the Turks would need 'to add . . . many more water wagons to their trains' to supply the garrison at Medina, further straining their resources and keeping their eyes away from Akaba.

Lawrence thought he could rush the station with 300 Arabs, which he hoped to raise along the way. For the journey, they would be joined by two British Army sergeants, Sergeant Yells, who would operate the Lewis gun, and Brooke, who would operate the Stokes trench mortar. The men were quickly given the imaginative nicknames of 'Lewis' and 'Stokes'. However, these red-faced, uniformed soldiers were novices when it came to the desert, and neither had operated alongside the Arabs before. They would need to adapt quickly.

On 7 September 1917, Lawrence and the Arabs rode out of Akaba and into the desert. With the temperature soon reaching 123 degrees, they tied their headdresses around their faces to protect them from the sun and rode slowly towards Auda's camp in the small village of Guweira, hoping to persuade the Howeitat to join them on their mission.

Arriving two days later, Lawrence found the camp in an angry mood. Besieged by a huge cloud of swarming flies, tempers were fraught. Some of the tribe accused Auda of keeping for himself most of the gold he was receiving from the British. Rather than deal with this issue, Lawrence found Auda more preoccupied with spending time with his young wife in his tent. Despite Lawrence's best efforts, it was clear that on this occasion the Howeitat would not move until Auda had satisfied them. As that didn't appear likely any time soon, he reasoned he would have to leave and hope to find other tribes to join them on their way.

Frustrated at this blow to his plans, Lawrence decided to ride south to Wadi Rumm, known as the Valley of the Moon because of its clear night skies. There they hoped to find a tribe known to be loyal to Feisal. Yet by now the sun was so ferocious that Lewis and Stokes found it difficult to continue. Even the Bedouin complained that it was far too dangerous to travel. Still, there was nowhere to stop. They had no choice but to carry on.

That night, as they set up camp, a Harithi sherif named Aid approached Lawrence in distress. 'In a chilled voice he said, "Lord I am gone blind."' Closer inspection revealed his retinas had been burned out by the sun's reflection off the sand. The desert was often just as dangerous as any enemy could be, and there was more to come.

Carrying the blinded Aid with them, they rode on the

following day through a steep, rose-coloured valley, passing huge boulders that had fallen from 2,000 feet above. It was a sign that a rock could fall and crush them at any moment. Moving on as fast as they could, they crossed a valley so wide that 'a squadron of airplanes could have wheeled in formation', before finally arriving at Wadi Rumm at sunset. There they saw several tents gathered around a spring. At last, they had reached the camp of the tribe known to be loyal to Feisal. Lawrence now hoped he could persuade them to join him in attacking Mudowwara.

Things were not as easy as Lawrence had assumed. The tribe believed the British were helping Auda assert his superiority over them. Lawrence tried his best to appease them, but then a fierce argument broke out with Gasim abu Dumeik of the Dhumaniyeh tribe. Gasim had previously led the daring attack on Abu el-Lissan which had proved so crucial to taking Akaba, yet such was his fury at the situation that he left the camp in a fierce temper, promising to join the Turks.

It was becoming clear that Lawrence would struggle to raise the numbers required to attack Mudowwara. Just as concerning was the fact that the tribes seemed more prepared to fight against each other. Lawrence therefore decided to hurry back to Akaba, along with a companion, to seek assistance. To help rectify the situation, Feisal provided Lawrence with Sherif Abdulla el-Feir, 'his best man present', who would ride with him to Wadi Rumm to calm tensions. He also promised Lawrence twenty more camels to carry explosives.

On returning to Wadi Rumm, Lawrence was relieved

when Sherif Abdulla won over some of the tribal leaders with a 'ready persuasiveness which was the birthmark of an Arab leader'. Gasim might have remained unhappy, but Lawrence was at least able to add around 100 men to his group, from the tribes of the Toweiha, Zuwieda, Darausha, Dhumaniyeh, Togatga, Zelebani, Howeitat and the Ageilat Beni Atiyah. It was still a third of the number he had hoped for, but he decided to proceed, aiming to modify his plans if necessary. Meanwhile, the extra camels Feisal had promised arrived, accompanied by four of Feisal's enormous Sudanese slaves, each armed with a rifle, sword, dagger, and pistol.

On 16 September, Lawrence and the Arabs recommenced their march towards Mudowwara. The atmosphere between the men was, however, uneasy. So many of them were from different tribes, and no one group would talk to the other. To keep some sort of harmony, and not be accused of any favouritism, Lawrence spent the day shuttling back and forth between them, trying to draw them together and ensure each clan felt valued.

He would later write in the *Arab Bulletin* about the issues he faced amongst the various tribes during just one of his raids. 'During the six days' trip I had to adjudicate in twelve cases of assault with weapons, four camel thefts, one marriage settlement, fourteen feuds, two evil eyes, and a bewitchment.' Commanding an army of Arabs from different tribes, Lawrence said, was 'not a job which should be undertaken by foreigners'. Thankfully, he was well versed in such matters and far from your typical foreigner.

Just a day's march away from Mudowwara, they camped

that night on a 'strange flat of yellow mud' and ate 'gazelle meat and hot bread'. When Lawrence was satisfied that all the tribal leaders were rested and well fed, he gathered them together before the dying embers of a fire and outlined his plan of action for the attack. He explained how he hoped to target the railway line 'in the early night' and that if they were successful, they would have some control over the Turks' water supply. This would allow them to protect Akaba and set their sights further afield. The tribal leaders seemed to understand their task and what was at stake for them all. If nothing else, Lawrence hoped this operation would bring them together as one.

The following morning the group made their way to the final well before Mudowwara. However, they found green slime floating on top of the water. Tasting a drop, Lawrence recoiled in disgust. Further examination revealed the Turks had tried to sabotage the well by throwing dead camels into it. Despite the taste, the group had no option but to fill their water-skins. It was too big a risk to hope they would have access to clean water once they had taken Mudowwara. Should things go wrong, then this was their only supply.

As the orange orb of the sun sank inch by inch behind the horizon, Lawrence called a halt to the march. The station at Mudowwara was close. Along with the two sergeants and the Arab leaders, Lawrence crawled across the sand mounds until he could see the buildings and tents of the Turkish garrison in the distance. It didn't look good. To succeed, Lewis and Stokes needed cover for their mortar and machine guns. As far as he could tell, there was none.

Lawrence was also beginning to realise that he did not trust his 116 divided and bickering men in a pitched fight with over 200 Turks. Reluctantly he decided that, for now at least, they would have to delay any attack and target Mudowwara when they were better prepared.

To keep up morale and still do some damage to the Turks, Lawrence decided to look for a quieter section of the rail track and blow up a Turkish train. The next morning, he found a convenient spot along the line to lay a mine. Burying blocks of gelatine in the stone ballast under the tracks, he ensured he left no footprints behind by brushing the sand with the hem of his cloak. Salem, Feisal's favourite slave, was then shown how to operate the exploder. When a train approached, all he had to do was push down on it and watch the train explode. He was honoured to be given such a role and excited to use it.

Against the setting sun, Lawrence returned to the area where the Arabs had taken their camels to graze. But they were not there. Instead, he found they had moved up to a high ridge, where they were highly visible. Unsurprisingly, this had attracted the attention of the Turkish outposts, who were taking shots at them from a distance. Lawrence was dismayed. They had needlessly given away their position.

Just as he feared, the Turks set out from the station in the morning light to hunt them down. As a firefight erupted, Lawrence hoped to keep them at bay until a train approached. However, as the sun grew fiercer and the fighting continued, a stronger Turkish patrol arrived and looked to overwhelm them. Lawrence was about to order his party to retreat when he saw the smoke of two locomotives in the distance.

Rushing to the scene, Lawrence quickly placed his Arabs behind a long ridge parallel to the track while Salem manned the exploder. Upon seeing the Arabs, the Turkish soldiers on the train stuck the muzzles of their rifles out of the windows, ready to open fire. But as the second locomotive began to cross the bridge, Lawrence raised his hand. At this, Salem pushed down on the exploder.

'Out of the darkness came a series of shattering crashes,' Lawrence recalled, 'and long loud metallic clangings of ripped steel, while many lumps of iron and plate, with one wheel of the locomotive, whirled up suddenly black out of the cloud against the sky, and sailed musically over our heads to fall slowly into the desert behind.'

There was silence for a few moments as the smoke cloud drifted away. Lawrence could then see that the mine had completely destroyed the bridge, while one of the locomotives was smashed beyond repair. At this, the Arabs opened fire, picking off the wounded Turks as they tried to escape. Positioned on a ledge above the wreckage, Lewis let rip with his machine gun, mowing down Turks as they tried to escape. Stokes ensured there were few survivors as he fired his mortar bombs to the far side of the train, killing those Turks that Lewis had missed. Meanwhile, Lawrence attached an explosive to one of the locomotive's boilers and detonated it. This ensured that the train was now damaged beyond all repair. Then the Bedouin hungrily searched for loot, tearing through the mangled and smouldering carriages.

The terrified surviving wives and children of Turkish officers hysterically gathered around Lawrence and begged for mercy. They were then pushed out of the way by their husbands, who tried to seize and kiss Lawrence's feet. He kicked them away 'in disgust'. He instead raced to help an old Arab woman who was having difficulty leaving the wreckage and looked bewildered, with soot covering her face and her clothes scorched. The woman was so grateful for Lawrence's assistance that she would later send him a valuable carpet from Damascus as a token of her gratitude.

Before the Turkish forces could descend upon them, the Arabs loaded their camels with as much booty as they could carry, then dispersed into the desert. However, as they fled, Lawrence could not see Salem. Asking if anyone had seen him, he was told that he had been wounded and left behind. Lawrence was furious. Salem had been left in his charge and was one of Feisal's favoured men. Despite knowing that Turkish reinforcements would be on their way, Lawrence asked for Zaal and twelve other tribesmen to join him on a rescue mission.

Nearing the site of the train attack, Lawrence raised his hand, causing his men to pull on the reins of their camels. The area was now swarming with over 150 Turkish soldiers. Not only would it be impossible for them to reach Salem, but it was very likely he was already dead; if not from his wounds, then the Turks would certainly have finished him off.

Returning to the main body of the tribesmen, Lawrence was still frustrated that he had not only lost a man, but one of Feisal's favourites no less. Then, suddenly, he saw a bloody and unconscious man strapped to the back of a camel. A closer inspection revealed it was Salem. He was told that the Howeitat tribesmen had stripped him as he lay wounded, taking his cloak, dagger, rifle, and headgear. After leaving him for dead, it was left to Mijbil, one of Feisal's men, to lift him onto the back of his camel and carry him to safety. Although Salem had been shot in the back, it looked like he would survive. Lawrence counted his blessings.

On 22 September, Lawrence and the men returned to Akaba, 'entering in glory, laden with all manner of precious things', with Lawrence keeping a red Baluchi prayer rug for himself. Lewis and Stokes were thrilled to have played their part and Lawrence ensured that once they returned to Cairo, Allenby decorated each of them.

While the Arabs celebrated their victory, Lawrence was conflicted. They might have destroyed two trains, but their real target had been the water station at Mudowwara, and that had failed. He was not to know that his attacks had inspired Turkish locomotive drivers to go on strike, further crippling supplies.

On top of this, Lawrence was now struggling to come to terms with the death and brutality of war. After all, he had initially been enlisted as a map-maker and was in no way prepared to fight. Although he was a keen student of military history, he was finding the reality of war a different matter altogether. And the more deaths he saw, the more of a toll it took on him. In a letter to an old friend at the Ashmolean Museum in Oxford, he wrote, 'I'm not going to last out this game much longer; nerves going and temper wearing thin, and one wants an unlimited amount of both . . . The killing and killing of Turks is horrible. When you charge in at the finish and find them all over the place in bits, and still alive many of them, and know you have done hundreds in the same way before and must do hundreds more if you can.'

When Feisal had gifted Lawrence the British Enfield rifle at the start of their adventure, he had meant to carve a notch into the stock for every Turk he killed. At the time, this had seemed a thrilling and worthy prospect to a novice of war. Now he had stopped in disgust after four.

I well recall suffering from similar feelings in Oman. Watching men die every day is a very difficult thing to deal with, even if they are the enemy. But rather than the countless deaths, your mind always focuses on one particular incident. And there was one that haunted me.

In an area controlled by the adoo, we saw four figures racing away, all wearing their signature dark cloaks. We opened fire on the group, killing three. However, when we went to investigate, we found the mutilated bodies were of women. The adoo had been recruiting women and children to fight on their behalf, often through intimidation, but this was the first time I had encountered them in battle. Even to this day, I can see their lifeless eyes staring accusingly back at me. I had killed many men in Oman, but it was this image my mind frequently returned to. It would also soon dramatically impact one of our most important operations.

Intelligence revealed that Salim Amr, the head of the

adoo execution squad, was staying in one of the mountain villages. This was our chance to take out one of the most wanted men in the country and strike a big blow against the adoo. After trekking through the night, we finally reached the enemy village. Peering through my binoculars, I saw a group of huts, and a man with a rifle, followed by four more men. It was the adoo, but they were six hundred yards away. The likelihood of hitting someone at that distance was remote. I should therefore call in the jets and have the village destroyed. But something held me back from the radio set. Sura rockets would make short work of anyone in the huts, but death and mutilation would not be selective. I knew that the innocent women and children there would also die. When I grabbed the radio, I could not bring myself to speak, the deaths of the three women we had previously killed running through my mind. My guilt overwhelmed me. The deaths of more innocents would be too much. I decided to wait for a better opportunity.

For forty minutes, we watched motionless as women and children moved about the village. Suddenly fourteen men appeared from a hut, wearing dark brown uniforms and floppy khaki hats. All were armed. Amongst them, I made out the skinny figure of Salim Amr. As they jumped in their vehicles and left the village, I flicked the switch on the BCC 30. 'Hallo, 57, this is 5. Target, over.' But by the time the Provost fighters arrived, Salim Amr and the adoo had scattered in all directions. My chance of a sure kill had gone. No innocents had been hurt, but one of the most notorious men of all was still alive, thanks to my own guilt.

As I had learned, the scars of war can soon add up. Slowly infiltrating your subconscious, they force you to hesitate, which is a very dangerous thing on the battlefield. Multiple events and tragedies had already taken their toll on Lawrence, and soon he would face an event that would mark him for the rest of his life, and significantly affect his judgement going forward.

16

After returning to Akaba, the Arabs, now with a taste for loot and killing Turks, were keen to continue attacking the Turkish railway. This certainly suited Lawrence. It not only helped to build morale but also kept the Turks from focusing their attention on Akaba. As such, over the next four months, the Arabs destroyed seventeen Turkish locomotives and miles of railway track.

Meanwhile, Lawrence was ordered back to Cairo to provide Allenby with an update. He found the general not in the best of moods. The Arab attacks on the railways were just a 'melodramatic advertisement', he told Lawrence, and didn't add up to much. Lawrence explained that he planned to disrupt the line to Medina continually, but not totally destroy it, to keep the Turks bottled up there and unable to strike against Akaba. Allenby wasn't convinced but decided to keep his faith in Lawrence, who so far had shown shrewd judgement.

Of far more concern to Allenby was the joint Arab and British operation that would allow him to take Jerusalem. After the previous failure under General Murray, the British were aware that Gaza was well defended, with trenches and fortifications. However, intelligence suggested that they were vulnerable at Beersheba. Allenby realised that this was a perfect opportunity. If he could take Beersheba, he could not only assure his troops of a reliable water supply, but they could also outflank Ottoman positions surrounding Gaza.

To help his operation, Allenby wanted the Arabs to destroy two bridges that crossed the Yarmuk River on 5 November 'or one of the three following days', to coincide as closely as possible with his own attack. 'To cut either of these bridges', Lawrence said, 'would isolate the Turkish army in Palestine, for one fortnight from its base in Damascus, and destroy its power of escaping Allenby's advance.'

The operation would be enormously difficult, not to mention hazardous. It first would require a 320-mile march from Akaba to the old Roman fort at Azrak. There, Lawrence and the Arabs would set up a base, before covering another 100 miles to reach Yarmuk. All the while, he would need to raise more tribes along the way, as well as seeking their permission for safe passage. Indeed, this was an area that was tightly held by the Turks and they could be betrayed or attacked at any moment. Nevertheless, Allenby and Lawrence agreed that the plan was worth all the risks.

While Lawrence returned to Akaba and made final preparations for the operation at Yarmuk, an unexpected ally arrived from Damascus. Emir Abd el-Kader was the grandson and namesake of the Arab hero who had fought against the French occupation of his native Algeria from 1830 to 1847. El-Kader the elder was revered throughout the Muslim world and beyond for his heroic deeds. Following his death, the family lived on in Damascus, with many of their Algerian followers settling close to the bridges Lawrence planned to destroy. El-Kader the younger was now seemingly ready to put himself and his tribe at Feisal's disposal. At face value, this appeared to be a piece of tremendous good fortune. With his Algerian followers on side, this would increase the strength of the Arab forces and, crucially, allow Lawrence and the Arabs access to the bridges.

Still, Lawrence was unsure about the man he described as 'an Islamic fanatic, half-insane with religious enthusiasm, and a most violent belief in himself'. He only became more uneasy when Colonel Brémond warned him that el-Kader was a spy and in the pay of the Turks. Yet Lawrence knew that el-Kader was vehemently anti-French and that this might have clouded Brémond's judgement. While Feisal was also unsure of el-Kader's loyalty, he recognised that if he was true to his word, he would be an enormous help. As such, he told Lawrence, 'Guard your head and use him.'

On 24 October, Lawrence and his group prepared to embark on the 320-mile journey to Azrak. From there, they could build a base to target the two crucial bridges on the Yarmuk River. A sherif from the Harith tribe named Ali joined Lawrence at the front of the camel train, hoping to persuade other tribes to join them en route. With his luxuriant black hair, washed in camel urine, Ali was a renowned warrior and a leader who 'could outstrip a trotting camel on his bare feet, keep his speed over half a mile, and then vault with one hand into the saddle, holding his rifle in the other'. With all of this, he was a vital and welcome addition.

For the initial part of the journey, they were accompanied by one of Lawrence's friends from the Arab Bureau, George Lloyd MP. Lloyd was curious to join Lawrence on one of his adventures, but had also been sent to keep an eye on him. In particular, Clayton could see that his role was 'well-nigh weighing him down'. The base engineer at Akaba, C.E. Wood, also formed part of the party. Wood had been wounded in the head in France and was marked 'unfit for active service'. Never one for convention, Lawrence thought he could be of some use, and Wood was more than eager to tag along. In addition, Lawrence added a company of Muslim Indian cavalrymen as a machine-gun section, under the command of Jemadar Hassan Shah, along with his two rambunctious young servants, Farraj and Daud. While others continued to find the pair troublesome, insolent, and too fond of practical jokes, Lawrence described them as 'capable and merry on the road'. They continued to be good for his morale if nothing else. Indeed, on the morning of their departure, Lawrence found they had been imprisoned for dyeing the governor of Akaba's prize camel with red henna. In punishment, they were also dyed red from head to toe, which caused Lawrence no end of amusement as he glanced at them, trudging forlornly by his side.

By now the Turks had put a significant bounty on Lawrence's head, said to be as much as £15,000 (about £1.3 million today). While he surrounded himself with a carefully picked bodyguard, he did not try to disguise himself. The man the Arabs called 'Aurens' had become known far and wide for his startling white robes and head cloth, from which peered his piercing blue eyes and clean-shaven face. This image had virtually become the face of the Revolt and had been imprinted on the minds of the Arabs. If they were to persuade other tribes to join them on their journey, then the mere sight of the slight Englishman in Arab robes might be enough.

At first, the group made slow progress, primarily due to the number of people new to camel riding. Some of the party quickly fell behind and got lost, while Lawrence rode on at a leisurely pace chatting pleasantly with Lloyd as they passed 'curved slopes of pink sandstone and tamarisk-green valleys'.

Lawrence was happy to have Lloyd with him. As fellow members of the Arab Bureau, they shared many of the same views, particularly their determination that France should not be allowed to claim Syria amongst its post-war spoils. Feeling relaxed in his company, Lawrence opened up about his pre-war escapades as an archaeologist. At the same time, he also displayed a more sensitive side, showing Lloyd a newspaper clipping from *The Times* about his dead brother Will. Lloyd was sympathetic. Almost everyone had lost a family member or close friend during this wretched war, including General Allenby, whose eighteen-year-old son Michael had been killed in France just one month after he arrived in Cairo. Keeping his grief to himself, he continued feverishly with his work, but those close to him saw he was a broken man.

That first night the party camped in the multicoloured landscape of Wadi Rumm, where the stars were splashed across the jet-black sky. Farraj and Daud were assigned to cooking duties and prepared a dish of rice and bully beef (the British Army's equivalent of canned corned beef). The saddle-sore Indians and British wolfed down their food before retiring early to bed, exhausted from the day's exertions.

In the middle of the desert, Lawrence no doubt felt safe to eat bully beef, but in the mountains of Dhofar I tried to avoid eating our British rations whenever I could. The smell was alien to the locals and therefore could be dangerous. I also saw first-hand how adept the locals were at using the smallest clues to their advantage. One of our guides knew the name of a camel's owner by the shape of the beast's hoof-print. Incredibly, he also knew where a camel had last drunk by the amount and frequency of the droppings, and by their texture in which wadis it had last eaten. He could also tell the spring from which any water came simply through a sniff and a taste. He was a true taster of 'desert wines'. For these reasons, the scent of something like bully beef would clearly give our position away.

As they rested, the group were eventually joined by Abd el-Kader and Ali, who had lagged behind and were arguing furiously. Lawrence sought to relieve tensions by inviting them to sit with him and Lloyd as they ate. For now, at least, el-Kader returned to his best behaviour, but it was clear that he was far from happy with the attention Lawrence paid Ali.

Setting off again for Azrak, they crossed the railway and cut telegraph wires near a Turkish blockhouse. However, as the sun set, Lawrence could hear Turkish rifle and machine-gun fire in the distance. Abd el-Kader and

Ali were again riding behind and had engaged in a brief firefight, losing two men, before disappearing into the darkness of the desert.

The next morning Lawrence and the Arabs continued to ride north. Keeping close to the rail track, they turned west to reach the flat plains around Jefer, soon finding Auda Abu Tayi and the Howeitat in their new camp, where they had moved to escape the attention of Turkish aircraft. Despite the change in location, the mood had not improved between him and his tribe. Still, they were grateful for Auda's hospitality as he served his guests a feast of rice, meat and dried tomatoes, which Lawrence described as 'luscious'.

The following morning, Lloyd left the group to return to Akaba. Lawrence immediately missed his company, as he went on to more 'war, tribes and camels without end'. He described Lloyd as 'the one fully-taught man with us in Arabia', and he appreciated his support.

Throughout the next day and night, Lawrence tried unsuccessfully to persuade Auda and the Howeitat to join him in destroying the bridges over the Yarmuk. However, that night, as they gathered around a fire eating and drinking coffee, Auda suddenly held up his camel stick for silence. Far away, they heard a noise 'like the mutter of a distant, very lowly thunderstorm'. 'The English guns,' Auda announced. It was 27 October 1917, and Allenby's attack on the Gaza–Beersheba line had begun.

The atmosphere in the camp suddenly became 'serene and cordial'. Here at last was some sign that a major offensive against the Turks was underway. It was also a sign that

Lawrence needed to get a move on. Yet as Lawrence said his goodbyes and prepared to leave the camp, Auda leaned close. 'Beware of Abd el-Kader,' he whispered, before moving away. Auda could say no more, but again Lawrence felt uneasy about el-Kader's presence.

If Lawrence was to commence the attack at Yarmuk on 5 November 'or one of the three following days', as he had promised Allenby, he knew he would have his work cut out. In rugged terrain, Lawrence's Indian machine-gunners could only march thirty or thirty-five miles a day at best. There were 150 miles to go before they reached Azrak, then another 100 miles to reach the bridges. It was going to be a close call.

Just as he urged greater speed and effort, they were stopped in their tracks near Bair. A dangerous gang from the Beni Sakhr tribe known as 'the Suhkuri' fired shots over their heads, then approached, ready to rob and kill them. But as they came close, they stopped at the sight of Ali. At once, they realised who he was. His reputation was known far and wide. This was not a man they wanted to fall out with. Trying to rectify the situation, they explained that they had been shooting into the air to welcome his arrival rather than aiming to rob and kill them. Whatever the reason, their chief was determined to prove his loyalty and put on a show in his esteemed guest's honour. Lawrence and the Arabs watched as the tribesmen rode around them on their horses, firing their rifles into the air, shouting 'God give victory to our sherif!' and 'Welcome, Aurens, harbinger of victory!' But the hailing of Lawrence and Ali again made Abd el-Kader furious. He shouted to his servants, who joined him galloping around in circles, spraying dust over the group while firing their rifles with wild abandon into the air. No one was impressed, especially the Beni Sakhr chief, who feared that one of his men might be shot. Not wanting to risk a tribal feud, Lawrence ordered el-Kader to stop.

Continuing on their way across the desert towards Azrak, the sound of the British guns boomed and rumbled in the distance. This only increased the pressure to move faster. For Allenby to finally take Gaza, he was relying on Lawrence destroying the bridges. But for Lawrence to proceed, he needed el-Kader to smooth the path with his Seraphin tribe. Without their help, reaching and taking the bridges would be almost impossible.

Upon reaching the Seraphin village, el-Kader seemed true to his word, and the tribe assured Lawrence that his route to Yarmuk would be unhindered. Lawrence was also desperate for more men and hoped they might join him. Gathering the leaders around a fire, he stated his case, admitting later that, in his tiredness, his speech was 'halting' and 'half-coherent . . . struck out desperately, moment by moment . . . upon the anvil'. Finally, 'as their worldliness faded', Lawrence persuaded the Seraphin to 'ride with us whatever the bourne'.

With this, the group marched for Azrak, where a Roman legion had once been garrisoned and left behind monuments dedicated to Emperor Diocletian. Here the Arabs could base themselves and strike out against the bridges at Yarmuk. Everything seemed to be on track, but their joy was short-lived: looking around the camp, Lawrence realised that Abd el-Kader was nowhere to be found. Asking questions about his whereabouts, it was reported that he was last seen riding away from the group and heading north to the village of Jebel Druse. Lawrence immediately knew what this meant. Abd el-Kader was indeed a traitor and was going to betray his plans to the Turks. If they continued their plan to attack the bridges, the Turks would almost certainly be waiting for them.

Yet Lawrence knew Allenby was relying on him. If the Arabs did not disable the bridges, the British advance on Gaza might fail. And this was the Arabs' first big test under Allenby's command. He did not want to let him down. Lawrence reasoned that, in the past, the Turks had proven incompetent, and he prayed that this might be the case again. They should at least attempt the attack, even if it was a suicide mission. One piece of unexpected good fortune was that el-Kader's Seraphin tribesmen were still keen to ride with him. But if they were to destroy the bridges, they had to move fast before the Turks had a chance to organise themselves. With Yarmuk a two-day ride, there was no time to waste.

17

Galloping at full speed to reach Yarmuk, the party only stopped to fill their water-skins at a half-mile-long hollow full of fresh rainwater. Gratefully gulping down the cool water, Lawrence saw something move in the distance. Closer inspection revealed a party of Circassian horsemen moving in the opposite direction. It appeared the Turks had sent them to look for the Arabs. Thankfully, their paths had not crossed, and they looked to be going the other way. For once, good fortune was on their side.

They set off on the final forty-mile dash with their water-skins full to the brim. Passing the railway as the sun began to rise, Lawrence sent scouts forward to report on the presence of any Turkish troops. To his delight, when they returned, they told him that only rail guards were present at the bridge. Better still, they didn't appear to be preparing for any great battle. He hoped that this meant that the Turks either weren't taking Abd el-Kader's report seriously or that they were displaying their usual incompetence.

Hiding in a ditch by the railway line, Lawrence waited for nightfall to begin their attack under cover of darkness. However, as he waited, he suddenly made a drastic, last-minute decision. He realised that speed rather than force would be essential if they were to succeed. Most of the

Indian machine-gunners were slow and clumsy riders and would be picked off as they tried to escape. With this in mind, he picked six of their best riders, while reducing their firepower to just one Vickers machine gun.

Despite previously thinking the manpower of the Seraphin tribe would be essential for success, Lawrence now decided that they were too much of a risk. After all, they were el-Kader's tribesmen and Lawrence had no idea if they were still loyal to him. Still, he did not want to offend them and cause an incident at this crucial juncture. He decided that while some would be left behind to guard the camp, those that joined him would be reduced to merely carrying some of the blasting gelatine.

Finalising his plans, Lawrence waited for the orange sun to disappear below the horizon and then set off with his much-reduced company into the darkness. With clouds gathering overhead, a steady drizzle turned the ground to mud. Toiling in the conditions, the camels 'sank fetlock in', dramatically slowing their progress. Lawrence worried whether the camels would be able to escape from the Turks if the rain continued.

Shortly after nine o'clock, they heard the sound of water in the distance. The Yarmuk Gorge was close. Dismounting from their camels, they descended a steep bank towards the bridge, trying to stay out of sight of the Turkish patrol. The Seraphin chosen to carry the bags of explosives were particularly nervous. If the bags were shot, they would explode in their arms.

Halting about 300 yards from the bridge, Lawrence peered through his binoculars. A sentry was standing in front of a fire, while on the far side was a guard tent. This was a relief. His scouts had been correct – there seemed to be no great Turkish armed presence. It was time to move.

Before setting off, he told the Indians that if the Turkish sentry heard anything, they were to rake the guard tent with the Vickers machine gun. As they moved into position, Lawrence and the Seraphin made their way down a steep construction path to where the bridge abutted, the river running far below them. All that remained was for Lawrence to scale the latticework of steel beams that supported the bridge, and fasten each thirty-pound bag of explosives. With these in place, they could blow the bridge to smithereens.

Yet just as Lawrence moved onto the bridge, one of the Indian machine-gunners slipped on the steep path and dropped his rifle. At the sound of the clatter, the Turkish sentry looked up from his post and saw their shadows on the opposite bank. Immediately he opened fire while also calling for help, as a fleet of Turkish guards came rushing out of their tents, brandishing their weapons. The Indians had not yet had a chance to put their Vickers gun in place. Under ferocious attack, they were unable to force the Turks back. As they scrambled to escape, the terrified Seraphin dropped their sacks of explosives into the river. This was a disaster. There was now no option but to retreat.

Fleeing into the darkness, with the Turks in hot pursuit, every village they passed on their way opened fire. Finally, after a breathless chase, it appeared they were at last safe. Lawrence counted his blessings that he had decided to leave his slowest riders behind at camp. Otherwise, they would have all surely been killed.

Eventually stopping for food, Lawrence recalled hearing the sound of 'Allenby's guns, still shaking the air away there on our right . . . bitter recorders of the failure we had been'. He was furious that something as basic as a dropped rifle had left the operation in tatters, and might also prove detrimental to Allenby's advance on Gaza, and therefore the whole war effort.

The mood in the camp was low. Lawrence could not face returning to Azrak, while the Arabs were determined to at least have something to show for the journey in the way of loot. There was still one sack of explosives left, and they wanted to blow up a train. Lawrence had already sent the Indian machine-gunners back to Azrak, along with Wood, who was suffering from pneumonia. Rations were also desperately low, as they had only taken enough to reach Yarmuk and back. Despite this, and against his better judgement, Lawrence decided to proceed.

In the orange tint of dusk, Lawrence and sixty Arabs made their way to the railway track at Minifir. It was raining and bitterly cold, which didn't help Lawrence's state of mind, nor did the fact that just as they arrived, they saw a train pass before they could lay the explosives. Who knew when one would pass again?

Due to the appalling conditions, it took Lawrence most of the night to prepare the mine. By the time he had finished, he was 'wet and dismal', and the sun was rising in the sky. There were also just sixty yards of insulated cable available. When he set the mine off, he would be uncomfortably close to it. None of this seemed like a good idea.

Finally, after hours of hiding from Turkish patrols in a tiny bush, Lawrence heard the sound of a train in the distance. Gathering the Arabs in expectation, they squatted on their heels in a ditch as the open-truck train came into sight, carrying a fleet of Turkish troops. This was the perfect target. Pushing down on the handle of the exploder, Lawrence waited. But nothing happened. Instead, the train continued on its way, and Lawrence was now in full view of it. Upon seeing the Arabs, the Turkish guards reached for their guns, leaving Lawrence no option but to act dumb, waving at them before running uphill to safety, carrying the defective exploder with him.

After this second failed mission, Lawrence and the Arabs were even more determined to see it through. This meant another night sleeping in the open, drenched in the rain, and with their rations all but finished. While Lawrence attempted to fix the exploder with a knife, and returned to the track in the dead of night to attach it to the wires, he knew that if a train did not arrive in the morning, they would have no option but to abandon the mine and leave for Azrak, haunted by their failure. The mood was slightly improved when Lawrence shaved slivers off a stick of blasting gelignite and lit a small fire, then ordered the Arabs to kill one of the weakest camels. For now, this meat was their last remaining rations.

In the morning haze, just as they were beginning to give up hope, they heard the sound of another train approaching. But if they were going to destroy it, Lawrence had to reach the exploder, which was half a mile away. Breathlessly racing towards the track, Lawrence reached the exploder just as the locomotive passed over the mine. Pushing down with all his might, the ground shook as a huge explosion buckled the track and derailed the train. Amidst the flames and the smoke, Lawrence saw 'in front of [him] . . . the scaled and smoking upper half of the body of a man'. The explosion had destroyed the culvert and damaged both locomotives beyond repair. Glancing down, he saw blood dripping down his arm. Just as he had feared, he had been too close to the explosion and a stray piece of iron had cut him. It was a lucky escape. The exploder, which had been positioned between his knees, was totally crushed by flying debris.

Approaching the wreckage, to his surprise Lawrence saw that one of the damaged carriages was a 'saloon, decorated with flags'. It was clearly carrying someone very important. He did not know until later that it was Mehmed Djemal, the general commanding the Turkish Eighth Corps, who was en route to defend Jerusalem against Allenby's advance. While Lawrence shot up the car and killed most on board, the general somehow escaped unharmed.

Before Turkish reinforcements arrived and those on the train regrouped, the Arabs happily looted the train and its victims while Lawrence tried to gather up those wounded who could be saved. This included one Arab who had been shot in the face. Somehow, he was still alive, although he had a hole in his cheek and had lost four teeth.

Taking as much loot as they could carry, the Arabs fled the smoking wreckage and roared away into the desert on their camels. Ensuring they didn't forget to take the remains of the slaughtered camel with them, that night they ate for the first time in three days, happily singing over and over, '*God forgive us, that we were victorious*.'

Lawrence did not share their joy. As the party finally returned to Azrak, he felt the whole venture had been an epic failure. Writing to Colonel Joyce about the debacle at Yarmuk, he said, 'If the Turks have not increased their guard we can do it later; but I am very sick at losing it so stupidly. The Bedu cannot take the bridge, but can reach it: the Indians can take it, but cannot reach it!'

He had promised Allenby that he would destroy the Yarmuk bridges to halt the Turks, and he had failed. Winter had now arrived, and there was little choice but to hunker down at Azrak and regroup. It should have been a time for rest and reflection. It was anything but.

18

It was now November 1917, and the hot days of summer, where the sun beat down like an inferno, were long gone. The temperature had dropped towards zero, while the rain, and sometimes even snow, fell from dark skies. The change in weather also suited the mood. After the Arabs' failure at Yarmuk, Lawrence had no idea if Allenby's advance on Gaza had been successful. But he thought it was unlikely due to the bridges still standing, and the horrendous weather curtailing their movement.

Living in the old Roman fortress, which was built on the edge of an oasis, Lawrence and the Arabs frequently received visits from tribal leaders based in Syria who wanted to pay homage to Feisal. In the evenings, they would gather around a great fire that had been lit in the middle of the floor, and with their ghostly shadows bouncing off the walls, they entertained each other with tales of their great battles, all to the sound of the rain rattling against the roof. Lawrence recalled, 'We dreamed ourselves into the spirit of the place; sieges and feasting, raids, murders, love-singing in the night.'

While Lawrence was ensconced in Azrak, another issue reared its head which threatened to complicate the position in the Middle East still further. After centuries of antisemitism in Europe and Russia, a group of European

Jews united around the dream of establishing a homeland in Palestine. This idea had first gained momentum in 1886 with the publication of Theodor Herzl's landmark book, *The Jewish State*. Herzl, a Viennese journalist, encouraged the spread of a new Jewish nationalist movement that came to be known as Zionism, with the aim of creating 'for the Jewish people a home in Palestine secured by public law'.

Before the war such a prospect appeared unlikely, but lately things had begun to change. The leader of the World Zionist Organization was a chemistry professor called Chaim Weizmann. After the war had commenced, there was a shortage of acetone, a key ingredient in the production of cordite, the smokeless explosive used in ammunition. In the middle of a war this was obviously a major concern. However, in a significant breakthrough, Weizmann found a way to produce acetone from starch. Without this, the British would have been in a perilous position. After Lloyd George awarded Weizmann the Order of Merit, Weizmann broached the subject of a Jewish settlement in Palestine. Lloyd George knew just how vital it was to keep Weizmann on side. He also thought that supporting Zionism might be useful in other ways. It would certainly appeal to the powerful and wealthy Jewish lobby in America, which had recently entered the war. Perhaps most importantly, it could help disguise his real ambition to turn Palestine into a British possession after the war, while simultaneously deflecting criticism of British imperialism. Like many others in government, Lloyd George believed that the British had fought too hard for Palestine to simply hand it over to France and Russia.

With all of this in mind, he put the wheels of Zionism in motion. On 11 November 1917, *The Times* published a letter from the foreign secretary, Arthur Balfour, to Lord Rothschild, a Member of Parliament and prominent British supporter of Zionism. In the letter, Balfour claimed to favour the establishment in Palestine of a national home for Jewish people. He then promised that the government 'will use their best endeavours to facilitate the achievement of this object'. It didn't matter that none of this had yet been discussed with the Arabs, let alone earned their approval. Unsurprisingly, the letter, known as 'The Balfour Declaration', caused significant controversy. Once more, the lands that the Arabs were fighting for were being carved up and given away without their consent.

While Sykes expressed enthusiasm for the declaration, Clayton was appalled. In a letter to Sykes, he wrote that the announcement in the Middle East was received with 'little short of dismay'. Those in Cairo would once again have to salve the Arabs' concerns while encouraging them to keep fighting for lands that might not end up in their hands.

At the time, Lawrence knew none of this. He was still preoccupied with the memory of his failure at the Yarmuk bridge, and frustrated with his enforced idleness at Azrak.

Becoming increasingly restless, he turned his thoughts to the town of Deraa, 'the vital junction of the Jerusalem, Haifa, Damascus-Medina railways . . . the only common point of all their own fronts'. The more he thought about it, the more he became convinced that if he could seize Deraa he could cut all Turkish lines of communication and supply. With that, Damascus would become vulnerable to an attack by the Arabs before the British, or more importantly the French, could claim it. This would go a long way towards convincing the British, and perhaps even the French, to accept an independent Arab state in Syria. He therefore decided to visit the town so that he could assess the strengths and weaknesses of the Turkish garrison there for himself, and then make a plan of action. Yet this was very dangerous.

Deraa was a Turkish-held town, and he not only had a price on his head, but it was also likely that the traitor Abd el-Kader had given the Turks an accurate description of him. They would be on red alert for a slight, fair-haired British officer in white robes. To proceed, he had to exercise extreme caution.

To avoid any Turkish patrols en route, he was led by Talal el-Hareidhin, Sheikh of Tafas, 'an outlaw with a price on his head'. Talal knew the approaches to Deraa like the back of his hand and could guide Lawrence away from any trouble. Lawrence was also joined by Faris, an elderly man who knew the town well, and, most importantly of all, would help Lawrence blend in.

After two days of travel, Lawrence and Faris entered Deraa as 'a lame and draggled pair', having disguised themselves as peasants. Thankfully, no one seemed to give them a second look. This only made Lawrence more confident. He wanted to gather as much information about the town as he could to ascertain whether it would be better to rush the railway junction first or to cut the town off by destroying the three railway lines that entered it. With this in mind, he approached the railway line nearest the Turkish aerodrome. Although there was a Turkish troop encampment nearby, Lawrence was not fazed. So far, the disguise had worked just as he had hoped.

Yet as they walked along the railway line, a voice shouted at them from behind. Lawrence froze. When he turned, he saw a Syrian soldier approach. Looking them up and down, the soldier asked where they were from. Not wanting to give himself away, Lawrence let Faris do most of the talking. Rather than them being in trouble, it seemed the soldier wanted to work out where he might gain safe refuge if he was to desert. But just as Lawrence started to relax, he was grabbed roughly from behind. 'The Bey wants you,' a Turkish sergeant growled before dragging him into a compound.

Inside a mud room, a 'fleshy' Turkish officer asked Lawrence his name. Quick as a flash, he replied 'Ahmed ign Bagr', and claimed he was Circassian, hoping this would explain his fair hair and blue eyes. 'He then turned around and stared at me cautiously,' Lawrence recalled, 'and said very slowly, "You are a liar. Keep him, Hassan Chowish, till the Bey sends for him."' This sent a chill through Lawrence. Did they know who he was?

Led to the guardroom, he was forced to wash himself and told that he might be released tomorrow, 'if [he] fulfilled all the Bey's pleasures this evening'. The smile on the guard's face, and the use of the word 'pleasures', left nothing to the imagination.

That evening Lawrence was taken upstairs to the bedroom of the Bey, 'a bulky man sitting on his bed in a nightgown trembling and sweating as though with fever'. The stubble-haired man inspected him for a moment as if he was a piece of meat, then roughly dragged him down onto the bed. Lawrence struggled against him, but it was no use. His small frame was no match for the much larger Bey. As he was held down, a sentry stripped him naked while the Bey began 'to paw' at him. Thrashing about, trying to release their grip, Lawrence launched his knee into the Bey's groin, sending him clattering to the floor. But before Lawrence could think of making any sort of escape, three guards roughly grabbed him. As they held him in place, the Bey walked towards him and spat in Lawrence's face. He was so close now that Lawrence could smell his stale breath and feel the prickles of his stubble against his skin. The Bey promised that before the night was over 'he would make me ask pardon'. At this, he kissed Lawrence on the lips and then thrust a bayonet into his ribcage. Twisting the bayonet, making Lawrence scream and swear, the Bey whispered in his ear, 'You must understand that I know: and it will be much easier if you do as I wish.' This confirmed Lawrence's worst fears. The Bey clearly knew who he was. Prolonged torture lay in store for him, and no doubt death.

Tying him down on the guard bench, a corporal began to whip him unmercifully. Lawrence immediately let out a howl but then gritted his teeth, determined not to show any pain. This only made the corporal whip him again and again, harder and harder, until the sweating and breathless corporal needed a break. Looking at Lawrence's quivering body, he told him he would make him 'beg for the caresses of the Bey'. Wiping the sweat from his brow, the corporal then tore the whip into Lawrence's skin with a renewed vigour. Come what may, he was determined to break him. Lawrence tried to count the blows to take his mind off the pain but lost count at twenty. Dark ridges now appeared on his back, dripping with blood. Finally Lawrence broke. He could hold back his cries no more. This admission of defeat seemed to satisfy the corporal. Yet the ordeal was not yet over.

Throwing Lawrence to the floor, he kicked him in the ribcage. Reeling back, Lawrence tried to catch his breath before the corporal cracked the whip and lashed him in the groin. Screaming and squirming in agony, Lawrence's bloody and naked body was then dragged to the Bey's bedside so that he could have his 'pleasure' at last. However, the Bey was disgusted by Lawrence's condition. He reprimanded his men for beating him too much and ordered them to take him away to recover. Only then would he see him again, and the true ordeal could begin.

Dragging Lawrence by his arms, his knees sagging against the floor, the men threw him into an empty wooden room, where an Armenian dresser was ordered to wash and bandage him. In the morning, he might then be ready for the Bey's pleasure. As Lawrence cowered back, still trying to ascertain his surroundings, one of the Turkish guards whispered to him that the door was not locked, before leaving the room.

Lawrence could not be sure if it was a trick. What if he tried to leave, and they were waiting on the other side to dish out more punishment? Nevertheless, he had to take the chance. He knew he would face death if he waited for morning to arrive. Struggling to his feet, he limped to the door and slowly turned the handle. Just as the guard had said, it was open. Tentatively entering the next room, his eyes darted around, looking for any sign of the guards waiting to pounce on him. But the room was empty, and in the far corner he saw a window had been left ajar. With no time to waste, he put on some old clothes left hanging on a door and quickly climbed outside.

It was still dark, but Lawrence knew the sun would soon be rising. He had to get away, and fast. With hardly anyone around, he hobbled and grimaced to the outskirts of the town, barely daring to look behind. At last he saw a Serdi tribesman riding a camel, heading toward Nisib, where his men had been camped. Lawrence explained he had business there and asked if he might ride on the back. Thankfully, the man took pity on him.

Soon after, Lawrence arrived, bloodied and bruised. His men were shocked to see him; they feared he had been captured and killed. Lawrence dared not tell them the truth, that he had been beaten and sexually assaulted. Instead, he made up a story of fooling the stupid Turks and escaping their clutches. And yet, as they all returned to Azrak and Lawrence battled with his wounds, he had far more than physical pain on his mind.

19

In Lawrence's autobiography, *Seven Pillars of Wisdom*, he reveals that 'some part of him had gone dead that night in Deraa'. In one of the most disturbing and lurid depictions of assault ever written, Lawrence claims to have been 'degraded' and reduced to 'beast level'. Perhaps most shocking of all, he admits that it had left him feeling 'like the striving of a moth towards its flame', as during the beating he felt 'a delicious warmth, probably sexual'. To his shame, while Lawrence had been beaten and sexually abused, he had found that it aroused him.

Although he wrote about the assault in such vivid and revealing detail, this might not have even been the whole truth. Richard Meinertzhagen, with whom Lawrence served in the Middle East, claimed in his memoirs that Lawrence told him that he had actually been 'sodomised by the Governor of Deraa, followed by similar treatment by the Governor's servants'. Lawrence said that he could not publish the complete account of the incident because it was too degrading and 'had penetrated his innermost nature'.

Before this event, Lawrence already had a complicated history when it came to his sexuality. In his Oxford days, he became friends with Janet Laurie Smith, and even asked her to marry him. They had never so much as kissed, and she saw him more as a brother than a lover. She therefore laughed in his face at such a ridiculous prospect. Soon after, she became engaged to Lawrence's brother Will, who sadly died on the battlefields of France.

From this point on, Lawrence appears to have made little attempt to engage in any sexual relationship with a woman. His brother Arnold even claimed that Lawrence remained a virgin until his death. There is, however, evidence to suggest that he might have had more sexual interest in men. Notes found in the private papers for his book have him admit, 'I take no pleasure in women. I have never thought twice or even once of the shape of a woman: but men's bodies, in repose or movement – especially the former, appeal to me directly and very generally.'

During his time working in the Middle East before the war, he had grown very close to a handsome teenage Arab boy named Dahoum. The pair did everything together, with Lawrence persuading him to pose naked so that he could carve his likeness in the soft local limestone. Lawrence even took Dahoum home to Oxford, where he met his parents. Whether or not they enjoyed a sexual relationship it is now impossible to say. However, as we shall see later, there is no doubt that Dahoum was one of the very few who left a lasting mark on Lawrence in this regard. Judging from all the evidence available, it is clear that Lawrence struggled with his homosexuality. The assault in Deraa left him more conflicted than ever. It was an event that continued to torture and excite him for the rest of his life, while it would also have significant repercussions for his remaining time in the Middle East.

Finally back at Azrak, the traumatised Lawrence retired to his room in the fort and tried to recover from the physical and mental scars. As he did so, further bad news made matters ever more difficult.

In November 1917, the Bolsheviks, led by Vladimir Lenin, seized power in Russia from Tsar Nicholas II. In doing so, they denounced the war as an imperialist project and pledged to withdraw and abandon all of the Ottoman territory they had gained. The Ottomans couldn't believe their luck. They had only entered the war in order to protect themselves from Russia. Now Russia had backed down and given back everything it had taken. Moreover, the Bolsheviks also provided the Ottomans with an invaluable propaganda tool.

To discredit the policies of the deposed tsar's government, the Bolsheviks published the terms of the Sykes–Picot Agreement. The Ottoman government seized on this immediately. On 4 December 1917, Cemal Pasha gave an impassioned speech in Beirut whereby he divulged the terms of the agreement to a stunned audience. In the process, he claimed Sherif Hussein and his sons were nothing more than British stooges. With this, Cemal urged the Arabs to abandon the Revolt and return to the Ottoman fold. He also dispatched a letter to Feisal and Hussein and offered them a deal. If they now called a halt to the Revolt, the Arabs would receive full autonomy within the Ottoman Empire.

These public revelations of the Sykes–Picot Agreement, along with the Balfour Declaration, suddenly left the Revolt hanging by a thread. To counteract the damage,

Lawrence's old professor, David Hogarth, immediately left Cairo and sought an audience with Sherif Hussein in Jidda. Reconfirming Britain's commitment to helping the Arabs claim their independence, he also addressed the Balfour Declaration. He claimed that while Britain did support a Jewish settlement in Palestine, it was on the proviso that the Arabs gave their permission.

Hussein saw this as an opportunity. If the Sykes–Picot Agreement had made provision for France to rule Syria, then the Balfour Declaration might help to counter this. By Hussein agreeing to accommodate the Zionist dream, he would earn favour with the British and Americans and thereby increase the chances of the Arabs ruling Syria for themselves. In the circumstances, Hussein believed that giving up a small piece of Palestine was a price worth paying. He was also aware that it would be impossible for the Arabs to now rejoin the Ottomans. There was no option but to forge ahead with the British and pray they were as good as their word. As such, he told Hogarth that 'he welcomed Jews to all Arab lands'.

For now, Lawrence knew very little of this. Ever since the failed assault on the bridges at Yarmuk, he had been cut off from news of the war. While Azrak continued to be hammered by sleet and snow storms, he spent most of his time in the Roman fort, wrapped in blankets, recovering from his ordeal in Deraa. But the trauma of the incident continued to plague him, and he became desperate to get as far away as possible. He therefore told Ali that he would return to Akaba, where he might get more news and help plan the next phase of the Revolt.

The march to Akaba was wet and cold, and the mud slowed their progress. Lawrence's injuries from Deraa didn't help as they left him 'curiously faint', with his muscles 'pappy and inflamed'. After stopping for a much-needed rest at Auda's camp, they 'toiled on doggedly' for the next few days, finally reaching Akaba at midnight. In his biography of Lawrence, Liddell Hart wrote that those who saw him as he arrived described him as appearing 'like a wraith, so white and remote. He said but the briefest word, just a mention of the bridge failure in the Yarmuk Valley, and then crept away to a tent.'

There was little time to rest. Awaiting Lawrence was an urgent message to fly to Palestine and report to General Allenby immediately. This surely wasn't good news. He feared that he would be reprimanded for failing to destroy the bridges. With this, Allenby's assault on Gaza must have also foundered. The failure was his and his alone, and it was now time to admit what he had long feared: he was a fraud.

20

Arriving at Gaza, Lawrence was immediately taken to see General Allenby, bracing himself to be reprimanded and sent back to Cairo, or even England. Either way, he was exhausted and would welcome putting all of this behind him. His dark, haunted eyes struggled to find much joy or optimism any more in the wilds of the Hejaz desert. He had come here to relieve his family's sins, but following the assault at Deraa, he was now carrying more guilt than ever.

Upon entering Allenby's office, he resolved to accept whatever punishment was in store without complaint. To his surprise, he found Allenby in excellent spirits. Rather than reprimand Lawrence for failing to destroy the bridges, he had other news to share. Just as Lloyd George had asked, he had captured Jerusalem before Christmas.

Lawrence might have failed to take the Yarmuk bridges, but his attempted attack had been enough in itself. Allenby had wanted his forces to be protected from the desert on his right. The Turks had been so worried about another attack on the bridges that they had loaded their forces there, leaving the path clear for the British to capture the wells at Beersheba. With this vital access to water, they could outflank the Turks, finally taking Gaza and Jafa. Following this, the British advanced on Jerusalem, where the Ottoman lines were destroyed after a series of battles in the Judean Hills. On 8 December 1917, with the British advancing, the Turks evacuated the city.

As a token of his appreciation, Allenby insisted that Lawrence should join him when he entered Jerusalem for the first time. Lawrence was honoured, albeit a little embarrassed. He still felt frustrated at the failure to destroy the bridges, while the events at Deraa played heavily on his mind. Still, he could not turn the opportunity down.

On 11 December, Lawrence put on a borrowed military uniform and proudly walked with Allenby through the Jaffa Gate and into the city. Aeroplanes circled overhead, and soldiers marched through the streets as Lawrence took in the smells of spices, herbs, and open drains, watching on as Allenby, to the crowd's cheers, received the surrender of the city from the acting governor. He later described these scenes as 'the supreme moment of the war', while back home, church bells heralded the conquest.

The French weren't quite so enamoured. Soon after Allenby entered the city, François Georges-Picot announced he would set up a civil administration in Jerusalem. Allenby told him this was out of the question. The city was under military government until he decided otherwise. Picot bristled with fury but had no choice but to accept the matter. As such, Ronald Storrs was installed as 'the first military governor of Jerusalem since Pontius Pilate', with the temporary rank of lieutenant colonel.

Meanwhile, an American journalist had arrived in the city looking for a story. Lowell Thomas had initially been sent to Europe by President Wilson to make a film that would drum up American support for the war. However, when Thomas, his wife, and cameraman Harry Chase arrived at the Western Front, they realised that the blood and horror of the trenches was not the feel-good propaganda Wilson had in mind. After learning about Allenby's campaign in Palestine, Thomas thought this sounded more promising. A Christian country like America would surely love a story that saw the Holy Land back in possession of the West.

Wasting little time, Thomas arrived just as Allenby made his grand entrance into the city. As Chase filmed the dramatic scenes, they would soon find another story that would make their fortune and resonate all over the world.

Thomas was buying dates on Christian Street when, amongst a group of Arabs, someone unusual caught his eye.

> [His] curiosity was excited by a single Bedouin, who stood out in sharp relief from his companions. The man was wearing an agal, kuffieh, and aba, such as are only worn by Near Eastern Potentates. In his belt was fastened the short curved sword of a prince of Mecca, insignia worn by the descendants of the Prophet . . . It was not merely his costume, nor yet the dignity with which he carried his five feet three, marking him every inch a king or perhaps a caliph in disguise . . . [but] this young man was as blond as a Scandinavian, in whose veins flow Viking blood and the cool traditions of fiords and sagas . . . My first thought as I glanced at his face was that he might be one of the younger apostles returned to life. His expression was serene, almost saintly, in its selflessness and repose.

Immediately seeking out Ronald Storrs, Thomas asked him, 'Who is this blue-eyed fair-haired fellow wandering around the bazaars wearing the curved sword of—?'

He did not even get to finish his question. Instead, Storrs opened the door to an adjoining room, where, 'seated at the same table where Von Falkenhayn had worked out his unsuccessful plan for defeating Allenby, was the Bedouin prince, deeply absorbed in a ponderous tome on archaeology'.

'I want you to meet Colonel Lawrence, the Uncrowned King of Arabia,' Storrs told him.

Thomas immediately recognised that Lawrence was a great story. The taking of Jerusalem would generate headlines, but now he had a unique personality to go with it. Better still, a personality and a character the world had never seen before. In the chiselled, clean-shaven face of the British officer who wore Arab dress and lived and fought amongst the tribes, Thomas saw a man the American public would love. This was just what Wilson had sent him across the ocean to find. When Lawrence told him, 'I wish you could come out and get a film of us blowing up trains. It's quite a sight to see one going up in the air,' it was an invitation Thomas could not turn down.

While Thomas made plans to join Lawrence in the desert, Allenby informed Lawrence that the British forces would settle in Jerusalem for two months to keep things under control. However, he had grand plans for February: to advance towards Jericho and the mouth of the Jordan River. At the same time, he wanted Lawrence to bring the 'Arab army' to the southernmost end of the Dead Sea.

Once again, this would distract the Turks from launching an attack against the flank of the British Army while also cutting off their supplies of food and ammunition.

To achieve this, Lawrence saw that the Arabs would need to take three small rural towns: Shobek, Tafileh, and Kerak. Yet this operation would require a fundamental change in tactics. The Arabs were now moving on from blowing up trains and disappearing into the desert to attacking heavily guarded Turkish-held towns and keeping them. To date, Lawrence had done all that he could to keep the Arabs from any large-scale battles. Now they appeared inevitable. But if they could succeed, it would help Allenby as well as put the Arabs within striking distance of Damascus.

As always, Lawrence required more supplies in the form of mountain guns, camels and automatic weapons, and of course more gold. In the aborted raid on Mudowwara, he had also noted how much of the desert consisted of smooth, flat, baked mud. He thought it was the perfect surface for a car, which was far quicker than a camel, and could also be fitted with guns. He therefore requested the support of Joyce's armoured cars, and a fleet of Rolls-Royce tenders to support them. All were granted without hesitation. Lawrence had more than proven his worth.

When Lawrence returned to Akaba on Christmas Day 1917, he soon had a new toy to play with. A Rolls-Royce had arrived, and Lawrence was eager to put it to the test. Along with Joyce, they drove it across the desert at more than sixty miles an hour, racing past a gazelle in the process. Marvelling at the new technology at their disposal, they decided to drive to Mudowwara along with eight other cars mounted with machine guns, and attack the station.

Such was their speed that, before the Turks could react, the cars had sprayed the trenches with their Vickers machine guns, and sped off into the desert. 'The novelty was most enjoyable,' Lawrence said. 'Armoured car work seemed fighting de luxe, for our troops, being steel covered, could come to no hurt.' At this time, Lawrence needed all the help he could get. The Turks' price for his head had risen to 'twenty thousand pounds alive or ten thousand dead'.

In 1969 the Marxists announced on Radio Aden that the freedom fighters of Dhofar had located a British officer corrupting the plains folk of Dhofar. They gave a detailed description of the man in question and announced that a reward would be given for his capture. To my horror, the man they were describing was me. At last, I had been put on Salim Amr's execution list. On the one hand, it was evidence that I had been doing my job well and that my men had made an impact. But of course on the other I was deeply concerned.

That week chance took us into the mountains to lay an ambush near the village of Darbat. At dusk, we drove to the plain above Taqa, where we scaled the hills with our rifles. But then I heard a twig crack above us. Raising my hand, the platoon stopped so I could listen closer. The noise grew louder. There seemed to be a host of people descending the mountainside, coming directly towards us. One of my men suddenly whispered, 'They can smell us in the dark, sahb. The wind blows behind us tonight. It will carry our smell unless we disguise it.'

One of the main reasons for our smell was that I had still not succeeded in preventing a man known as 'Taj' from using a potent Indian hair cream called Jungle Petal. He loved it so much that he even brought a jar of it on patrol. Now it could result in Salim Amr capturing me and getting us killed. We needed to do something and fast.

On the floor all around us was the liquid green spattering of cattle. Quickly I ordered the men to smear it on their faces, arms, shirts, and trousers. They weren't enthusiastic, and we smelt evil, but I prayed it would disguise our scent. As always, Taj had his bottle of Jungle Petal with him. I told him to wipe it all over the rocks around us, hoping to put the adoo off our trail. Following this, I signalled to my men to follow me to a cave on the opposite side of the hill.

Racing away, but careful not to make much noise, we soon reached our hiding place. With my binoculars, I scoured the landscape and finally saw some movement. There were at least twenty men on the hillside, but now moving in the opposite direction. I exhaled with relief. For now I had escaped the grasp of Salim Amr, but I knew this would not be the last of it. I had to get him before he got me first.

Although I could only rely on my Recce Platoon to protect me, Lawrence decided to enlarge his personal bodyguard, with members loyal only to him. This was seen as a real position of privilege and Lawrence soon had the choice of the toughest warriors in the land. However, he purposely ensured the group consisted of men from different tribes so that they would never plot against him. With ninety men at his disposal, each was then provided with a rifle and dagger, while every two men were armed with a Lewis or Hotchkiss light machine gun. 'The British called them cut-throats,' Lawrence smiled, 'but they cut throats only to my order.' 'Like a bed of tulips,' they surrounded Lawrence in their colourful robes, while he stood out in the middle, dressed in white, as always.

Yet one of his bodyguards soon put Lawrence in a difficult position. At Akaba, a man from the Ageyl tribe by the name of Ali was 'caught in the open enjoyment of a British soldier'. For this sin, he was sentenced to be lashed fifty times, as was expected and accepted by the Arabs. Lawrence also had to decide on the punishment the British soldier, Carson, 'a very decent A.S.C. lad', should receive. Making matters more complex, this incident occurred just six weeks after Lawrence had been assaulted in Deraa.

Homosexual acts committed by a member of the British armed forces were strictly prohibited. Indeed, it was a criminal offence. After much thought, Lawrence eventually decided that he would have to inform Carson's officer about the incident so that he would receive the appropriate military punishment.

Not all of the Brits felt this was fair. In particular, Corporal Driver, the British NCO in charge of the cars, pleaded with Lawrence to keep the matter to himself. He explained that Carson 'was only a boy, not vicious or decadent', and 'had been a year without opportunity of sexual indulgence'. Surprisingly, Lawrence refused to show him

Lawrence and Feisal meeting with American journalist Lowell Thomas, who would come to play a major role in Lawrence's fame.

It was Feisal who originally presented Lawrence with the white, gold-threaded robes that made him stand out from the other tribesmen, who typically wore brown. These robes indicated his esteemed status among the men.

Feisal and Arab tribesmen at Wadi Ithm. Lowell Thomas is driving, while Lawrence may be seen seated in the back. According to Lawrence, using these armoured cars in battle was 'fighting de luxe, for our troops, being steel covered, could come to no hurt'.

Lawrence reading in his tent at Guweira, 1918. After successfully cutting off Turkish traffic in the Dead Sea, Lawrence and his men were in urgent need of supplies. They returned to Guweira, where food and gold coins from Akaba brought them one step closer to the ultimate conquest: Damascus.

A city square in Damascus in 1918, before it was captured. The fall of the Syrian capital signalled Arab liberation, but was quickly tempered by the Sykes–Picot Agreement coming into effect.

Lawrence enters Damascus in a Rolls-Royce, greeted by cheering crowds.

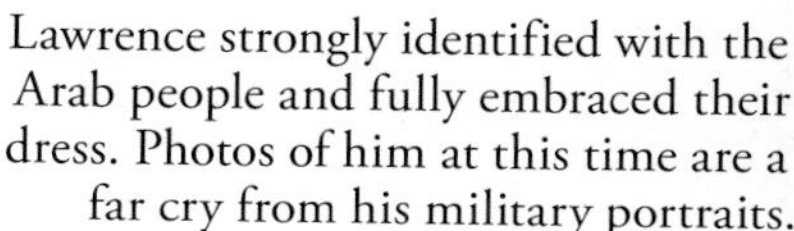

Lawrence strongly identified with the Arab people and fully embraced their dress. Photos of him at this time are a far cry from his military portraits.

A weary Lawrence on the balcony of the Victoria Hotel in Damascus, shortly after resigning his position. With the French gaining control of Syria, to Feisal's fury, Lawrence was left to doubt the value of his whole mission.

Feisal, Lawrence and the Arabian Commission at the Paris Peace Conference, 1919.

The crowded great hall at Versailles. Lawrence and Feisal addressed the ten leaders of the Allied governments, Lawrence translating from Arabic into English and then French, which earned him a round of applause.

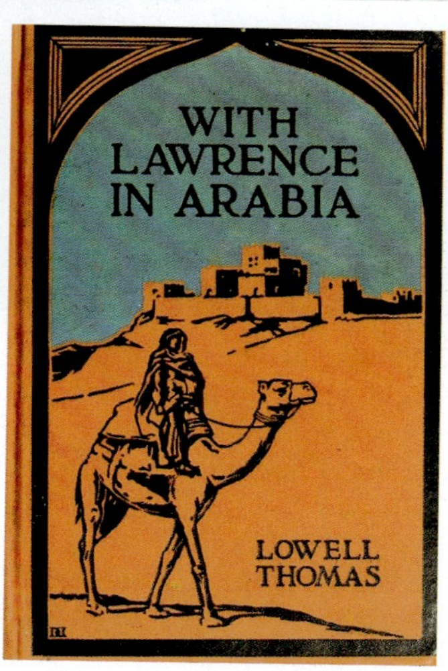

American journalist Lowell Thomas *(above right)* first met Lawrence in Jerusalem and was immediately struck by the potential of Lawrence's story.

Lowell Thomas's 1919 show *With Allenby in Palestine and Lawrence in Arabia*, and subsequent book, caused a sensation.

The show used photos of Lawrence in Arabia, and posed portraits taken in a studio in London.

THE MANCHESTER PROGRAMME

Entertainments and Pleasure.

The Official List and Recognised Medium for the Manchester Amusements

No. 1916 WEEK COMMENCING APRIL 19, 1920.

PEOPLE OF TO-DAY.

"THE UNCROWNED KING OF ARABIA" COLONEL T·E·LAWRENCE

THE MOST ROMANTIC CAREER OF MODERN TIMES. By Lowell Thomas

While Lawrence had hoped to retreat from the limelight following Paris, the show brought him enormous notoriety.

In 1920, Lawrence began working for Churchill as his political adviser in the Middle East, as well as his emissary to the Arabs. Both men can be seen in this photo from the 1921 Cairo conference *(Churchill centre front and Lawrence just behind in a dark suit)* – along with two lion cubs in the foreground.

Mr & Mrs Winston Churchill, T. E. Lawrence and Gertrude Bell on camels in front of the Sphinx. Egypt, 1921.

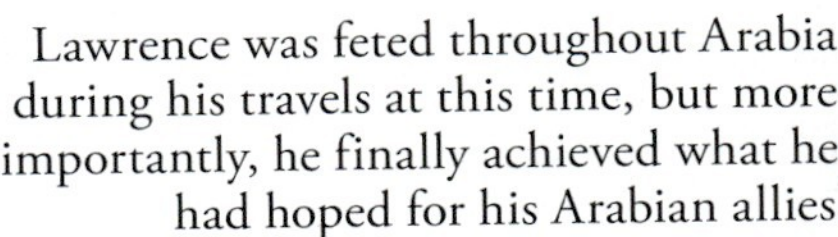

Lawrence was feted throughout Arabia during his travels at this time, but more importantly, he finally achieved what he had hoped for his Arabian allies.

A keen motorcyclist, on his return to Britain Lawrence got his thrills by driving at speed through the Dorset countryside. The pastime was to spell disaster however.

Lawrence's account of his adventures, *Seven Pillars of Wisdom*, caused him considerable debt to publish.

When Lawrence advised on the redrawing of borders in 1921, a new country, Jordan, was created, with Sherif Hussein's son Abdullah taking the throne.

Feisal's coronation, 1921. With Britain having the mandate for oil-rich Iraq, Lawrence ensured that Feisal was crowned as its king.

DAILY SKETCH, MONDAY, MAY 20, 1935

WHAT 50 YEARS ON STAGE HAS TAUGHT ME—MARIE TEMPEST WIRELESS: P. 20

DAILY SKETCH

THINGS I HATE BY BERNARD SHAW

No. 8,131 (Registered as a newspaper.) MONDAY, MAY 20, 1935 ONE PENNY

TOO BIG FOR WEALTH AND GLORY

LAWRENCE THE SOLDIER DIES TO LIVE FOR EVER

Having lingered for six days, Lawrence of Arabia (Mr. T. E. Shaw) died in hospital at Bovington Camp, Dorset, yesterday from injuries received when he crashed with his powerful motor-cycle at Moreton. He was 46. When the war broke out Lawrence was excavating Hittite ruins near Carchemish on the Euphrates. Two years later he organised and virtually commanded the Arab Army that gave such powerful help to the British campaign in Palestine. In this rôle he became famous the world over as Lawrence of Arabia (right). Scorning notoriety and wealth, he declined an offer of £10,000 to appear in a film.

On 13 May 1935 Lawrence was thrown from his motorcycle after swerving to avoid two boys. He died in hospital six days later, aged forty-six.

A legend in his own lifetime, Lawrence's fame has only grown since his death. This plaque adorns his alma mater, Oxford High School.

The stone tomb effigy of Lawrence in Arab dress at St Martin's Church, Wareham.

any leniency. He told Driver that he could not 'let our man go free . . . We shared good and ill fortune with the Arabs, who had already punished their offender in the case.' As far as Lawrence was concerned, both the Arabs and the British should be punished equally for the offence.

Corporal Driver had the perfect response to this. Asking Lawrence to visit Private Carson at the British camp, he then pointed to a huddled figure sitting in front of a fire, surrounded by his fellow soldiers. Lawrence recalled that he was covered with a blanket, looking 'drawn and ghastly'. Driver then pulled off the blanket to reveal a score of deep red welts across Carson's back. The men had decided that he should receive the same punishment as Ali, 'even giving him sixty instead of fifty, because he was English!' The whipping had also been carried out in front of an Arab witness from Lawrence's bodyguard. They 'hoped I would see they had done their best and call it enough,' Lawrence recalled. He agreed with the punishment. Justice had been served. In his eyes, Carson and the Arab had been treated equally. But after his own experience of being raped and whipped in Deraa, Lawrence might have also felt that the punishment equated with his own.

For Carson, the punishment might have stopped such behaviour from ever occurring again. For Lawrence, it was just the beginning of a complex and tortured form of psychological and physical punishment that would soon explode.

21

Before Lawrence could take the three Turkish-held towns for Allenby, he needed to cut the railway line at Jurf to sever communications and prevent the Turks from sending reinforcements.

As night fell and temperatures dropped below freezing, the Arabs set off. Led by Sherif Nasir, they opened fire on the station with a mountain gun, following which the Beni Sakhr charged over the frosty ground on their camels. Overwhelming the Turkish garrison with their ferocity, they killed 20 Turks and took nearly 200 prisoner.

Following the news from Jurf, the Arabs made quick work of taking Shobek. The Iraqi officer Nuri Said then rode on to Tafileh through the night, arriving at the edge of a cliff above the mist-covered town as dawn broke. Shouting below, he demanded the Turks surrender or be shelled. They refused. They knew of the capture of Jurf and Shobek, but they were 150 men, all well-armed, and fancied their chances. That was until Auda Abu Tayi appeared alongside Nuri and bellowed, 'Dogs! Do you not know Auda?' In Liddell Hart's words, 'The defences of Tafila collapsed before his trumpeting voice as those of Jericho had once collapsed before Joshua.'

So far, things had gone like clockwork. Two of the three key towns were now occupied by the Arabs. However, when Lawrence, Zeid, and Jaafar Pasha arrived at Tafileh things were not running as smoothly as they hoped. Although most of the townspeople were Arab, they were divided in their loyalty to different clans. Now the Turks were gone, bitter feuds had erupted between the tribes. Gunshots rang out up and down the streets as each clan sought to assert their dominance. For now, the gift of gold temporarily put a stop to the violence, but it wouldn't take much to set it off again.

Just as Lawrence regained some order, news reached him that a sizeable Turkish force was marching from Amman to retake Tafileh, consisting of 'three . . . battalions of infantry, a hundred cavalry, two mountain howitzers and twenty-seven machine guns . . . led by Hamid Fakhri Bey, the commander of the 48th Division'. The town was quickly sent into a state of chaos and terror. In Lawrence's vivid description, people 'rushed to save their goods and their lives . . . It was freezing hard, and the ground crusted with noisy ice. In the blustering dark the crying and the confusion through the narrow streets were terrible.'

There was no time to waste. Lawrence needed to defend the town but the decision was not his alone. In the desert Lawrence had often asserted command. Yet in this instance, Feisal's younger half-brother Zeid was supposedly in charge, even though he had minimal experience in military strategy. Jaafar Pasha, commander of the Arab regulars, was perhaps the most experienced military man in Tafileh, and understandably expected to direct the defence, while tribal leaders such as Auda also wanted their say. With time short, and so many different voices, it was a recipe for disaster.

Ultimately, Zeid, as Sherif Hussein's son, had the final say, and he was therefore besieged from all sides with conflicting strategies. He thought the townspeople were probably pro-Turk, and would welcome the Turks back, making it very difficult for the Arabs to operate from within the town. He therefore gave the order for the tribesmen to leave Tafileh. Lawrence disagreed with this. He had spoken to the local people. Whether Arab, Armenian, or Senussi, he found that they were united only by their hatred of the Turks. They were also terrified by the Motalga tribesmen firing their rifles into the sky as they clattered out of town at full gallop, apparently abandoning the locals to their fate.

Lawrence also disagreed with Jaafar Pasha's tactics to move his regulars onto high ground to the west of the town in order to defend it. There was plenty of 'dead ground' in front of Jaafar, which would allow the Turks to easily work their way around his flank. While they were stranded on the high ground, the Turks could then take the town.

Working on Zeid, he managed to persuade him that Jaafar was wrong. As such, Zeid quickly ordered the regulars to move to the triangular plain in front of the town, ready to fight 'a pitched battle'. Lawrence might not have had the right to lead when compared to Zeid, or the military experience of Jaafar, but his unique blend of skills meant he understood this situation better than anyone. When this quickly became apparent, they all stood aside and let him direct matters.

To buy them some time to reorganise their defence, he

suggested that Abdulla, a Mesopotamian machine-gun officer and some of his men should march ahead on mules to engage with the Turks. While the enemy was kept at bay, Lawrence then stationed Zeid's personal camel-men and some of his own bodyguards on a steep ridge on the eastern side of a ravine. He told them to stay in full sight, so as to give the impression that the ridge was strongly held. He wanted to force the Turks across from there, and towards the triangular plain, where they would meet the full might of the Arab forces.

In the distance, Lawrence heard the screeching and explosions of Turkish howitzers. They were still too far away to do any real damage, but he saw the shells were falling on a ravine. Making his way there, he picked up a shell fragment to examine it. It was a Skoda eleven-pounder. If the Turks got much closer, he did not think the town could hold out under such a barrage of shell fire.

With the Arab regulars now engaging with the Turks, Lawrence joined the Motalga tribe on the hillside as they came under attack from machine guns. Sheltering behind a rock, Lawrence recalled that 'The bullets slapped off it deafeningly, and the air above it so hummed and whistled with them and their ricochets and chips, that it felt like sudden death to put one's head over the top.'

But Lawrence knew that despite being under heavy fire he could not afford to hide for long. The Turks were getting closer to the town and he needed to push them across to the triangular plain. To the surprise of the Motalga, Lawrence suddenly emerged from his hiding place and, under heavy fire, carefully counted his paces.

It seemed an act of lunacy, but Lawrence knew what he was doing. With this he could work out the exact range to set the sights of his machine guns and his mountain gun. Still, it was a miracle he was not shot.

As the Motalga held their position, Lawrence mounted a camel and galloped back across the icy plain while gunshots and shells rained down upon him. With the Arab machine guns opening fire on the Turks, he sent Rasim – 'a Damascene, a sardonic fellow, who rose laughing to every crisis and shrunk around like a sore-headed bear . . . when things went well' – to lead about eighty horsemen to attack the Turks' left flank. At the same time he ordered 100 armed villagers to attack the Turkish right.

Suddenly the Turks found themselves under ferocious attack from all sides, and having no option but to move exactly where Lawrence had wanted them. Watching on, Lawrence saw that they were about to face the full might of the Arab forces.

The massacre that followed was unrelenting. Over 200 Turks were killed, including the commander, Hamid Fakhri Bey, while the Arabs took 250 prisoners, as well as 2 mountain howitzers, 27 machine guns, and 200 horses and mules. In the words of Liddell Hart, it was a victory 'in the purest classical tradition . . . it was Cannae, or still more, Ilipa, adapted to modern weapons', a 'gem' which placed Lawrence among 'the Great Captains'. Indeed, he would be promoted to lieutenant colonel for these exploits.

With Tafileh once more under Arab control, Lawrence wasted no time in ordering the attack on Kerak to commence. Seventy Bedouin rode through the night and attacked the unsuspecting Turks at dawn. The men trying to defend the town were from the Turkish Navy and were not equipped to fight a rampaging cavalry. Kerak therefore fell quickly, with the Arabs looting and burning the town and taking sixty Turks prisoner.

Two weeks ahead of Allenby's schedule, the Arabs had brought a stop to Turkish traffic in the Dead Sea. Yet Lawrence realised that if they were to hold out and continue, they urgently needed supplies, particularly food and gold. He needed to travel to Guweira at once.

Conditions were treacherous. The temperature had dropped dramatically, while the air swirled with snow storms and ice. But he had no choice. Without food and gold, they could not hope to continue. The journey would take him to the very edge.

22

For the 150-mile journey to Guweira, Lawrence was joined by five of his men as the wind howled around them, 'and the slabby stones of the valley-slopes became sheets of ice'. The camels struggled on the frozen ground, which 'broke rottenly beneath their weight and let our camels in, four or five inches deep, at every stride'. The men had no choice but to hurry their poor beasts on for fear that they might freeze to death.

Finally, the camels became so weak that the men had to walk alongside them. In the face of a blizzard, some of the men seemed resigned to their fate. They would have died in the desert if Lawrence had not urged them on. Freezing, exhausted, and hungry, they finally reached Guweira in a bedraggled state.

For the next three days, Lawrence and his men took the opportunity to rest, and hoped that conditions would be more favourable for their return. Lawrence spent the time catching up with Joyce and Feisal and regaling them with the dramatic story of how Tafileh had been taken. Finally, £30,000 in gold coins (approximately £2.1 million today) arrived from Akaba. This was what Lawrence had been waiting for. He could now return to Zeid in Tafileh, and they could continue to hand out gold coins to those tribesmen who pledged their loyalty to Feisal and the Arab

Revolt. With this, the march to Jericho, and then Damascus, could begin.

For the return to Tafileh, Lawrence took fourteen tribesmen with him to share the load, with each man carrying two bags of gold. However, the return journey was as cold and difficult as the journey down. Departing into a rainstorm, the men were soon drenched, while the camels once more struggled in the mud. Rain turned to snow, and with wind continuing to buffet them, some of the men finally flung themselves to the ground and refused to continue. 'I, too, was very near crying,' Lawrence admitted.

Pushing on as the rest of his men lagged behind, Lawrence found himself alone in a blizzard when his camel lost its footing and sent them both hurtling down a hillside. Lawrence was unharmed, but he could tell the camel was shaken. When he tried to mount her, she dropped to her knees and collapsed to the ground. No amount of encouragement or hitting her from behind would get her to move. Lawrence began to panic. He was all alone and could not be sure if his tribesmen would reach him. The conditions were so bad that if he were to stay out in the open, he would surely die. Yet if he were to try to walk to Tafileh, the gold would be too heavy to carry and he would have to leave it behind. After more pleading, prodding, and cajoling, his camel finally rose unsteadily to its feet. Although still shaken, and trudging slower than usual, it was able to carry Lawrence to Tafileh, where the remaining tribesmen eventually joined him. Traumatised, and suffering from hypothermia and frozen limbs, it was a miracle that no one had died.

After a good night's sleep, Zeid told Lawrence that,

while he had been away, another English officer had joined them in Tafileh. Lawrence went at once to meet Lieutenant Kirkbride, a young intelligence officer who was fluent in Arabic and had been sent to report on the progress of the Arab Front. Feeling re-energised, Lawrence decided to show Kirkbride his plans for the next stage of the Revolt. Together they rode north on a reconnaissance mission, 'as far as the edge of the Jordan valley'. From there they could hear Allenby's guns attacking Jericho. It was now time for Lawrence to bring the Arab army north of the Dead Sea, just as he had promised.

They duly rode back to Tafileh to spread the good news. However, Zeid was not convinced. He told Lawrence it would require a lot of money if they were to proceed. Lawrence was confused. Just that very morning, he had handed Zeid the £30,000 in gold coins. Zeid looked shamefaced. He told Lawrence that he had been persuaded, or browbeaten, by the local sheikhs to pay them for their support. The gold was all but gone. Lawrence was incredulous. These men had done little to help the Revolt and offered little going forward. Despite this, Zeid had paid them all he had. Without the gold, the plan of advancing north was impossible.

'This meant the complete ruin of my plans and hopes,' Lawrence said. He also realised that it might prove fatal to the British advance. Suddenly, he found that his 'will was gone' and thought he had 'made a mess of things'. He blamed himself for 'that pretence to lead the national uprising of another race', and 'the daily posturing in alien dress'. He therefore decided to ride to Allenby at once and resign.

23

By camel, car, and then train, Lawrence travelled north through the night to Bir Salem, the General Headquarters of the British forces. His mind raged with thoughts of the Arabs' incompetence, the Allies' duplicity, the Turks' sexual assault in Deraa, and the conflict within himself. Finally, it had all become too much to bear. His hands were soaked in blood, and his morals were in the dirt. All he wanted to do was to escape this unrelenting nightmare once and for all. Rather than wait for Allenby to relieve him of his duties, this time he would beg to go home.

However, when he arrived at Bir Salem station, he was surprised to find David Hogarth waiting for him. Somebody had passed on the message that Lawrence was on his way to Allenby in a desperate state of mind, and Hogarth was there to intercept him before he did something rash. Hogarth knew that nobody could replace Lawrence and the missing gold was an insubstantial amount in the great scheme of things.

The frail Lawrence told Hogarth that he was 'a very sick man, almost at breaking point', and was 'sick of responsibility'. He was angry that 'Cairo had put on him the moral responsibility for buoying up the Arabs with promises that might never be fulfilled.' But more than that, after the incident with the gold at Tafileh, he had now lost faith in the

Arabs' ability to handle their own affairs. For this, he blamed no one but himself. All of it had been a sham of his own design.

Hogarth let Lawrence speak without interjecting. Clearly he was tired and emotional and needed to blow off some steam. When he was finished ranting, Hogarth suggested they have breakfast in the officer's mess with General Clayton. Hopefully, some good food and sage advice might make him think again.

Over toast and marmalade, Hogarth told Lawrence to forget about the £30,000. It was but a drop in the ocean, and the equivalent to the cost of the war for a seven-hour period. Besides, Lawrence couldn't be blamed for how Zeid had used it. Clayton also tried to appeal to his ego, pointing out that Lawrence was indispensable, no one could do what he did, and Allenby had great things in store for him.

Clayton went on to tell Lawrence that General Jan Smuts of the Imperial War Cabinet had paid a visit to Allenby on behalf of the prime minister. Smuts had emphasised the crucial importance of victory over the Turks and urged Allenby to be even more aggressive. Allenby was therefore about to embark on the final big push. At last, the end was in sight. At such a crucial juncture, Clayton bluntly told Lawrence, there was no question of 'letting him off'. He had to stay around and finish the job he had started. Lawrence didn't say much, but it was clear that he had calmed down considerably. Satisfied that Lawrence again saw reason, Clayton took him straight from the breakfast table to meet Allenby.

Even if Lawrence was still in the mood to share his

concerns with Allenby, he didn't have a chance to speak. Barely acknowledging Lawrence's dishevelled state, which was by now par for the course, Allenby instead launched into his plans for the next phase of the Revolt. He told Lawrence that his orders were to take Damascus and Aleppo as soon as possible and to knock Turkey out of the war once and for all. He therefore needed the Arabs to become his right wing, taking on the Turkish Fourth Army to the east of the Jordan River.

To achieve this, he first wanted the Arabs to concentrate on cutting the railway north of Maan. Meanwhile, the British would cross the Jordan, occupy the hillside town of Salt, just ten miles west of Amman, and destroy as much of the railway as possible south of the city. Following this, they would secure Amman, severing the Hejaz permanently from the Turks, while opening up the route to Damascus.

Lawrence had come to Allenby to resign, but at such a crucial stage there was no question of that. He had no option but to once more take up his 'mantle of fraud in the East' and return to the fold. Yet, to achieve Allenby's plan, Lawrence required 700 camels, more weapons, and, as usual, a lot more gold. Allenby did not hesitate to agree. The war was reaching its most critical moment, and now was the time to strike.

Soon after, Lawrence returned to Akaba, where American journalist Lowell Thomas and his cameraman Harry Chase were waiting for him. After gaining the permission of Allenby, Thomas was determined to shadow Lawrence and spread his incredible story across the globe.

It seems from the resulting photographs that the usually publicity-shy Lawrence was not only cooperative but enthusiastic. Despite his dark mood, he appeared relaxed and good-humoured, allowing them to take pictures as he went about his work. He certainly did not look like a man being harassed by American journalists. This suited both Thomas and Lawrence. From Thomas's point of view, it made the whole story more of a scoop, while for Lawrence, it freed him from the accusation of seeking publicity. Lawrence also understood the value the photos might have. Thomas told him that the American public would love him, and in turn, this would result in even more people supporting America's involvement in the war. For now, Lawrence thought this could only be a good thing, but in time he would come to regret it.

Returning his focus to the real business at hand, Lawrence began to prepare for the Arabs' operation to support the British raid on Amman. As supplies started to arrive in Akaba, so did some newcomers. Lieutenant Colonel Alan Dawnay headed up the Hejaz Operations Staff and was someone Lawrence greatly admired, calling him 'Allenby's greatest gift to us'. He did not, however, feel the same way about Captain Hubert Young of the Indian Army, a fluent Arabic speaker who had been sent to serve as Lawrence's 'understudy'. The two men had a mostly civil relationship and had known each other before the war, but each was suspicious of the other and neither entirely convinced the other was adequately fulfilling his role.

In analysing the job in hand, Lawrence thought it would require three separate operations. Jaafar Pasha's Arab regulars would need to seize the railway north of Maan, while Dawnay would attack Mudowwara with the armoured cars, and cut the railway line to Medina once and for all. Meanwhile, Lawrence, Zeid and Nasir would join Allenby at Salt, raising the local Beni Sakhr clans along the way. Salt would then become the centre of operations for both the British and Arab armies. Together they could then advance to the north and take Damascus. This was it, the big push at long last.

As Lawrence waited for the go-ahead for the Maan operation from Allenby, he received some bad news. Daud, one of his high-spirited servant boys who had amused and annoyed him in equal measure, had frozen to death in Azrak. Lawrence was devastated, as was Daud's partner in crime, Farraj. The pair 'had been friends from childhood, going about hand in hand, for the happiness of feeling one another, and diverting our march by their eternal gaiety'. Lawrence reflected on the 'openness and honesty in their love, which proved its innocence; for with other couples we had seen how, when passion had thrust in, it had not been a friendship any more, but a half marriage, a shamefaced union of the flesh'.

Worse news was soon to come. The British assault on Amman had been hampered by appalling weather, which not only prevented the movement of heavy artillery but saw camels slip and break their legs in the quagmire. Without the necessary firepower to take on the Turks, they were soon in full retreat and fleeing from Salt. More than 1,200 British soldiers were killed in the aborted operation, while Cemal Pasha soon arrived and publicly executed any Arabs who had backed the British. Through sheer fear, most of the townspeople now joined the Ottoman Army. Such was the desperate state of affairs that some thought the Turks might even retake Jerusalem. Things were beginning to look bleak.

Dismayed at this turn of events, Lawrence decided to examine for himself what had happened in Amman, but he wasn't going to make the same mistake as in Deraa. This time he needed a much more convincing disguise to enter a Turkish-held town. He and Farraj therefore hired three Gypsy women, dressed them in long robes and flowered veils, then did likewise in an attempt to blend in.

Walking around the town in disguise, Lawrence reached the depressing conclusion that the British had not done enough to damage the railway, and the Turks had easily been able to receive supplies. He also realised just how heavily defended the town was. It would not be taken quickly. His thoughts were suddenly cut short when they were approached by Turkish soldiers. Thankfully, they only thought they were prostitutes, though this was enough to persuade Lawrence to leave the town as soon as possible.

On their return journey to Akaba, Lawrence's small group of Arabs saw a patrol of Turkish soldiers in the distance. Lawrence saw no reason to bother with them – they could easily continue their march without becoming embroiled in an unnecessary fight – but his men, including Farraj, wanted to attack. Lawrence argued it was pointless, but they went ahead anyway, at a deadly cost.

In the brief fight that followed, Farraj was shot and fell from his camel. A bullet had passed through his spine, and he could not move. Lawrence rushed to his side while the Arabs shouted that fifty more Turkish soldiers were coming towards them. The tribesmen tried to pick Farraj up, but he screamed in pain so terribly that they had to put him down. It was no use: they would have to abandon him.

Lawrence knew he could not leave Farraj alive for the Turks to find. They tortured Arabs unmercifully, sometimes mutilating them or burning them alive. 'For this reason,' Lawrence wrote, 'we were all agreed before action to finish off one another if too badly hurt to be moved away, but I had never realised that it might fall upon me to kill Farraj.'

Kneeling beside him, Lawrence's finger rested on the pistol by his side. He looked at Farraj, struggling to do what he knew he had to.

'Daud will be angry with you,' Farraj grimaced, indicating to Lawrence that he must proceed and reunite him with his friend.

Lawrence picked up his pistol and replied, 'Salute him from me.'

Farraj shut his eyes and said, 'God give you peace.'

At that, Lawrence shot one of the few people on this earth he could truly call a friend.

It was a devastating moment. Daud and Farraj had given him so many moments of joy and had brought laughter in even the toughest situations. They had more than played their part in the success of the Arab Revolt, but now they were both dead. It was yet another tragedy Lawrence would have to put to the back of his mind and one day try to process. In a letter home around this time, Lawrence wrote about being surrounded by so much blood and death: 'After four years of this sort of thing I am become altogether dried up, and till the business ends I can't do anything else either here or there. It will be a great comfort when one can lie down and sleep without having to think about things; and speak without having one's every word reported in half a hundred camps. This is a job too big for me.'

24

There was no time to grieve for Farraj. As Lawrence and his men set off to rejoin Feisal in Akaba, they heard gunshots coming from the direction of Maan. Heading towards it, Lawrence recalled, 'The road was littered with crumpled khaki figures, and the eyes of the wounded, gone rich with pain, stared accusingly at us.' Something was wrong.

Stopping at Jebel Semna, a 3,000-foot hill overlooking the town, Lawrence could see the Arab regulars' operation to attack the station was already well underway. But the Turks manfully defended it and refused to surrender. In response, the French bombarded the station with their guns, but they soon ran out of ammunition, while the Arabs surrounded the station but could not break through. Over 90 men had already been killed and 200 injured. It was just the sort of result Lawrence had long hoped to avoid in sending the Arabs into battle.

Dawnay's operation at Mudowwara thankfully met with more success. Lawrence joined him as a joint force of Egyptian soldiers and Arab tribesmen, aided by British cars and aircraft, attacked the station. After some particularly aggressive looting (in which Lawrence managed to walk off with the station bell), Dawnay took his armoured cars and the Egyptians south. There they destroyed nearly eighty miles of railway track, seven stations, and numerous causeways and bridges. This finally severed the link to Medina. Now unable to receive any supplies or reinforcements, the Turks were left to rot there until they chose to surrender.

At this, Lawrence and Dawnay raced to the Dead Sea and set sail to meet with Allenby at British headquarters. On arrival, Lawrence found a hive of frenzied activity. Everything seemed set for another big push on Salt and Amman, and confidence was high that this was finally their moment to break the Turks. However, when Allenby told Lawrence that the Beni Sakhr tribe had joined forces with the British and had promised to raise 20,000 men, Lawrence knew something was seriously wrong. Farhud, the leader of the Beni Sakhr, could not raise 400 men, let alone 20,000.

This sadly proved to be the case: not one tribesman from the Beni Sakhr arrived for the second assault on Amman, and the British were once more forced to retreat, suffering an additional 1,500 casualties in the process. It was another humiliation. Lawrence was infuriated that instead of going through him, as had always been the case, Allenby's staff were now dealing with the Arabs directly. It was no surprise that it had been an unmitigated disaster. They had no idea how the Arabs operated, nor did they understand which tribes could be relied upon.

The failure to take Amman for a second time had severe consequences. The new Russian Bolshevik government had recently signed a peace deal with Germany. This allowed the Germans to withdraw fifty divisions from the

Eastern Front and set them loose on the British in France. In March 1918 they commenced the biggest artillery barrage of the war, firing 1.1 million shells on British positions in five hours, resulting in 38,000 casualties. After four years of trench warfare, the Germans quickly breached the British line and sent them reeling back to Amiens, gaining eight miles in the process.

In the circumstances, the British government felt that Allenby's plan to cross the Jordan River was no longer a priority. To repel the Germans, reinforcements were urgently needed on the Western Front. Allenby was therefore stripped of two complete British divisions, numbering 60,000 experienced infantrymen in total (as well as numerous artillery, cavalry, and machine-gun units). In return, he was promised the men would be replaced by some of the Indian divisions in Mesopotamia. Not only were these inexperienced men who required significant training, but they would not arrive for many weeks. Until then, the best Allenby could do was to try to hold Jerusalem.

This left the Arabs in a precarious position. Lawrence told Allenby that without the British pressing on Amman, the Turks would send reinforcements to Maan, from where they could drive the Arabs back. Allenby certainly didn't want to concede any more ground while he waited for the Indians to arrive. He therefore promised a British operation at a vast bridgehead across Jordan, which would keep the Turks at Amman occupied, for now at least. He also promised the Arabs more supplies in the shape of more air raids on the Hejaz railway. Better still, as the Imperial Camel Corps Brigade was being abolished, over

2,000 camels were now free for the Arabs to utilise. Despite all the bad news, this was 'an immense, a regal gift', Lawrence recognised, 'the gift of unlimited mobility'.

When Lawrence returned to Akaba and told Feisal this news, he was also astonished. Calling all of the tribal heads to his tent, he announced that, with this gift, 'Our war was to march unchecked to freedom, its triumphant end.' The British might currently be bogged down, but that didn't mean the Arabs couldn't move on Damascus themselves.

Better yet, an influential group of seven Syrians had been meeting with the Arab Bureau to gain some reassurance over their country's future and the situation in Palestine. The British government finally gave a commitment, known as 'The Declaration to the Seven', which ensured 'the complete and sovereign independence' of territories that had been in Arab hands before the war, and which had been liberated since. Any territory that the Allies subsequently took would then be governed according to the 'principle of the consent of the governed'. To avoid this being misconstrued, the document ended by stating that 'the oppressed peoples . . . should obtain their freedom and independence'. Despite these good intentions, France was not a party to the agreement and would certainly not agree to what the British proposed. Still, it was a clear sign that the British were prepared to do all they could to support the Arabs.

Before the Arabs could make any moves towards Damascus, however, the new camels would have to adapt to a new diet. In Palestine they had been fed barley, while in the desert they would need to subsist on scrub. This process could take many weeks. Nevertheless, while the Arabs waited for the camels, there was still plenty of work to be done. To ensure the Turks were cut off in Medina and Maan, there continued to be a steady succession of raids, train and bridge demolitions, and hit-and-run attacks. Yet it also became apparent that the Turks were growing stronger. If the Arabs were to continue to keep the Turks occupied in Medina and Maan, and then strike out towards Damascus, they urgently needed more men.

Lawrence suggested that Feisal ask his father to transfer Ali and Abdulla's regular units to Akaba. This would provide over 10,000 men in uniform who could be divided to retain Maan and attack areas around Deraa and Damascus. The rest could then connect with Allenby's forces at Jericho. In principle, this sounded like a good idea, but King Hussein refused to grant his consent.

Lawrence therefore made his way to Cairo to meet Allenby in the hope that the general could change Hussein's mind. He explained that with Abdulla's and Ali's forces at his disposal, they could commence moving towards Damascus, with Allenby joining in later to offer further support. Allenby explained this would not be necessary: at long last, his reinforcements had arrived from India. By late September, they would be ready for a new offensive on Damascus and Aleppo.

After the two failed attacks on Amman, Allenby knew that the Turks would be waiting for them. But this meant that the coastal sector would be poorly defended. With this in mind, Allenby needed Lawrence and the Arabs to attack Deraa, which would keep the Turks focused on the Jordan Valley, while the British attacked along the coast.

Allenby told Lawrence that he planned to commence his attack on 19 September. He therefore needed the Arabs to make their move 'not more than four but no less than two days before he did'. As Allenby put it, 'Three men and a boy with pistols in front of Deera on September the sixteenth would fill his conception; would be better than thousands a week before or a week after.'

However, as Lawrence commenced plans to return to the scene of his rape and assault, intelligence arrived that the Turks were planning a raid on Abu el-Lissal which could block their path. Lawrence and Dawnay immediately leaped into action. To proceed, they needed something to distract the Turks. Allenby agreed to lend them two companies from the recently disbanded Imperial Camel Corps, led by Colonel Buxton, to lead the Turks in the wrong direction. But it was 'on the condition that they should avoid casualties'. This presented an obvious problem. If they were going anywhere near the Turks, then there was a risk some might be killed.

Lawrence decided that 'Buxton should march from the Canal to Akaba; thence, by Rum, to carry Mudowwara by night-attack; thence by Bair, to destroy the bridge and tunnel near Amman; and back to Palestine on August thirtieth.' Joyce and Young disagreed with Lawrence's plan. They calculated that there were not enough provisions or water available to the men and their camels. But Lawrence held firm. He insisted that the force, just 500 strong, could live off the land, while forage could be obtained easily for the camels after an abundant season. Young was still unconvinced. Lawrence recalled that 'In riposte, he became aggressively regular. I prosed forth on my hoary theorem that we lived by our raggedness and beat the Turk by our uncertainty. Young's scheme was faulty, because [it was] precise.' Lawrence knew from experience that his Arab irregulars were able to cover hundreds of miles with little in the way of food or drink. However, many of Buxton's men had never engaged in such a long, arduous journey in the desert. His presumption that they could do the same as the Arabs was a considerable risk.

With Lawrence refusing to budge, he greeted Colonel Robin Buxton and his 300 men as they arrived in Akaba. That night he gathered them around a blazing campfire and gave a rousing speech. He recognised that for many of these Englishmen, this foray into the desert would be an entirely new experience. He told them they were entering 'a part of Arabia where no white man had ever set foot'. Some of the Bedouin they might encounter were 'none too friendly', and would see them as the enemy. To succeed in their mission, they must 'turn the other cheek'. They were not there to score points but to occupy the Turks. He had promised Allenby there would be no casualties and didn't intend to lose any men to needless squabbles with the Bedouin. Colonel Stirling, later to become the famed author of *Safety Last*, called the speech 'the straightest talk I have ever heard'. He recalled that the men 'retired for the night fully convinced that they were about to embark on the greatest jaunt in the history of war'.

25

Lawrence accompanied the Camel Corps on the first stage of their journey to ensure their safe passage through lands held by the Howeitat. However, he also needed to persuade other tribes to let them pass unhindered. He therefore flew to Jefer to meet with Feisal, Nuri Shaalan, and the rest of the Rwala sheikhs. 'Many times in such councils had Feisal won over and set us aflame new tribes,' Lawrence recalled; 'many times had the work fallen to me; but never until today had we been actively together in one company, reinforcing and relaying one another, from our opposite side of the poles.'

Along with more gold and Feisal bringing 'nationality to their minds', Lawrence proceeded to settle any doubts with another rousing speech, this time 'emphasising the mystical enchantment of sacrifice for freedom'. Staring at the tribal leaders one by one, Lawrence felt the flame of excitement ignite within them as they became desperate to do their bit and make history. With this, the Rwala tribe agreed to facilitate Feisal and Lawrence in any way they could.

But as Lawrence returned to Akaba, he was racked by guilt. Once again he had persuaded Arab tribes to back the Revolt when they would probably only exchange living under Ottoman rule for life in a French colony. 'I cannot put down my acquiescence in the Arab fraud to weakness of character or native hypocrisy,' he admitted, 'though of course I must have had some tendency, some aptitude, for deceit, or I would not have deceived men so well, and persisted two years in bringing to success a deceit which others had framed and set afoot.' Despite these misgivings, he reassured himself again that if he could just help the Arabs take Damascus and prove themselves as a military force, then there was still a chance they might be able to have their independence.

It seems Allenby could read his mind. When Lawrence arrived in Akaba, Dawnay presented him with a message from headquarters. Allenby warned Lawrence not to do anything rash, such as trying to rush Damascus alone. He reminded him that if any attack were to be a success, he would need British assistance.

Yet Feisal remained undeterred. He told Lawrence that 'he would try this autumn for Damascus though the heavens fell, and, if the British were not able to carry their share of the attack, he would save his own people by making separate peace with Turkey.' Cemal Pasha had long been sending Feisal 'secret correspondence', making various peace offers. Feisal therefore knew that this was still an option if his plans did not materialise. Either way, the time to move on Damascus was fast approaching, with or without the British.

Good news arrived via aircraft soon after. On 8 August, Lawrence was informed that the 300 troopers of the Imperial Camel Corps had destroyed the watering station at Mudowwara, and had taken 150 Turkish prisoners. On the same day, the defeat of the German forces was also underway on the Western Front at the Battle of Amiens. In a surprise attack, the Allies overwhelmed the German defences with a barrage from tanks, aircraft and artillery, and were able to advance more than seven miles. After the war, the German chief of staff, Erich von Ludendorff, wrote in his memoirs that it was 'a black day of the German army'. At last, the tide was turning in both theatres at the same time.

With the Camel Corps on the move to Jefer, Lawrence rode to join them in his Rolls-Royce tender, 'Blue Mist'. Following their victory, Lawrence found the men in good spirits and fast adapting to life in the desert. The next morning, he rode ahead of Buxton's troopers to 'smooth the way' for them among the tribes they would soon pass, going all the way to Azrak.

As more gold and promises were exchanged, Lawrence rejoined Buxton and the Camel Corps, which had now moved on to Bair. It was 16 August 1918, Lawrence's thirtieth birthday. In his quest to relieve his family burden, he admitted that 'he had meant to be a general and knighted, when thirty'. While he had not yet hit those heights, he was well on his way to achieving them, even being put forward for the Victoria Cross. And yet, the war had changed Lawrence and how he saw things. In what seems to have been a day of introspection, he wrote:

> Such temporal dignities (if I survived the next four weeks) were now in my grasp – only that my sense of the falsity of the Arab position had cured me of crude ambition:

> while it left me my craving for good repute among men . . . Here were the Arabs believing me, Allenby and Clayton trusting me, my bodyguard dying for me: and I began to wonder if all established reputations were founded, like mine, on fraud . . . The truth was I did not like the 'myself' I could see and hear.

It seems that after two years of immersing himself with the Arabs, he had lost sight of who he was. 'A man who gives himself to be a possession of aliens', he wrote in *Seven Pillars of Wisdom*,

> leads to a Yahoo life, having bartered his soul to a brute-master. He is not one of them. He may stand against them, persuade himself of a mission, batter and twist them into something which they of their own accord, would not have been. Then he is exploiting his old environment to press them out of theirs. Or, after my model, he may imitate them so well that they spuriously imitate him back again. Then he is giving away his own environment: pretending to be theirs; and pretences are hollow, worthless things.

His unique ability to shift seamlessly between being an Arab and a British officer was now threatening to unravel him. Was his mission to give the Arabs their independence just an attempt to soothe his own traumas? Did that even matter? He no longer knew.

Indeed, Lawrence not only felt guilt at deceiving the Arabs. He was also deceiving Allenby and the British with his plans to take Damascus without them. Wherever he turned, he saw that he could not be completely honest with anyone. And when he admitted his deceit to himself, it tortured him. The constant conflict between himself and others saw him write in a letter: 'I change my abode every day, and my job every two days, and my language every three days, and still remain always unsatisfied. I hate being in front, and I hate being back, and I don't like responsibility, and I don't obey orders. Altogether no good just now. A long quiet like a purge, and then a contemplation and decision of future roads that is what to look forward to.'

His head swirling with such questions and contradictions, Lawrence continued on with the Camel Corps, reaching Muaggar a few days later. Now just fifteen miles south-east of Amman, their final target was within reach. But as they prepared to attack the railway bridge and tunnel, a Turkish plane circled above them. They had surely been spotted.

Calling a halt, Lawrence despatched a scouting party into the nearby villages to ascertain the position. They soon returned with unwelcome news: Ottoman mounted infantry were nearby. There was therefore no chance of a surprise attack. Lawrence estimated that if they were to proceed, he might lose up to 50 men, and he had promised Allenby there would be no casualties. There was no choice to be made. Reluctantly, Lawrence decided to send the Camel Corps back to Azrak. However, he rationalised that the purpose of the mission was to distract the Turks from the Arabs' planned attack on Deraa. While they could not destroy the bridge, they could certainly keep them looking the wrong way.

To persuade the Turks that they were still out in the

desert, and in a large force, they left behind evidence of fires, empty meat tins, and car tracks. Lawrence also encouraged some of the tribal chiefs to spread the word that the Camel Corps was actually Feisal's Arab army and was preparing to attack Amman.

Following this, Lawrence led the Camel Corps on the fifty-mile journey to Azrak. The men were disappointed that their adventure in the desert was over, but they were delighted once they arrived at the old oasis to bathe in the 'shining pools', having not had the chance to wash since leaving Akaba.

After resting for a few days, and satisfied that Buxton and his men were safe, Lawrence returned to Abu el-Lissan to check on preparations for the Arab assault on Deraa. Joyce, Dawnay, and Young reported that everything was now ready. But then another matter reared its head that threatened to bring the Revolt crashing to a halt. And this time, the trouble came from within.

26

While Lawrence had been away, Jaafar Pasha had received a British decoration whereby he was referred to as 'the general commanding the Arab Northern Army'. In response, King Hussein issued a royal proclamation announcing that no rank higher than captain existed in the Arab Army. This might have seemed petty, but Hussein feared that should Jaafar become too powerful and renowned for his brave deeds, he might be a real threat to his sovereignty. There might have been some merit to his paranoia, but unsurprisingly his statement caused grave offence, as Jaafar and his fellow senior officers immediately offered their resignations to Feisal.

Feisal was furious with his father. Refusing to accept the resignations, he telegraphed Mecca, hoping King Hussein would recognise the error of his ways. Yet the king didn't back down. Instead, he called Feisal a 'traitor and an outlaw'. At this insult, Feisal resigned his own position. In response, Hussein tried to promote his brother Zeid to succeed him, but Zeid refused. In this void of Arab leadership and senior officers in Akaba, all preparations ground to an abrupt halt.

In a telegram to Cairo, Lawrence wrote: 'Owing to Feisal's resignation demoralisation is spreading from regular army amongst Bedouins. According to plan, convoy and advanced guard of Sept scheme are going forward on our orders, without Sharifian approval, and I think that situation can be held together another 4 days. If Feisal can be satisfied by then, operations may continue, if not will do all possible to withdraw to advanced posts.' At its most crucial moment, the Arab Revolt was hanging by a thread.

Day and night, Allenby and Wilson frantically worked on King Hussein, in the vain hope he might back down. If he did not, then the Arab Revolt would collapse. When this situation was made clear to him, Hussein only responded by sending more poisonous telegrams to Feisal. Luckily, Lawrence managed to intercept them. He then edited them to avoid Feisal taking further offence and things crumbling for good.

Finally, after days of this charade, a half-apology arrived from Hussein. While it still contained traces of venom, Lawrence removed as much as he could and handed the rest to Feisal. 'He was astonished,' Lawrence recalled, 'and gazed wonderingly at me, for the meek words were unlike his father's querulous obstinacy.' Finally, he announced, 'This telegraph has saved all our honour.' The Revolt was back on.

Lawrence could now return his focus to attacking Deraa on Allenby's behalf. Thanks to Buxton's Camel Corps, the Turks believed that the Arabs were aiming for Amman and had reinforced it accordingly. 'Our formidable talk of advance by Amman had pulled their leg nearly out of socket,' Lawrence recalled, 'and the innocents were out to counter our feint. Each man they sent south was a man, or rather ten men, lost.'

Allenby compounded their confusion west of the Dead Sea by 'creating dust columns with mule-drawn sleighs moving eastward by day, while troop columns marched [back] westward by night'. Fifteen thousand dummy horses made of canvas also 'filled the vacant horse lines in the interior'. All this forced the Turks to conclude that the British were preparing to attack in force to the east and take Jericho.

With the Turks occupied, and looking in the wrong direction, Lawrence and the Arabs now prepared to move on Deraa, and then at last, Damascus. 'I could feel the taut power of Arab excitement behind me,' Lawrence wrote. 'The climax of the preaching of years had come, and a united country was straining towards its historic capital.'

On 14 September 1918, an army of 1,200 Arabs made their way to Umtaiye, 'a great pit of rainwater fifteen miles below Deraa and five miles east of the railway to Amman'. Meanwhile, Lawrence and the recently recovered Colonel Joyce set out in a Rolls-Royce tender, 'crammed to the gunwale with gun cotton [an explosive] and detonators', aiming to destroy the railway track and a bridge near Umtaiye, to prevent the Turks from receiving any reinforcements. Captain Lord Edward Winterton, an officer from the disbanded Imperial Camel Corps, also joined them in a second tender, escorted by two armoured cars.

Upon reaching 'the cover of the last ridge before the railway', Lawrence got into one of the armoured cars and took 150lbs of gun-cotton with him. While he drove straight to the bridge to lay a mine, the other cars attacked the Turkish redoubt protecting it. Quickly, Lawrence placed his six charges and stood back as the ensuing explosion left 'the skeleton of the bridge intact, but tottering', so the enemy would 'first have to tear down the wreckage before they could begin building a new bridge'. While he admired his work, Lawrence saw Winterton and Joyce frantically signalling. They had to leave at once – Turkish back-up was on its way.

However, after travelling just 300 yards, one of the springs on Lawrence's car broke. He was stranded, with the Turks on their way. Frantically, he jacked the car up and repaired the spring as best he could. Looking up, he saw the Turks were now within sight. There was no time to do any more. Jumping back into the car, he was relieved to find his quick repair job had worked, leaving him to race away across the desert, rejoicing at his good fortune.

After this breathless escape, Lawrence eventually rejoined the main force at Tell Arar the next morning. With the Arabs already attacking the redoubt that guarded the bridge there, Lawrence was set loose on the railway. Laying over 600 charges, he destroyed over six kilometres of track, cutting off the Damascus and Hejaz Railways. But to ensure Deraa was completely isolated, Lawrence also wanted to destroy a bridge over the Yarmuk River at Tell el-Shehab.

It seemed the Turks could read his mind. On arrival at Tell el-Shehab, Lawrence saw that they were doing all they could to protect their last available approach to Deraa. The bridge was under heavy guard, and a train filled with German reserves had just arrived. In the circumstances, it would be impossible to attack the bridge. However,

Lawrence realised he could still delay the Germans reaching Deraa.

As such, he targeted the track and the station at Nisib, and a bridge north of it. Machine-gun fire made quick work of the station, while Lawrence set about the bridge. Packed with explosives, the resulting explosion produced a 'lurid blaze' and sent 'the whole mass of masonry sliding slowly down into the valley below'.

The speed with which Lawrence moved and the unexpected direction of his attacks convinced the Turks that Allenby's offensive would be directed away from the coast and towards the east. This was just what Allenby had wanted, and he was now ready to capitalise on it.

27

In the early hours of 19 September 1917, 385 British guns opened fire on the Turkish front line in Palestine, followed by a full-scale infantry assault. Just as Allenby had planned, the Turks had been so convinced that the attack would be towards the Jordan River that they had left the coastal plain wide open. It was a crucial mistake, and their defences quickly crumbled.

Just twenty-four hours later, forty miles north of their starting point, the Thirteenth Brigade of the British Fifth Cavalry Division charged into Nazareth. General Liman von Sanders, the commander of the Ottoman Army, was shocked. With his lines of communication cut by Lawrence, he had no idea the British forces were so close, let alone in Nazareth. Without any time to gather his belongings, he was forced to flee from his headquarters to avoid capture. As a sign of the total breakdown in his communications, just before Liman von Sanders fled, he received a telegram asking if he was willing to offer a prize for a sack race in Constantinople.

From here, Allenby's cavalry continued almost unopposed, reaching the Jordan River just south of the Sea of Galilee. Meanwhile, Allenby's infantry ventured into the hills of Samaria and captured the city of Nablus.

By 21 September, the Turkish Seventh and Eighth

armies, west of the Jordan, were in total disarray. Fleeing for their lives, they were left without weapons or food, and became desperate to surrender to end their misery. The Fourth Army, east of the Jordan, still tried to put up a fight, but they were also beginning to realise it was a hopeless cause. Without food or water, they also tried to retreat, but thanks to Lawrence, the railway was out of action. Exposed in the wilds of the desert, the Bedouin attacked without mercy.

Such was Allenby's rapid advance and the Turkish collapse, just four days after his attack had commenced, every major city in Palestine was now in British hands.

All the while, Lawrence and the Arabs continued to hold on to Umtaiye, which gave them control of Deraa's three railways. If they could hold it for a week, then the Turkish army would be all but stranded and impotent. However, this wasn't easy. While the Turks desperately tried to repair the rail track, hoping to flood the area with Turkish and German reserves, they bombarded the Arabs, and any supporting villages and tribes, from the air to force them back.

The Arabs were an easy target because they had based themselves in the open desert, which offered the only available water supply for their large numbers of camels and horses. As a result, the Turkish aircraft were able to pick them off at will, with the Arabs now living in terror of the regular attacks. Lawrence noted that the aerial bombardments had been enough to 'disquiet the irregulars who were our eyes and ears. Soon they would break up and go home, and our usefulness be ended.'

As such, he immediately flew to General Allenby's headquarters in Palestine, and informed him of the situation. Fresh from his victory, Allenby was in no mood to let the Turks off the hook. Two Bristol fighters were ready to head to Umtaiye the next day, along with a Handley Page bomber, and a DH9 carrying more fuel, spares and supplies. In Oman we were extremely fortunate to have air cover, with Provost fighters able to drop 250lb fragmentation bombs on enemy positions, followed later by Strikemaster jets firing rockets. Without such cover, we might have found it impossible to push back the adoo, who were so adept at hiding in the mountains.

In his cool, whitewashed office, Allenby briefed Lawrence on the next stage of his advance. He told him that the Australian Mounted Division and the Fifth Cavalry Division would now turn north of the Sea of Galilee and advance on Damascus. Meanwhile, the Fourth Cavalry Division, under Major-General George de Symons Barrow, would strike east to capture Deraa, and then turn north towards Damascus.

All of this should have been very welcome news to Lawrence. Allenby would shortly reach Damascus, very likely forcing the Turkish government to sue for peace. However, this British advance meant that Lawrence's hope for an independent Arab state in Syria depended on the thin prospect of getting Feisal and the Arab forces into Damascus before Allenby's cavalry divisions arrived. Allenby was not naive and was undoubtedly aware of the danger of this. He once again warned Lawrence against attempting an 'independent coup'. The Arab forces should instead solely focus on cooperating with Barrow and the British Fourth Cavalry Division. Any thought of getting to Damascus first was to be put out of Lawrence's mind.

'It seemed to me that in the Arab hands lay an option,' Lawrence said. 'Whether to let this victory be just one more victory, or, by risking themselves once more, to make it final.' And for Lawrence, the chance to make amends to the Arabs, and to restore his family honour in the process, was finally reaching the most dramatic of conclusions.

28

Following his meeting with Allenby, Lawrence quickly flew to the Arab camp, now situated at Um el-Surab to help avoid detection by the Turkish aircraft. Alongside him were the two Bristol fighters that Allenby had promised. The Handley Page bomber would also shortly arrive, along with '[DH]9s like fledglings beneath its spread of wings'. The arrival of the British aircraft at the camp caused quite a stir. Before long, they had a chance to prove their worth.

As Lawrence and his men sat at breakfast, the low drone of Turkish aircraft could be heard coming from Deraa. Wasting no time, an Australian pilot immediately jumped into his fighter and set off to engage. Lawrence and the Arabs watched in awe as the Turk was quickly shot out of the sky. The encounter had, in fact, been so quick that the Australian pilot returned to the camp while his breakfast was still hot. If optimism was high before, then now it was bubbling over.

Throughout the day, the British fighters continued to retaliate whenever the Turks dared to rear their heads, while a landing ground was prepared for the Handley Page bomber. When it finally arrived, the Arabs were amazed by its size. This was beyond their wildest dreams. Such was their excitement that they were prompted to say, 'At last they have sent us THE aeroplane.'

That night the Handley Page bombed Mafrak and Deraa, further destroying the railway while also disrupting the Turkish Fourth Army's line of retreat. In their desperation to escape, some Turks cut the horses loose from carrying the guns so they could ride them. They were the lucky ones. The others were left at the mercy of the British aircraft and the Arabs. It finally felt as if the war was turning decisively against the Turks.

Our turning point in Oman came when a villager walked over forty miles to tell us where we could find Salim Amr. No large army group could hope to penetrate the area undetected, so it fell on the Recce Squad to take him, dead or alive. For too long, he had terrified the villagers with his extreme methods, and after he had put a price on my own head, I was only too keen to get to him before he got to me. It was also made clear to me that his removal, one way or the other, might do permanent damage to the adoo.

Putting everything we had learned into practice, we set off into the mountains at night, heading deep into adoo territory. Heavily camouflaged, using hand signals as we moved, we didn't know if we were walking into a trap. No one was really sure just how trustworthy the intelligence was. To top it all, we had no reinforcements if things went badly wrong. We were all alone.

At any moment I expected to be ambushed, so urged my men on to greater speed as it was imperative that we were in and out before dawn. As soon as the sun rose, we would be in deep trouble. The valleys were growing more frequent, falling away steeply to either side and visible only as dark shadows of indeterminate size and depth. We skirted above them, keeping to the high grassy shoulders below the skyline. Finally, we saw wooden huts rising sharply on the side of a hill. It was our destination: Mahra village.

Moving like ghosts, we entered Mahra on a precision raid. The villager had told us what Salim Amr's hut looked like, and in the light of the moon we were soon able to locate it. As my men stood ready in case any adoo should come out of their huts, I moved towards the far end and into the shadows. Taking a deep breath, I kicked down the door and shouted in Arabic, 'We have you surrounded! Come out with your hands on your head.' The room was too dark to see anything, but I heard something quickly move in the corner. Against a sliver of moonlight, I then saw a flash of metal. It was a gun. Without hesitating, I pulled the trigger and heard the thud of a body hit the floor. Racing to its side, I knelt and pulled the figure into the light. The scarred face of Salim Amr stared back at me open-eyed. He was dead.

Suddenly, I heard gunfire erupt outside. The adoo had raced out of their huts at the sound of my gunshot, and my men were now forcing them back with phosphorous grenades. These provided smoke to screen our getaway, and burned the adoo's flesh if they tried to follow. We only had a short period to escape before the sun rose and exposed us, so for four hours we ran, barely stopping to break. Somehow we emerged from the mountains safe and having achieved our goal. It was the most significant moment of my time in Oman. Just months before, my team had been a shambles. Now they had executed our guerrilla strategy to perfection.

With the Turks in a desperate state of retreat, more and more tribes came flocking to join the Arab cause, including Nuri Shaalan's Rwala camel-men, which increased their numbers to 4,000-strong. Now the momentum was truly with the Arabs. No longer fearful of Turkish troops or aircraft, they again moved their camp to Umtaiye. Not only were they confident that Deraa would soon fall, but talk quickened about the prospect of getting to Damascus before the British. Yet not everyone thought this would be sensible.

The likes of Young felt that it was too great a risk for the Arabs to attempt to take Damascus by themselves, as they would still be outnumbered. They should therefore wait for the British to arrive, then claim Damascus together. Even some Arab officers agreed with this point of view. They believed that they had achieved their goal and should now put their faith in Allenby to finish off the Turks. But Lawrence was determined to get to Damascus first, no matter the cost. 'Damascus meant the end of this war in the East,' he later wrote, 'and I believed, the end of the general war too; because the Central Powers being inter-dependent, the breaking of their weakest link – Turkey – would swing the whole cluster loose. Therefore, for every sensible reason, strategical, tactical, political, and even moral, we were going on.'

At dawn, Lawrence and the Arabs set off on their final steps towards taking Damascus. Along with Lawrence's bodyguard, they were joined by Auda, Nasir, Nuri Shaalan, Talal el-Hareidhin, and their large bodies of irregular Bedouin. Almost every village en route heralded their arrival and provided them with food and water, with ever more men joining their growing ranks. The Arabs were now on a date with destiny, and everyone wanted to be part of history.

On the way, they continued to blow up the railway, rounded up Turkish prisoners, and targeted any villages that might oppose their march or help the Turks. One such village, Ezra, was held by the traitor Abd el-Kader, but he fled before he could be captured. Perhaps now he regretted betraying the Arabs to the Turks.

While camping at Sheikh Saad, about seventy miles from Damascus, a British aircraft dropped the message that Bulgaria had surrendered, the first of the Central Powers to do so. As the crucial land-bridge between Germany and Turkey, this effectively severed the railways, and cut off supplies that the Germans had been providing to prop up the Turks. At last, their vital lifeline had been cut, and the meagre sources remaining would soon be exhausted. The Allies had them by the throat.

Soon after, word reached Lawrence that the Germans had set fire to their aeroplanes and storehouses in Deraa, and that 4,000 troops were now evacuating the town. The dominos were beginning to fall in Europe and the Middle East. But this also presented a problem.

Thousands of Turks were now fleeing Deraa, determined to raze to the ground any villages that they passed that had supported the Arabs. When Lawrence heard that the Turks were moving on Talal's village, Tafas, he quickly led a contingent to try to defend it.

Sadly, they were already too late. With smoke rising from the village in the distance, bloodied men, women, and children staggered away from the carnage, screaming and wailing or silent in shock. They told of a massacre, which was still ongoing.

As they entered the smouldering village, dead bodies lined their path in all directions. Throats had been slit, limbs cut off. Amongst the dead were the bodies of four babies, while a naked, pregnant woman lay sprawled in the mud, a bayonet stuck between her legs.

It seemed the Turks had left no one alive, but then Lawrence saw a small child, about three years old, stagger away. Tentatively approaching her, the little girl cried in fear, 'Don't hit me, Baba.' She thought they were Turks. Now that he was closer, Lawrence saw blood pumping from a large wound between her neck and shoulder, the result of a Turkish lancer. When the Arabs tried to comfort her, the child let out a chilling scream and then collapsed to the floor, dead.

At the sight of so much brutality, some Arabs heaved, while others, on the edge of madness, could not help but laugh. No one felt this more than Talal. This had once been his village, and now all of his friends and family had been slaughtered. Feeling a rage unlike anything he had felt before, Lawrence suddenly cried, 'The best of you brings me the most Turkish dead!' These men deserved no mercy.

Racing away from the village, the Arabs shot down any fleeing Turks they came across before seeing the main body of their army. The Arabs halted for a moment as if to work out how to proceed, but Talal did not hesitate. Crying out the name of his village – 'Tafas! Tafas!' – he thundered towards them, shooting his rifle from his saddle. In return, the Turks took aim and shot him from his camel. Auda gritted his teeth and turned to the tribesmen. 'God give him mercy,' he cried. 'We will take his price!' At this, he led the tribesmen charging towards the enemy, wielding their weapons and screaming into the air. The Turks weren't prepared for the savagery that greeted them. Like a swirl of rampaging devils, the tribesmen shot, hacked, and jabbed at those who tried to stand their ground, while pursuing those who attempted to flee with relish. Even the Turkish horses were shot in the head.

When Lawrence saw that a group of Arabs had gathered over 200 Turkish prisoners, he might have been inclined to show some mercy. But then he saw an Arab man nearby, pinned to the ground, bayonets piercing his shoulder and thigh, blood pumping and pooling over the soil. Asking him who had done such a thing, the stricken man glanced towards the prisoners. At that, their fate was decided. None of these men deserved to live. Without saying a word, Lawrence and the Arabs aimed their Hotchkiss rifles and opened fire until they were all dead.

The Turks had been routed. Not a single one was left alive. Bloodstained, and with the stench of death and misery all around them, the men returned to Sheikh Saad in silence, traumatised by what they had seen.

Unsurprisingly, Lawrence struggled to sleep that night. His mind was tormented by the evil he had witnessed, having yet more blood on his hands, and knowing that further atrocities lay in store on the road to Damascus. Author and psychiatrist John E. Mack believes that Lawrence's thirst for vengeance at Tafas might also have been the result of his assault at Deraa. 'His apparent loss of control at Tafas', he wrote, 'was linked to and perhaps made possible by the humiliation he had experienced ten months before, and the desire for revenge it left within him.' Whether or not the trauma of Deraa was on his mind when he gave the order to massacre the Turks is impossible to say. Such an order was certainly out of character, and we know the assault at Deraa had a detrimental effect on him. And yet, such was the savage brutality of the Turks at Tafas that this alone might have been enough to make him snap.

There was little time to rest or reflect on such matters. Just after midnight, a message arrived that Deraa, the town that had caused Lawrence so much misery, was at long last in Arab hands. Lawrence decided he wanted to see this for himself.

Mounting a camel, he joined Nuri Said and the Rwala and raced towards Deraa at full canter, arriving in the first flickers of daylight. While some Turks still tried to defend the way, the Rwala made quick work of them, eager to reach the town and get their hands on as much loot as possible. But there would be competition for this. On arrival, they found the locals were already plundering the burning Turkish camp and storehouses, trying to grab whatever they could. Some even entered smoking buildings as the roofs looked set to collapse, while wounded Turks were stripped naked and their possessions torn from their dying hands. Others were whipped and chased as they tried to flee.

Lawrence was shocked at what he saw. 'The whole place was indescribably filthy,' he wrote,

> defiled and littered with smouldering cinders and the soiled leavings of loot. Turks, some dead and some dying, lay about the railway station or sat propped against the houses. Those still living gazed at us with eyes that begged for a little mercy of which it was hopeless of them to ask of the Arabs, and some cried feebly for water . . . In all this there was nothing that was uncommon in war. But a revolting scene was being enacted at the moment we entered, far exceeding in its savagery anything that has been known in the conflicts between nations during the past 120 years and happily rare even in earlier times.

Upon reaching the station, Lawrence found Nasir trying to establish an administration to restore some order. Soon after, the Fourth Cavalry Division under General Barrow arrived. He was appalled at the horrific scenes, and ordered Lawrence to end the savagery and looting. Lawrence told him it would be impossible. He knew this was an accepted Arab practice, while some were so scarred by their treatment by the Turks that they now barely saw them as fellow human beings. After his treatment in Deraa, there must also have been a part of him that was happy to see the town razed to the ground.

Barrow was disgusted and told Lawrence that he had been ordered to take control of the town. In return, Lawrence insisted that the Arabs were already establishing an administration and the British should leave them to it. Barrow was not impressed. Nevertheless, he acceded to

Lawrence and prepared to march his troops towards Damascus instead. It seemed Lawrence had won the first showdown between the British and the Arabs over their right to govern, but there would be far bigger battles to come.

That night, Lawrence and his men camped in the shadow of Deraa's charred aerodrome while he ran things over in his mind. 'In front was our too-tangible goal,' he wrote, 'but behind lay the effort of two years, its misery forgotten or glorified. Names rang through my head, each in imagination a superlative: Rum the magnificent, brilliant Petra, Azrak the remote, Batra the very clean.' Many battles had already been won, and the final one now lay ahead.

Unable to sleep, his mind whirring under the moonlight, Lawrence wanted to get as close to Damascus as possible to ascertain the situation. Together with Major Stirling, he hopped into a Rolls-Royce, and they set off at dawn.

At noon, Lawrence saw Barrow and his staff, also en route to Damascus, watering their horses in the distance. He hadn't forgotten their fraught exchange at Deraa, so he decided to play a game. Getting out of the car, he jumped onto a camel and rode across. Barrow was shocked to see him. While he had left Lawrence in Deraa the day before, it seemed he had somehow caught up with him, riding a camel no less. Confused, he asked Lawrence when he had left Deraa. 'This morning,' Lawrence replied, somehow maintaining a straight face. 'Where will you stop tonight?' Barrow asked. 'Damascus,' Lawrence smiled, watching Barrow's face fall.

However, Lawrence would soon need Barrow's help. Remnants of the Turkish Fourth Army were still trying to block the way to Damascus and had turned their mountain guns and machine guns on Nasir, Nuri Shaalan, Auda, and their tribesmen. To fend them off, Lawrence needed support from Barrow's leading cavalry regiment. Yet his request for help was met with disdain by an 'ancient, surly' colonel of the Indian army.

Lawrence was furious. Thankfully, one of Barrow's brigadier generals was more cooperative. Ordering the horse artillery and the Middlesex Yeomanry to attack the Turks, they were soon sent fleeing into the desert, where Auda and his men were waiting. At this, the Turkish Fourth Army was all but destroyed, and the road to Damascus was finally clear.

That night Lawrence rested in Kiswe, only a few miles from Damascus. But with victory within his grasp, he had plenty on his mind. As he mixed with British and Indian troops in his Arab dress, he remarked, 'I could walk as I pleased, an unconsidered Arab: and this finding myself among, but cut off from, my own kin made me strangely alone.' He had been an outsider all his life, playing different roles to fit in but never truly feeling like he belonged to the English or the Arabs. Now he felt 'alone', with nothing left to fight for but his own purposes.

From the direction of Damascus, he suddenly heard a series of shattering explosions. It was the Germans blowing up their ammunition dumps and stores. Along with the Turks, they were fleeing the city, knowing Allenby's forces were on their doorstep. But this also represented a problem. It was clear that the Arab army would not get into the city before the British. Lawrence, therefore, consulted with Nasir and Nuri Shaalan and formulated an alternative plan.

So long as they installed an Arab government in Damascus before the British troops arrived, this might be enough to stake their claim. Lawrence therefore 'decided to send the Rwala horse galloping into town' to alert Feisal's supporters to take control of the administrative affairs of the city, raise an Arab flag and proclaim Feisal 'King of the Arabs'.

Lawrence was soon in hot pursuit. Jumping into his Rolls-Royce, he drove to a ridge that looked out over the city. All of a sudden a horseman galloped towards him. Upon seeing Lawrence, he announced, 'Good news: Damascus salutes you.'

29

On the morning of 1 October 1918, Lawrence entered Damascus in his open-top Rolls-Royce. Taking in the extraordinary scenes, he wrote, 'A movement like a breath, in a long sigh from gate to heart of the city, marked our course.' Wherever he looked, people were packed solid along the road, on the pavement, on the roofs and balconies of the houses, and at every window. Such was their joy that while some danced, threw flowers, and fired rifles into the air, others cut themselves with swords and daggers and yelled themselves hoarse. The mass of people was so great in places that the roads were nearly impassable. When the crowd caught sight of the diminutive Brit, dressed in his trademark white robes and headdress, they hoarsely shouted his name – 'Aurens! Aurens!' – welcoming him to the city and thanking him for saving them from the Turks. Lawrence tried to take it all in but could scarcely believe the scenes. He had long dreamt of this moment, and now it was all true.

However, when Lawrence entered the town hall, a very different scene was taking place in the antechamber. Lawrence's old enemy Abd el-Kader, along with his brother Mohammed Said and their armed followers, had broken into the room. Shouting at the top of his voice, el-Kader announced that he had formed a provisional government and, without a hint of shame, proclaimed Hussein as king of the Arabs.

Lawrence was enraged at this shameless attempt to switch sides and grab power. But before he could do anything about it, a furious fight broke out. Old enemies Auda Abu Tayi and the Druse leader, Sultan Hussein el-Atrash, tore and clawed at each other until Lawrence 'jumped in to drive them apart'. Sultan el-Atrash was pushed out of the room while Lawrence dragged Auda, 'blind with rage', into the empty state room. With gritted teeth and popping eyes, Auda told Lawrence he was determined 'to wash out the insult with Druse blood'. Tensions were high, and they were about to get much higher.

After Lawrence finally managed to calm Auda down, he returned to the antechamber and announced that, until the governor, Ali Riza Rejabi, returned to the city, Major General Shukri Pasha el-Ayubi would serve as the temporary military governor of Damascus. In response, Abd el-Kader, 'in a white heat of passion', lunged at Lawrence with a drawn dagger. Only the intervention of Auda stopped him from being wounded, perhaps fatally.

Amidst more shouting and fighting, Lawrence briefly contemplated having the two brothers arrested and shot. However, with tensions already running high, a political execution was the last thing the city needed. Instead, the brothers were allowed to leave unharmed. Storming out of the town hall, swearing revenge, they remained hell-bent on seizing control before Feisal or the British reached Damascus.

In his report for the *Arab Bulletin*, Lawrence wrote: 'Abd

el-Kader called together his friends and some leading druses, and made them an impassioned speech, denouncing the Sherif as a British puppet, and calling on them to strike a blow for the Faith in Damascus.' At midnight, Abd el-Kader and Mohammed Said again tried to seize control of the city. With their followers shooting rifles into the air, looting shops and homes, they attempted to approach Central Square. There they found the Arabs waiting. Shooting down twenty el-Kader supporters, they sent the rest fleeing into the darkness. By morning Mohammed Said was arrested, and Abd el-Kader had escaped to the countryside. Lawrence was desperate to race after him, but for now more pressing matters needed to be dealt with.

At lunchtime, an Australian army doctor came to Lawrence to complain of the appalling conditions in the Turkish military hospital. Lawrence rushed to the barracks, where he found a distressing scene. It was 'squalid with rags and rubbish', while a room was crammed with dead Turkish soldiers, their oozing yellow and black bodies gnawed at by a flock of red-eyed rats. When Lawrence entered a ward, he saw scores of wounded men in soiled beds or on the floor, their filthy unchanged bandages smelling of gangrene. Those who could speak cried out, 'Aman, aman!' ('Pity, pity'). Some had dysentery, while others were desperate for water or food. Many of them would have welcomed death.

Heading upstairs, Lawrence was shocked to find the Turkish commandant and a few doctors 'boiling coffee over a spirit stove'. Barely able to conceal his fury, he ordered them and a few of the less seriously sick Turkish soldiers to clean up the hospital at once. Holding them at gunpoint, he watched as they dug a six-foot-deep trench in the garden, gathered up the rotting corpses, and dumped them into it. Such was the state of decay that some of the corpses had to be scraped off the floor with shovels.

After overseeing this clean-up operation and ensuring the survivors were being tended to, Lawrence left another British officer in charge. Finally, at midnight, he went back to the Hotel Victoria. He was now running on empty. Since leaving Deraa four days before, he had slept less than three hours. However, General Harry Chauvel, one of the first British senior officers to arrive in the city, was waiting for him at the hotel. In a long list of complaints, he reprimanded Lawrence for the Arabs' failure to salute his Australian officers properly. Lawrence promptly ignored him and retired to bed.

The next morning, 3 October, Lawrence returned to the Turkish military hospital. Conditions had improved dramatically, but as he was leaving, a flustered major of the Royal Army Medical Corps showered Lawrence with abuse, calling the situation at the hospital 'scandalous, disgraceful, outrageous, ought to be shot'. Lawrence could take no more. In response, he 'cackled like a duck, with the wild laughter that often took me at moments of strain'. The major finally brought a stop to this by slapping Lawrence across the face. This somewhat brought Lawrence to his senses. He wrote that the major 'stalked off, leaving me more ashamed than angry, for in my heart I felt that he was right, and that anyone who had, like me, pushed through to success a rebellion of the weak against the master, must come out of it so stained that nothing in the world would make him clean again'.

The following morning, the arrival of General Allenby only complicated things further. Lawrence was unsure how Allenby would react to him having imposed an Arab government in Damascus. Yet when he met with him at the Victoria Hotel, Allenby didn't reprimand him. He merely ratified the decision. By now, he was already eager to push on with the next stage of his offensive and take Aleppo and Beirut. He therefore asked to meet with Feisal – who was in the process of travelling to Damascus – as soon as he reached the city.

Soon after, Feisal arrived at the hotel suite still giddy at the waves of excitement that had greeted him as he rode into the city on horseback, but his mood was quickly tempered. With Lawrence sitting alongside him, Allenby informed Feisal that the Sykes–Picot Agreement was now being brought into effect. Feisal was confused. He had repeatedly been told that the agreement was dead. Despite Feisal's victorious entrance into the city, Allenby now told him that France 'was to be the Protecting Power over Syria'. In return, Feisal was to have 'the Administration of Syria' on behalf of his father, but under French 'guidance'. He was also not 'to have anything to do' with Lebanon, which was reserved for France. Finally, Allenby announced that he would need to exchange Lawrence for a French liaison officer.

Feisal was furious and objected 'very strongly'. If he was to be under anyone's rule, he told Allenby, he wanted it to be the British. Moreover, if Lebanon was not joined to Syria, 'a country without a port was no good to him'. He also 'declined to have a French Liaison Officer or to recognise French guidance in any way'.

Allenby was confused by Feisal's intense fury. He turned to Lawrence and said: 'But did you not tell him that the French were to have the Protectorate over Syria?' Lawrence replied, 'No, Sir, I know nothing about it.' This was somewhat disingenuous. Both Lawrence and Feisal certainly knew of the intentions of the Sykes–Picot Agreement, and the details had been published in newspapers worldwide. Despite this, the Arabs had never agreed to fight on those terms. Indeed, Feisal's father had been told something very different in his correspondence with Henry McMahon, both before and during the war. As far as the Arabs were concerned, the agreement was a 'dead letter', superseded by the events of the war. Lawrence was also dismayed. He had hoped that, in reaching Damascus, common sense would prevail. The Arabs had fought their way there and had helped knock the Turks out of the war. Now he was being told that, despite all of this, the Sykes–Picot Agreement still stood.

A moment of silence followed as all parties tried to somehow pick up the pieces. Then Allenby put them both straight. Whatever Feisal's aspirations, as things currently stood he was a lieutenant general under Allenby's command and would have to obey his orders. Feisal somehow bit his tongue and stormed out of the room.

After Feisal's departure, Lawrence told Allenby that he would not work with the French and that perhaps it was time he returned to England. Exasperated, Allenby replied,

'Yes! I think you had!' At this, Lawrence left the room. His adventure was over.

The next evening, Lawrence left Damascus. He had spent the previous two years fighting to get there, but after just forty-eight hours he was leaving, never to return. The capture of Damascus was meant to be a triumph whereby he gave the Arabs their freedom, alleviated his guilt, and restored his family's honour. But as he left the city behind, he realised he had achieved none of these things. In fact, he felt more worthless and consumed by shame than ever before. 'I had been born free, and a stranger to those whom I had led for the two years,' he wrote, 'and tonight it seemed that I had given them all my gift, this false liberty drawn down to them by spells and wickedness, and nothing was left but to go away. The dead army of my hopes, now turned to fact, confronted me, and my will, the worn instrument which had so long frayed our path, broke suddenly in my hand and fell useless.'

Lawrence was now left to doubt the value of his whole mission, riddled by shame and doubt. I felt similarly conflicted when my two-year contract in Oman ended in 1970. As I boarded a plane back to England, one of my men said to me, 'We are your brothers, sahb. Do not forget us, where you go to.' There was no chance of that. These men had been my closest companions for two years and together we had grown to become much better soldiers and people. Yet as I left Oman behind and looked down below at the mountains, I not only felt a keen sense of loss, but I also felt empty. What had I actually achieved? Had any of it been worth it? The Sultan was still in power, and the people of Oman and Dhofar were still living in poverty. There was nothing more I could now do about it. Time would tell if any of it had been worthwhile.

But as Lawrence prepared to return home, he was not willing to leave such matters to fate.

30

On 24 October 1918, Lawrence was finally back at his family home in Oxford after four years away. In that time, both he and the world had changed considerably. He had lost almost 40lbs on his adventures, now weighing little more than 80lbs, appearing gaunt and emaciated. If he had been somewhat tortured by his past before the war, now he was tormented by his perceived deceit and failures. He also struggled to process the many traumas he had experienced, including the countless Turkish deaths, killing Farraj with his own hand, and the massacre at Tafas. The assault at Deraa also continued to trouble him. The incident itself had been horrific, but it had again made him question his sexuality. All of this and more left him feeling worn down and haunted.

While he had been away, millions had died fighting in France, including his two brothers, casting a pall over the family. And yet one particular loss hurt him more than any other.

He now found that Dahoum, the young Arab boy with whom he had enjoyed a close relationship before the war, had died of typhus in 1916. While they might never have sexually consummated their relationship, there is little doubt that he was one of the few people that Lawrence truly loved. Indeed, this was revealed years later when Lawrence released his memoirs. The dedication to the book reads:

To S. A.

I loved you, so I drew these tides of men into my hands
and wrote my will across the sky in stars
To earn you Freedom, the seven pillared worthy house,
that your eyes might be shining for me
When we came.

Death seemed my servant on the road, till we were near
and saw you waiting:
When you smiled, and in sorrowful envy he outran me
and took you apart:
Into his quietness.

Love, the way-weary, groped to your body, our brief wage
ours for the moment
Before earth's soft hand explored your shape, and the blind
worms grew fat upon
Your substance.

Men prayed me that I set our work, the inviolate house,
as a memory of you.
But for fit monument I shattered it, unfinished: and now
The little things creep out to patch themselves hovels
in the marred shadow
Of your gift.

It appears that 'S. A.' was Dahoum, whose real name was Selim Ahmed. This passage not only helps us to understand

Lawrence's love for him, but provides another motive for his intense dedication to the Arab cause before, during, and after the war. He had been saddled with his mother's ambitions to redeem his family and do great things, while he had also been fascinated with military history. Thanks to both, he had hoped to become a hero and set a people free. When he fell in love with Dahoum and the Arab culture, he found the cause he was long looking for. And judging by the strength of feeling in the dedication, he was not just fighting for Arab independence in the desert. He was also fighting for Dahoum. Now the failure of the Revolt, and Dahoum's death, left him devastated.

Despite this, Lawrence realised there was still a chance to resolve all these issues and finally be at peace with himself. He wrote that his aim was not just to 'defeat the Turks on the battlefield, but my own country and its allies in the council chamber'. As such, when the Turks surrendered on 31 October, with Beirut, Homs, Hama, and Aleppo also in British hands, Lawrence realised that a peace conference would urgently need to be called in order to determine the distribution of the Arab lands. Now back in England, he was determined to speak to anyone who might have any influence, and to have a seat at the table.

Within five days of his return, Lawrence addressed the Eastern Committee of the War Cabinet. Much to Lawrence's embarrassment, Lord Curzon began the meeting by outlining his achievements. Lawrence was not there to receive any praise or official recognition, so when Curzon asked if he wanted to add anything, he simply replied, 'Yes, let's get to business. You people don't understand yet the hole you have put us all into.'

He then bluntly explained the situation in the Middle East, and all of the promises made to the Arabs which had inspired them to fight in the first place. Now they had fought on those terms, and had been betrayed. In a letter to Robert Graves in 1927, Lawrence claimed that 'Curzon burst promptly into tears, great drops running down his cheeks, to an accompaniment of slow sobs.' It is debatable whether or not this is true, but he had certainly set a few people straight. In a letter to his sister around this time, Lawrence outlined what he believed would happen if the British should fail to keep their promises:

> The results will be as follows – If we keep our part with the French the Arabs will rightly say we have sold them, that we have raised them up only to cast them down . . . News of this will spread through the Mohammedan World and do us unutterable harm. Also it will entail certain interior chaos and probably war between the French and the Arabs. If we don't keep our pact with France the world will say 'Oh Yes! England land grabbing again.' We don't in the least want any of this country but we simply cannot let the Arabs down. If only we could buy French interests out by the session of land say in the Cameroons it would save so much. Otherwise our name will be mud.

There were, thankfully, some who needed no persuading of this position. Since the capture of Damascus, many in the British government held the view that the Sykes–Picot Agreement should be discarded in its entirety. Many still hoped that the Arabs and Zionists would cooperate in Palestine under the protection of a British administration. If that was the case, the Arabs should be allowed to rule for themselves in Syria. The French would surely object to this, but the British believed that the American president, Woodrow Wilson, would look favourably on the British and Arab position.

A few days later, Lawrence was invited to a private audience with King George V. Allenby had recommended that Lawrence be awarded a knighthood, but Lawrence had informed the king's military secretary that he would not accept the honour. Instead, he would be grateful to speak to the king about the issues facing the Arabs in the Middle East. King George later revealed that when he tried to pin medals on Lawrence's chest, Lawrence immediately removed them. As if to explain his continued loyalty to the Arabs, he explained that 'if a man has to serve two masters it was better to offend the more powerful'. Thankfully, the king was not offended, especially when Lawrence presented him with a gift: the inscribed Lee-Enfield rifle that Enver Pasha had once given to Feisal, and Feisal had then gifted to Lawrence to fight the Turks. In a remarkable journey, it had come full circle.

There was enormous respect between the two men, but Lawrence did not hold his tongue. He explained to the king that if the government now reneged on its promises to King Hussein and the Arabs then they were 'crooks', and he again made clear his opposition to the Sykes–Picot Agreement.

Lawrence did not let the matter rest there. He was

determined to speak to all levels of government in order to make his case. After presenting a long paper on his views to the War Cabinet committee, the minister of munitions, Winston Churchill, became particularly beguiled by Lawrence. He agreed with much of what he had to say, and became one of his greatest supporters. In time, this relationship would reap enormous dividends for both men.

It seemed Lawrence had made significant headway when, on 7 November 1918, the British and French governments signed a declaration agreeing to implement 'a complete and final liberation' of countries that had been part of the Ottoman Empire. This seemed to indicate that countries like Syria would be allowed to choose their own governments.

However, matters became more complicated just four days later, on 11 November, when Germany asked for an armistice, and the war finally came to an end. Suddenly, it wasn't just the issue of control in the Middle East that needed to be thrashed out, but also in much of Europe, as well as the German colonies in Africa. Such matters needed to be dealt with quickly to prevent any chaos from spiralling.

A peace conference in Paris was subsequently scheduled, and Lawrence wasted no time in ensuring that the Arabs were present. Upon writing to King Hussein, he urged him to send Feisal to appear in Paris on his behalf. Lawrence would be there as 'advisor on special subjects' for the British delegation, while also serving as a member of Feisal's staff. Once more, he was attempting to serve two masters.

Despite the Anglo-French Declaration just a few days

before, the French contended that the Sykes–Picot Agreement was still in force. At the same time, the Americans were on their way to the conference, planning to exert their own power in the region. Indeed, many in the British delegation realised that, if they were to hold on to Mosul and its oil reserves, they might very well have to let the French keep Syria, despite any promises made to the Arabs.

Unsurprisingly, the French did not want the Arabs to state their case at the conference and were outraged when Feisal arrived in Marseille. To keep him away from Paris for as long as possible, they arranged for him to tour the French battlefields and factories while Prime Minister Clemenceau met with Lloyd George in an attempt to reach a backroom deal.

Meanwhile, Lawrence and Feisal were attempting to broker deals of their own. In London, Lawrence helped state Feisal's case to A. J. Balfour, the foreign secretary, and the Zionist leader, Chaim Weizmann. Feisal remained determined that the Arabs should keep Syria, but in return he was open to a limited Jewish settlement in Palestine. He was quoted as having told a Reuters' correspondent:

> The two main branches of the Semitic family, Arabs and Jews, understand one another, and I hope that as a result of the interchange of ideas at the Peace Conference, which will be guided by ideals of self-determination and nationality, each nation will make definite progress towards the realization of its aspirations. Arabs are not jealous of Zionist Jews, and intend to give them fair play,

> and the Zionist Jews have assured the Nationalist Arabs of their intention to see that they too have fair play in their respective areas.

In principle, Feisal hoped this would encourage an influx of Jewish finance into the region and keep the British and the Americans on side in the peace conference. However, Lawrence and Feisal made it clear that this was all on the proviso that the Arabs gained their independence in Syria.

Continuing to speak to anyone in a position of power, Lawrence also realised that British public opinion was important. He therefore wrote an article for *The Times* explaining the sacrifices the Arabs had made based on the promises of the British. In doing so, he detailed the McMahon–Hussein correspondence, the Sykes–Picot Agreement, the Declaration to the Seven, and the Anglo-French Declaration from just a few weeks before.

Perhaps his biggest coup was securing a meeting with President Wilson, who seemed aligned to his way of thinking. When America first entered the war, Wilson attacked 'the little groups of ambitious men who were accustomed to use their fellow men as pawns and tools. We have no selfish ends to serve. We desire no conquest, no dominion.' The United States would 'fight for the things we have always carried nearest our hearts – for democracy, for the right of those who submit to authority to have a voice in their own governments, for the rights and liberties of small nations'. In their subsequent meeting, Wilson told Lawrence that 'the powers will attach more importance to the bodies and souls of the Arabic-speaking peoples than to their own material interests.' He also agreed that there should be an inquiry into the wishes of the Syrian people. Confidence was now high that the Arabs might get what they had been promised after all.

After many meetings and proposed deals, the Paris Peace Conference began on 18 January 1919. With the borders of Europe, the Middle East, and Africa on its agenda, it would become one of the most important meetings of the twentieth century. More than thirty national delegations attended, along with thousands of others, all pushing their own cause. Yet most of the focus now appeared to be on Germany and Europe, with the issue of the Arabs almost an afterthought. Indeed, the French initially left Feisal off the list of official delegates, with the issue only rectified when the British objected.

On 6 February, Lawrence and Feisal finally addressed the ten leaders of the Allied governments. In making Feisal's case for an independent Syria, Lawrence translated his Arabic into English and then French, which earned him a round of applause. Then the other delegations, including Chaim Weizmann, were permitted to have their say. As he had discussed with Feisal, Weizmann asked for a Jewish national home in Palestine, with annual immigration of 70–80,000 Jews.

While this debate continued for the rest of February and into March and April, the Spanish flu pandemic started to spread worldwide, killing over 100 million people over the next two years. On 16 February 1919 it claimed the life of Sir Mark Sykes, while just weeks later Lawrence's father also succumbed to the illness. This prompted Lawrence's return to England to visit his mother. Unlike so many other deaths he experienced, Lawrence never spoke about his father's. They had enjoyed a complicated relationship, but there was no evidence that Lawrence was ever bitter towards him. Perhaps the strength of Lawrence's feeling for him can be seen by his determination to redeem his family's honour, and return it to noble status.

So far he had failed to do that, and, away from Paris and grieving for his father, Lawrence began to realise that the Arabs were fighting a losing cause. The Americans might have advocated for an inquiry into the wishes of the Syrian people, but Wilson was prepared to do no more than that. The French and then the British refused to accept the findings anyway, which only led to the 'surprising' conclusion that the United States should occupy Syria instead. With just the French and the British left to fight it out, Lawrence knew it was a fait accompli.

Ultimately the British wanted to keep their spoils, and their oil in Iraq. A contemporary British intelligence report outlined just how vital access to oil was for the British Empire: 'Fuel oil is now essential to the maintenance of British sea power,' it began. 'Our power to control the world's shipping in time of war is likely in the future to be measured largely by the proportion of the world's oil supply that we shall command.' In order to achieve this, the British would have no option but to concede Syria to France. What the Arabs were promised, or wanted, didn't come into the matter. Winston Churchill said, 'The idea that France, bled white in the trenches of Flanders, should emerge from the Great War without her share of conquered territories was insupportable to [Clemenceau] and would never have been tolerated by his countrymen.'

The issue only became more confused when Ibn Saud's forces clashed with King Hussein's over his right to rule in the Hejaz. This conflict significantly weakened Feisal's hand in Paris. As if this was not enough, the British colonial government of India backed Ibn Saud, while the British Foreign Office backed King Hussein. It was starting to look increasingly likely that, rather than be king of all the Arabs, neither King Hussein nor his sons would have any land to rule at all. Indeed, most delegations at the peace conference were happy to let Ibn Saud keep the lands in Saudi Arabia while they fought over Syria and Iraq. No one yet realised the vast reserves of oil that lay beneath its desert.

Soon after, Britain came to an agreement with France. Just as Lawrence had predicted, the British would leave Syria and it would now fall under French rule. If Feisal wanted any say in the matter, he would have to deal with the French alone. The Union Jack was duly pulled down in Damascus and replaced by the Tricolore. All that Feisal and the Arabs had fought for looked to be in vain. The French had merely replaced the Turks, and the Arabs found themselves with no more independence than when they had started.

In his memoirs, Lawrence would write: 'We lived many lives in those whirling campaigns, never sparing ourselves: yet when we achieved and the new world dawned, the old men came out again and took our victory to remake in the likeness of the former world they knew. Youth could win, but had not learned to keep: and was pitiably weak against age. We stammered that we had worked for a new heaven and a new earth, and they thanked us kindly and made their peace.'

And yet, Lawrence was not finished. There was still one final chance to make things right.

31

Following the Paris Peace Conference, Lawrence initially tried to retreat from public life. He turned down a number of honours and job offers and instead commenced a research fellowship into 'the antiquities and ethnology, and the history (ancient and modern) of the Near East' at All Souls College, Oxford. This allowed him the modest sum of £200 a year and a set of rooms from which he could study. He also started to write his memoirs, hoping to get the horror of the war out of his system while continuing to make the case for Arab independence. He no doubt also hoped to free himself of much of the guilt he continued to carry.

However, in March 1919, Lawrence's hope for seclusion was blown apart when Lowell Thomas opened his long-awaited show in New York, titled 'With Allenby in Palestine and Lawrence in Arabia'. Containing Harry Chase's slides and film footage, Lowell began the show by grandly stating, 'Lawrence of Arabia . . . a young man whose name will go down in history beside those of Sir Francis Drake, Sir Walter Raleigh, Lord Clive, Charles Gordon, and all the other famous heroes of Great Britain's glorious past.'

The show caused a sensation. The epic story of Lawrence riding alongside the Arabs regularly filled Madison Square Garden and was seen by more than two million people. Soon after, it was transferred to Britain, where it was greeted with even greater enthusiasm, first at the Royal Opera House in Covent Garden, and then throughout the country. Underneath the poster ran a quote from Lloyd George, no less: 'Everything that Mr Lowell Thomas tells us about Colonel Lawrence is true. In my opinion Lawrence is one of the most remarkable and romantic figures of modern times.'

Lawrence hated all of the publicity and the scrutiny that followed. For someone who was trying to avoid the limelight, he was now unable to walk down the street without being mobbed. Although it seems that Lawrence was at the same time curious to see what the fuss was about: he went to see the show no less than five times, but always in disguise. On one occasion, when Mrs Thomas spotted him, he turned bright red in embarrassment, laughed in confusion, and then hurried away, stammering his apologies.

Thomas made over $1.5 million from the show, as well as from a subsequent biography of Lawrence (more than $23 million today). In return, Lawrence didn't receive a penny. Not that he would have accepted any monetary reward. He always felt too ashamed to profit from his failed efforts. More than anything, Lawrence despised being heralded as a hero when he felt anything but.

Indeed, just a year on from the Paris Peace Conference, Feisal's forces were at war with the French in Syria. After heavy losses, Feisal was forced to flee to Egypt, seeking the protection of the British. The British were also engaged in a battle of their own as they sought to quell rebellions in both Egypt and Iraq.

In 1919, Winston Churchill became secretary of state for war and therefore in charge of policy in the Middle East. He immediately turned to Lawrence and offered him the chance to become his political adviser, as well as his emissary to the Arabs. Lawrence could not resist. This was yet another chance to help the Arabs and keep his promises to them. On 18 February 1920, Lawrence began working for Churchill on a salary of £1,200 per annum and was soon back in the Middle East trying to conjure a solution that might satisfy everybody. Despite his reservations regarding the part he had played in the Revolt, Lawrence was still a hero to the Arabs. Detective Inspector Walter Thompson, Churchill's bodyguard, remembers the scenes when Lawrence, dressed in Arab robes, made his way to a mosque in Gaza:

> No Pope of Rome ever had more command before his own worshippers in the Palazzo. And Colonel Lawrence raised his hand slowly, the first and second fingers lifted above the other two for silence and for blessing. He could have owned the earth. He did own it. Every man froze in respect, in a kind of New Testament adoration of shepherds for a master. It was quite weird and very comforting.
>
> We passed through these murderous-looking men and they parted a way for us without a struggle. Many touched Lawrence as he moved forward among them. Far off, drums were beating, and a horse neighed. A muezzin's cry fell sadly among us from the single minaret in the mosque.

When Lawrence visited Abdulla at his desert camp, the artist Eric Kennington, who accompanied him, recalled the rapturous welcome he received from the Arab tribesmen: 'Their cries . . . became a roar, Aurens – Aurens – Aurens! It seemed to me that each had need to touch him . . . Recreating the picture, I see him as detached as ever, but with great charm and very gracious . . . They loved him, and gave him all their heart.'

Lawrence was grateful for such receptions, but he was also determined to put things right. He reasoned that, first and foremost, Hussein and his sons must somehow be satisfied, and that this might then calm tensions in the region. Arab rule in Syria remained out of the question, but if they could not rule the lands they had been promised, Lawrence had another solution in mind. With the British having the mandate for oil-rich Iraq, Lawrence ensured that Feisal was crowned as its king. At the same time, he advised on redrawing the borders, which created a new country known as Jordan, with Abdulla being put on its throne. This not only placated him, but also stopped him from carrying out a planned attack on the French in Syria.

Lawrence and the British now believed that their promises to the Arabs had somewhat been upheld: Feisal and Abdulla were kings of their own countries, albeit under a British mandate. At the same time, Hussein continued to rule from Mecca (although by 1924 Ibn Saud had forced him out of the Hejaz altogether, creating modern-day Saudi Arabia in the process). In the current circumstances, these arrangements appeared to be a sensible compromise for everyone. Indeed, Lawrence believed Iraq was a far greater prize for Feisal than Syria, particularly due to its oil-rich lands. No one yet realised the trouble all of this was storing up for decades to come.

With his work complete, Lawrence left his post in 1922, satisfied that he had done all he could. 'We were quit of the war-time eastern adventure, with clean hands,' he said, while in his formal letter of resignation to Churchill, he wrote that he was 'very glad to leave so prosperous a ship'.

Once again, Lawrence was feted for his achievements. He had apparently helped to solve the great conundrum of the Middle East and saved a lot of blood, money, and reputations. His suggestion to pull the British Army out of Iraq and replace them with the RAF also saved over £38,500,000 per annum (around £2.7 billion today). Churchill and Lawrence had grown to greatly admire each other, with Lawrence exclaiming that he was 'an employer who had been for me so considerate as sometimes to seem more like a senior partner than a master'. Finally it seemed that Lawrence could be at peace with himself and no longer carry such a burden of shame.

His tremendous exploits leading the Arabs in the war, and his diplomatic success following it meant that Lawrence could now have almost any job of his choosing. Few men in history could have had such prosperous and glittering opportunities. But no one could have predicted what he did next.

32

Despite his success, more than anything Lawrence wanted to completely disappear from public life. He was tired of being a supposed leader of men, making life-and-death decisions that often impacted whole continents. The weight of it all had become far too much, especially amidst the hysteria of becoming an icon now known around the world as 'Lawrence of Arabia'. While he might have believed that he had kept his promises to the Arabs and had redeemed his family's honour (although still no one yet knew he was an illegitimate child), the scars of the war tormented him.

After weighing up his options, Lawrence decided to return to the armed forces, but under an assumed name. He had climbed to the rank of lieutenant colonel but no longer had any great military ambitions to become a general. Instead, he wanted to start again at the bottom and be a simple private, following orders and doing simple things. He would spend the next decade attempting to achieve this.

With the help of his superiors, he initially enlisted in the RAF as an aircraft hand called John Hume Ross. Following this, he joined the Royal Tank Corps as Private Thomas Edward Shaw, and then returned to the RAF as AC2 Shaw, spending time in India, where he worked as a clerk in the

Engine Repair Section. He then returned to Britain to work on rescue boats for the marine branch of the RAF in southern England, with his final posting at Bridlington in 1934.

At the time Lawrence made the decision to return to the forces, he was clearly physically unwell. Indeed he failed his RAF medical, being 15lbs underweight and suffering from extreme nervous exhaustion. The scars on his back from Deraa were also still present. Lawrence later said, 'If I had known I was such a wreck I'd have gone off and recovered before joining up, now the cure and experiment must proceed together.' He was clearly not physically fit for service but he was allowed to enlist regardless.

While he was still not well physically, he was also unwell mentally. Many of his colleagues recall him waking in the night suffering from nightmares and needing to be consoled and calmed down. In a letter to Charlotte Shaw, wife of famed author George Bernard Shaw, he wrote: 'The war is so long over, that we should all be recovered from it now, only we aren't. It wakes me up in the early hours, sometimes, in a terror.'

Lawrence also found that disappearing and becoming a simple private again was far more difficult than he had envisaged. He might have enlisted under an assumed name, but he was still one of the world's most famous men. If his superiors or men in his barracks didn't recognise him, then the media were trying to chase him down. Indeed, this was a sensational story in itself. Lawrence could have had fame and fortune, but was instead trying to do his best to disappear, in the military's lower ranks, no less. Unsurprisingly, when the media did track him down, it became a feeding frenzy and only made things more difficult.

At times, Lawrence didn't help himself. While he wanted to be a lowly private, this was very difficult after all of his experiences. Doing menial tasks such as delivering messages and cleaning offices was all well and good, but sometimes he couldn't help but declare his dissatisfaction. When his superiors worked out who he was, this also caused some difficulty. Some found it embarrassing to give orders to a living legend. In contrast, others wanted him removed altogether, believing it to be nothing more than catering to Lawrence's whims and a distraction to their goals. Charles Findlay, an RAF adjutant, later wrote that it was 'a heavy responsibility to have a world-famous character on our hands as an AC2, and many times I saw his slight, blue-uniformed figure engaged in some menial task I tried with difficulty to reconcile it with the romantic soldier who had inspired the grim, desert peoples to fight so audaciously.' David Hogarth, Lawrence's old professor and companion at the Arab Bureau in Cairo, also remarked to George Bernard Shaw that 'Some RAF officers disliked commanding him and thought he laughed at their instructions.'

Although there were clearly many difficulties, there were also a number of positives. His report card from the RAF reveals that his character was assessed as 'exceptional', while he also had a considerable impact on the men whom he served alongside. During his research for his book *The Life of T. E. Lawrence,* John E. Mack spoke to many of these men and wrote: 'Several of his former companions have told me of the difference he made in their lives. Some spoke of being shown aspects of the world they had been ignorant of, while others stressed a kind of moral lift or turn their lives took following the association with Lawrence. Some he introduced to literature, which then became a lifelong interest for them. All experienced an increased confidence and an ability to think things out for themselves as a result of knowing him.'

Alec Dixon, who was a corporal in the Tank Corps with Lawrence, described him as being 'as good a soldier as any man in the Depot'. According to Dixon:

> He never leaned or lounged, and I never saw him to relax. He was surely a man with 'ants in his pants' if ever there was one. When walking about the Camp his normal bearing was very noticeable for, except when on a drill parade, he did not swing his arms as he walked in the approved manner – an oddity which singled him out from all of us. He walked 'all of a piece' as it were, with an air of tidiness; his arms were close to his body and his toes well turned out, though not exaggeratedly so. As he walked, he appeared to see no one about him; his head was slightly tilted and the blue-grey eyes steady, looking neither to the right nor to the left.

Helping individual soldiers with their issues was one thing, but Lawrence did not hesitate to press his argument for service reforms in areas he found unsatisfactory. Amongst the many causes that he promoted were the elimination of bayonets from airmen's rifles; the abolition of the death penalty for cowardice and desertion in the face of the enemy; the abolition of compulsory church parades; the elimination of swagger sticks for officers and men; change from monthly to yearly kit inspection; weekend passes; posting of servicemen to stations nearer their homes; permission to leave the service voluntarily; encouraging the wearing of civvies; less arbitrary deprivation of leaves; and permission for pillion-riding on motorcycles.

Despite all of this, many felt that Lawrence was merely running away from his issues and himself. George Bernard Shaw perhaps best summed up Lawrence's predicament in a letter to him:

> Like all heroes, and I must add, all idiots, you greatly exaggerate your power of moulding the universe to your personal convictions . . . It is useless to protest that Lawrence is not your real name. That will not save you . . . You masqueraded as Lawrence and didn't keep quiet: and now Lawrence you will be to the end of your days . . . Lawrence may be as great a nuisance to you sometimes as G.B.S. is to me, or as Frankenstein found the man he manufactured; but you created him, and must now put up with him as best you can.

Ever since he had learned of his illegitimacy as a child and borne the weight of his mother's unrealistic expectations to save the family's reputation, Lawrence had struggled with his identity. This was only furthered during the war when he flitted between British soldier and Arab guerrilla fighter, caught between two goals and two loyalties. There were also his feelings about his sexuality, which became more complex after being tortured and sexually assaulted in Deraa.

This was revealed in a letter to Charlotte Shaw in 1924, when he wrote: 'About that night, I shouldn't tell you . . . I gave away the only possession which we are all born into the world with – our bodily integrity. It's an unforgiveable matter, an irrecoverable position; and it's that which has made me forswear decent living and the exercise of my not contemptible wits and talents . . . It will hang about me while I live and afterwards if our personality survives. Consider wandering among the decent ghosts hereafter, crying "Unclean, unclean!"'

No matter where Lawrence went or what name he called himself, the events in Deraa continued to haunt him. In the years following the war, there continued to be no romantic interests, whether male or female. In another letter to Charlotte, he admitted that he did not follow his colleagues to brothels due to his fear of 'seeming a novice in it . . . it's because I wouldn't know what to do, how to carry myself, where to stop'. Instead, Lawrence seems to have become preoccupied with the beating at Deraa, to a destructive degree.

While stationed at Bovington with the Royal Tank Corps, he met a nineteen-year-old Scotsman named John 'Jock' Bruce. He told young Bruce that he was being blackmailed and 'the old man' behind the affair had ordered him to be punished to avoid disclosing any secrets. Despite this incredulous story, Jock did not question it. Instead, for the next twelve years, he subjected Lawrence to brutal whippings, for which he was paid. To further satisfy 'the old man', he also detailed the exact punishment he had inflicted on Lawrence, which he passed to Lawrence to hand to the supposed blackmailer.

Of course, there was no old man. Jock must have realised this, yet while he was being paid and keeping Lawrence happy, he did not question it. It is difficult to say whether Lawrence wanted to be whipped for pleasure, punishment, or both. His description of the whipping at Deraa made it clear he was sexually aroused, and he might therefore have wanted to try and repeat this. Alternatively, he might have wanted to punish himself for his perceived failures. Perhaps he believed that being whipped and beaten were what he deserved. After all, that was what his mother had done to him when he had displeased her as a child.

There is no record to suggest the truth. Like so many things with Lawrence's complex character, it is open to interpretation. What does appear to be definite is that there remained no loving relationship in Lawrence's life until the day he died. In a letter to Lady Astor, he said, 'Probably it would be wholesome for me to lose my heart . . . if that monstrous piece of machinery is capable of losing itself: for till now it has never cared for anyone, though much for places and things. Indeed, I doubt these words of hearts . . . If only one might never come nearer to people than in the street.'

Throughout this time, Lawrence continued to write his memoirs, a prolonged and torturous affair, not helped when he lost the manuscript at Reading Station and had to rewrite it. However, with other authors releasing books about him, he wanted to tell his story in his own words to set the record straight. Yet he had no ambition for the book to become a bestseller nor to profit from it.

Therefore, in 1926, he released a 250,000-word self-published book to just 200 subscribers, titled *Seven Pillars of Wisdom*. Although it allowed him to tell his story in detail for the first time, it also plunged him into considerable debt. The books cost £13,000 to publish and only earned £3,000 in return. Matters weren't helped by him giving away a number of copies to close friends who had served alongside him, such as Allenby, Joyce, Newcombe, Young, Stirling, and Winterton.

Following demand for a more widespread release, in 1927 the book was published as an abridged 130,000-word version called *Revolt in the Desert*. After selling 90,000 copies in the UK and over 130,000 copies in the USA, Lawrence withdrew the book. Despite being in debt, he ensured that all proceeds went to an RAF charity fund, while he also freely gave money to help fellow colleagues in need. He remained determined not to profit from his deeds in any way.

However, Lawrence was pleased that the book was heralded by critics and readers alike. *The Times* called it 'a masterpiece', while the *Daily Telegraph* said it was 'one of the most stirring stories of our times'. Even General Allenby was moved to write to Lawrence and call the book 'a great work'. While it was a story full of blood and adventure, many in high literary circles also found the prose impressive. George Bernard Shaw was particularly complimentary, as was E. M. Forster. Later, Winston Churchill was moved to say, 'It ranks with the greatest books ever written in the English language. As a narrative of war and adventure it is unsurpassable.'

The book also ushered in a new type of hero for the twentieth century. Lawrence had fought many battles and had shown extraordinary courage and bravery in doing so. Yet in his book, he chose to reveal in detail his complex character, laying bare his defects, his capacity for deceit, and most shockingly of all, the events of Deraa, where he admitted he had been sexually aroused. In his review of the book, E.M. Forster wrote that it displayed 'a sexual frankness which would cause most authors to be run in by the police'. When writing that specific chapter, Lawrence admitted to Charlotte Shaw, 'Working on it always makes me sick. The two impulses fight so upon it. Self respect would close it: self-expression seeks to open it. It's a case in which you can't let yourself write as you could.'

Rather than be repulsed or to turn Lawrence into a villain, it seems that the public was willing to welcome a flawed hero. The carnage of the war, and the deaths of millions, had perhaps persuaded them that conflict was not romantic and that the men who fought were often tragic figures who carried a heavy burden and battled on regardless. The character of Lawrence in *Seven Pillars of Wisdom* subsequently became the template for fictional heroes that endures to this day.

Despite the acclaim, Lawrence was determined that there would be no further publication of his memoirs until after his death. It would not be until 1997 that the unabridged version would finally be released. That is not to say that he stopped writing altogether. During this time, he also wrote a book about the early days of the RAF, and his own experiences within it, called *The Mint*. Again, due to Lawrence's instructions, the book would not be published until 1955, and some of the names within it were changed to avoid causing embarrassment or offence. He also accepted offers to anonymously translate the Odyssey under the name of T. E. Shaw, but turned down further opportunities to write anything original. It seemed he had said all he had to say. He admitted as much in a letter, saying, 'I'm all smash inside . . . there was never an orange squeezed dryer than myself. Not a kick in the entire body. I'll write nothing else I'm sure.'

He nevertheless continued to assist writers who wanted to write about his adventures, including Lowell Thomas and military historian Captain Basil Liddell Hart. In the early 1930s, Liddell Hart wished to write a full-length biography on Lawrence, as well as to analyse his military strategies. Lawrence did not want to encourage any more attention, but was happy to provide certain information and correct proofs to ensure nothing unsubstantiated was written. As a further sign of how conflicted he was, he wrote to the book's publisher, 'My reading Liddell Hart's effort does not imply either approval or collaboration. I regret it and apprehend it keenly.' When the book was published in 1934, it was widely acclaimed and, just as Lawrence had feared, led to ever more interest in him. Again, Lawrence tried to shun it, and was particularly scathing of the praise Liddell Hart lavished on him. He wrote, 'It fails to criticize anything. One could swallow praise, if it was moved with a reasonable amount of blame;

but as one knows that not everything was well done, one cannot trust his judgement.'

On 25 February 1935, Lawrence was finally discharged from the RAF, with his final report describing him as 'an exceptional airman' whose conduct and character at all times had been 'very good'. However, he was no closer to finding himself than when he began. Perhaps that was the point. To stop searching for himself and become consumed by simple affairs. In a letter to Robert Graves, he said of his time in the forces: 'I went into the RAF to serve a mechanical purpose, not as a leader but as a cog of the machine. The key word, I think, is machine. I have been mechanical since, and a good mechanic, for my self-training to become an artist has greatly widened my field of view. I leave it to others to say whether I chose well or not: one of the benefits of being part of the machine is that one learns that one doesn't matter!'

Soon after, he returned to his small cottage in Dorset, Cloud Hill, and wondered what he would do with the rest of his life. He was not to know that he had already entered his final chapter.

33

In 1935, Lawrence found himself at a crossroads in his life. Still searching for validity and meaning, there was talk of more travel, where he might 'wander for most of this year about England'. He also debated starting a printing press, which had long been an ambition. Yet nothing seemed to grab him. After all his adventures, he was tired and described himself as 'grey-haired and toothless, half-blind and shaking at the knees'. At just forty-six, he confided, 'the active part of my life is over.' Indeed, when he found his friend Frederick Manning had died, he wrote to his publisher, 'I find myself wishing all the time that my own curtain would fall.'

The only thing that seemed to occupy him was his Triumph motorcycle, which he enjoyed riding at high speeds through the country lanes without a crash helmet. While in the Royal Tank Corps he had admitted: 'When my mood gets too hot and I find myself wandering beyond control I pull out my motorbike and hurl it top speed through these unfit roads for hour after hour. My nerves are jaded and gone near dead, so that nothing less than hours of voluntary danger will prick them into life.' Such danger seemed to be the only thing that got his blood pumping any more. When he was told by a friend that 'You will be breaking your blinking neck on it,' Lawrence merely replied, 'Well, better than dying in bed.' He would soon get his wish.

On the morning of 13 May 1935, Lawrence set off on his motorcycle to deliver a parcel to the local post office. As he rode over a dip at 50–60mph, he was suddenly confronted by two boys riding their bicycles across the road. Pressing hard on the brakes, he swerved to avoid hitting them and lost control. Thrown over the handlebars, his head smacked against the road, before he was thrown into a tree, his head smashing again into the trunk.

Lawrence was immediately taken to Bovington Camp Hospital, unconscious and in a critical condition. For the next six days doctors did all they could to save him, but it was useless. At 8 a.m. on Sunday 19 May, the man known around the world as Lawrence of Arabia passed away. He was just forty-six years old.

After so many years of fighting in the desert, facing all kinds of life-and-death situations, it was a simple motorbike accident which finally got the better of him. Some could not accept that a legend could succumb to such an end, and thought he had been murdered by unseen forces. There is no proof of this. Instead, it is one of life's curiosities that a man who had faced so many bullets should perish in such a manner. He had always been more mindful than most about the need to preserve lives. In swerving out of the way of the two boys, he had ensured that they lived.

On 21 May 1935, Lawrence was buried in the small local churchyard at Moreton, with Ronald Storrs as one of his pallbearers. In attendance were the likes of General

Allenby, Alan Dawnay, Winston Churchill, Siegfried Sassoon, Lionel Curtis, and Lawrence's brother Arnold. Unsurprisingly, a mob of photographers had also gathered. In a letter to Arnold, King George wrote: 'His name will live in history.'

Although he had tried to escape his famous name since the war, he could no longer escape it in death. His tombstone was simply engraved 'T. E. Lawrence'. It is ironic that he had tried on many names and identities, and yet never had the chance to fit comfortably into the one he was given at birth. As he wrote to Charlotte Shaw in 1925, 'The Lawrence thing hasn't any better foundation than my father's whim.'

While Lawrence never truly accepted his identity, his death hasn't stopped an army of scholars, authors and fans from trying to work out who he really was, and what truly inspired him to join the Arab Revolt. Over the years, scholars have pored over his papers, while countless books have been written about him, as well as several documentaries released. Then, in 1962, director David Lean released his movie *Lawrence of Arabia*. Starring Peter O'Toole in the lead role, it won seven Oscars and was acclaimed as a masterpiece. This only served to introduce Lawrence to a new generation and invite more research and speculation about him.

To this day, the fascination with Lawrence continues. Including my own, there have now been over 300 books written about him, with no one able to say definitively what made the man. There is far too much ambiguity and complexity for that. But isn't that the case for most of our idols? No man is unblemished, particularly those who reach for greatness. It takes many forces and influences to inspire a man to achieve such goals. And yet Lawrence continues to have a far-reaching influence to this day, both good and bad.

Lawrence is perhaps most famous for attempting to provide the Arabs with independence during and after the war. However, the remarking of the borders in Iraq has caused significant controversy and bloodshed right up until the present day. The Kurds in Kurdistan were subsumed against their will into the new Iraq, and have fought bitterly over this ever since. The fact that Iraq was predominantly a Shi'ite Muslim country and their new King Feisal was from the Sunni faith also caused resentment. Following the removal of Sunni president Saddam Hussein in 2003, there followed an explosion of violence as Shi'ites became determined to return to power. Moreover, carving Kuwait out of Iraq meant that the latter had no access to the sea. When in 1990 Saddam Hussein sought to reclaim both Kuwait's oil and its coastline, it set in motion the Gulf War. As far as President Hussein and others saw it, Iraq had only been denied these assets due to a British pen over a map.

The discovery of oil in the Middle East, and the wars to own it, also affected my time in Oman. Not long after I had left, in July 1970, a coup by the Sultan's son Prince Qaboos saw him finally seize power. The deposed Sultan was left to live the rest of his days in a suite in London's Dorchester Hotel. As had been hoped, Qaboos immediately used the oil revenues to instigate an ambitious industrial programme, helped when world oil prices doubled, leading to Oman's oil income reaching £300 million in 1975 alone.

While I had long been troubled by my time in Oman, I soon felt a lot better when I returned in 1973 to film a documentary. In just a few short years, the country was unrecognisable from the one I had left behind. Tarmac roads, harbours, new towns, lighting and piped water had arrived in lightning succession. Hospitals, schools and employment had also mushroomed, while cars, newspapers and cafes suddenly appeared. In just three short years, Sultan Qaboos had pulled Oman from the Middle Ages into the twentieth century. He also whipped the carpet from under the revolutionaries, who had lost their most vital propaganda tool. I now look back with pride at the small role I played in helping to keep the communists at bay so that the people of Oman and Dhofar could live under such prosperous conditions and still be able to peacefully practise their religion to this day. Without Lawrence's example, I might never have been able to mould my men into a capable force and, in turn, take out a monster like Salim Amr, who had caused so much misery.

Of all the issues with which Lawrence was involved, it is perhaps Zionism that has been the most controversial. Jewish emigration to Palestine was initially as Chaim Weizmann had predicted. Abdulla, the son of King Hussein, admitted that some Arabs were 'annoyed and insulted by Zionist immigration but not alarmed by it. It was steady, but fairly small, as even the Zionist founders thought it would remain. Indeed, for some years, more Jews left Palestine than entered it – in 1927 almost twice as many.'

However, this all changed after the Second World War. The rampant antisemitism and mass murders of Jews in Nazi Germany encouraged millions to flee to Palestine for safety. The state of Israel was subsequently founded in 1948 and continued to grow thereafter, offering a safe haven to Jews all over the world. It is now thought to control as much as 85 per cent of historic Palestine, with a never-ending conflict between the Jews and Palestinians. In Lawrence's defence, much of this was difficult to foresee when he and Feisal welcomed the Zionist project. To this day, it remains a complex and violent situation that shows no sign of being solved.

In some quarters, Lawrence has faced much criticism for encouraging the Arabs to fight for their independence. But again, this is not entirely fair. Before Lawrence had anything to do with the Arab Revolt, it was already well underway. In addition, he was not made aware of the details of the Sykes–Picot Agreement, nor the Balfour Declaration, until it was too late. If he had not urged the Arabs on to claim Damascus, they would have had nothing to bargain with at the subsequent Peace Conference, or thereafter. Things might, in fact, have been far worse. Had the Turks won, then the retribution against the Arabs would have been bloody and merciless, as evidenced in the Armenian genocide, where they stand accused of murdering over one million people. In leading the Arabs to victory, Lawrence's guerrilla strategy also saved many Arab lives. Under anyone else's leadership, they might have been forced into direct battle and perished in their thousands.

After sending Herbert Samuel, the former high commissioner of Palestine, a copy of his book, Lawrence attempted to explain himself. 'I find myself pleading that I was in a horrible position in Arabia, throughout, with the choice of no more than evils before me: and that I tried to do the least harmful of them, and to do it so that the fewest small people were harmed by it.'

There can be no denying that Lawrence's strategy in the Hejaz continues to inspire military operations and guerrilla rebellions throughout the world, including my own in Oman. Indeed, military author and biographer Liddell Hart ranked him alongside the greatest generals of history, as he helped to create a new form of hybrid warfare, with modern weapons operating alongside irregular forces. Lawrence's ideas and strategies can be seen in the Second World War, with Churchill employing a number of successful guerrilla operations. The Vietnamese forces successfully utilised many of his tactics during the Vietnam War, as did rebel leaders such as Fidel Castro and Che Guevara in Latin America. They were also highly influential in 2001, when US forces invaded Afghanistan using a combination of US air strikes and Arab tribesmen on the ground. As a result, Lawrence has been added to the military curriculum of the United States Army, where he remains a considerable authority in irregular operations.

In trying to free the Arabs, Lawrence also tried to free himself. Ultimately, neither goal was reached, certainly not in his lifetime. And yet this conflict within him, and not knowing who he really was, might have been the key to his success.

The author and psychiatrist John E. Mack wrote, 'I have little doubt that his extraordinary capacity to move flexibly among peoples of other classes and races, to understand or intuit their needs and hopes, their feelings and dreams, derived to a large degree from the complex and unsettled elements of his own identity. This capacity seemed to know no bounds. He could be what people needed him to be, for he knew what they felt, what they were.'

This search for himself in the desert brought enemies together, forged new countries and ensured that the name of Lawrence of Arabia shall live on for ever. Through his actions, he displayed an extraordinary capacity for empathy and a rare respect for the value of life during warfare, redefining the values of what we expect from our leaders and heroes. He remains a symbol of opposition to oppression, and of how one man's dream can achieve miracles against all odds. He might not have set the Arabs free as he had wished, but he continues to inspire freedom movements all over the globe. His initial goal to redeem his family honour was to 'free a people'. Until the end of time, his example will do just this.

Acknowledgements

My sincere thanks to my Publishers, my Family, the Ashmolean Museum in Oxford, especially Robert Johnson and Xa Sturgis, and to all the brave soldiers of Fiend Force. There are also many individuals who helped over the years in my long search for the Lost City of the Queen of Sheba – my version of Lawrence's Carchemish.

Bibliography

Adlington, Richard, *Lawrence of Arabia: A Biographical Enquiry*, London: Collins, 1955

Barr, James. *A Line in the Sand*, New York: Simon and Schuster, 2011

—, *Setting the Desert on Fire: T. E. Lawrence and Britain's Secret War in Arabia, 1916–1918*, London: Bloomsbury, 2007.

Brown, Malcolm, and Cave, Julia, *Touch of Genius: The Life of T. E. Lawrence*, London: Dent, 1988

Graves, Robert, *Lawrence and the Arabs*, London: Doubleday Doran Co., 1927.

—, and B. H. Liddell Hart, *T. E. Lawrence to his Biographers*, New York: Doubleday, 1963

Faulkner, Neil, *Lawrence of Arabia's War: The Arabs, the British and the Remaking of the Middle East in WW1*, New Haven, CT: Yale University Press, 2017

Fiennes, Ranulph, *Atlantis of the Sands: The Search for the Lost City of Ubar*, London: Bloomsbury, 1992

—, *Where Soldiers Fear to Tread*, London: The Travel Book Club, 1975

Johnson, Rob, *The Great War and the Middle East*, Oxford: Oxford University Press, 2016

Jolley, Alison, *Lawrence of Arabia's War Day by Day*, Great Britain: Dreadnought Publishing, 2018

Knightly, Philip, and Colin Simpson, *The Secret Lives of Lawrence of Arabia*, London: Nelson, 1969

Korda, Michael. *Hero: The Life and Legend of Lawrence of Arabia, London: Arum Press, 2012*

Lawrence, T. E. *Correspondence with Bernard and Charlotte Shaw, 1922–1926, Vol. 1,* Jeremy Wilson and Nicole Wilson (eds.). Fordingbridge, England: Castle, 2000

—, *Seven Pillars of Wisdom,* London: Jonathan Cape,1935

Liddell Hart, Basil, '*T. E. Lawrence' in Arabia and After,* London: Jonathan Cape, 1934

Mack, J. E., *Prince of Our Disorder: The Life of T. E. Lawrence,* Boston: Little Brown, 1976

Meinertzhagen, Richard, *Middle East Diary,* London: Cresset, 1959

Murphy, David, *The Arab Revolt 1916–1918,* Oxford: Osprey Publishing, 2008

Rogan, Eugene, *The Fall of the Ottomans,* New York: Basic Books, 2015

Storrs, Ronald, *Orientations,* London: Reader's Union, 1939

Thomas, Lowell, *With Lawrence in Arabia,* New York: Doubleday, 1967

Wilson, Jeremy, *Lawrence of Arabia: The Authorized Biography of T. E. Lawrence,* New York: Atheneum, 1990

Picture Credits

Chronicle / Alamy Stock Photo: page 9, middle

Crown Copyright: page 4, top middle & bottom; page 5, middle; page 6, bottom left & bottom right; page 7, top, middle & bottom; page 8, top & bottom; page 9 top & bottom; page 11, top left & bottom; page 12, bottom; page 13 top left; page 14, bottom right; page 15, top right

Fremantle / Alamy Stock Photo: page 14, bottom left

John Frost Newspapers / Alamy Stock Photo: page 16, top left

Marist College Special Collections IMG_0419 Scrapbook, IMG_0404 Scrapbook, IMG_0412 Scrapbook: page 13, bottom left

Pictorial Press Ltd / Alamy Stock Photo: page 3, top right

Public Domain: page 1, top right & bottom right; page 13, top right

Ranulph Fiennes: page 2, middle

Unknown / Public Domain: page 2, bottom left & bottom right; page 5, bottom; page 16, bottom

Wikimedia Commons: page 1, top left & bottom left; page 2, top left; page 3, top left & bottom; page 4, top left & top right; page 5, top; page 6, top; page 10, top, middle & bottom; page 11, top right; page 12, top; page 13, bottom right; page 14, top; page 15, top left, bottom left & bottom right; page 16, top right

Every effort has been made to trace copyright holders and to obtain their permission for the use of copyright material. The publisher apologizes for any errors or omissions and would be grateful to be notified of any corrections that should be incorporated in future editions of this book.

Index